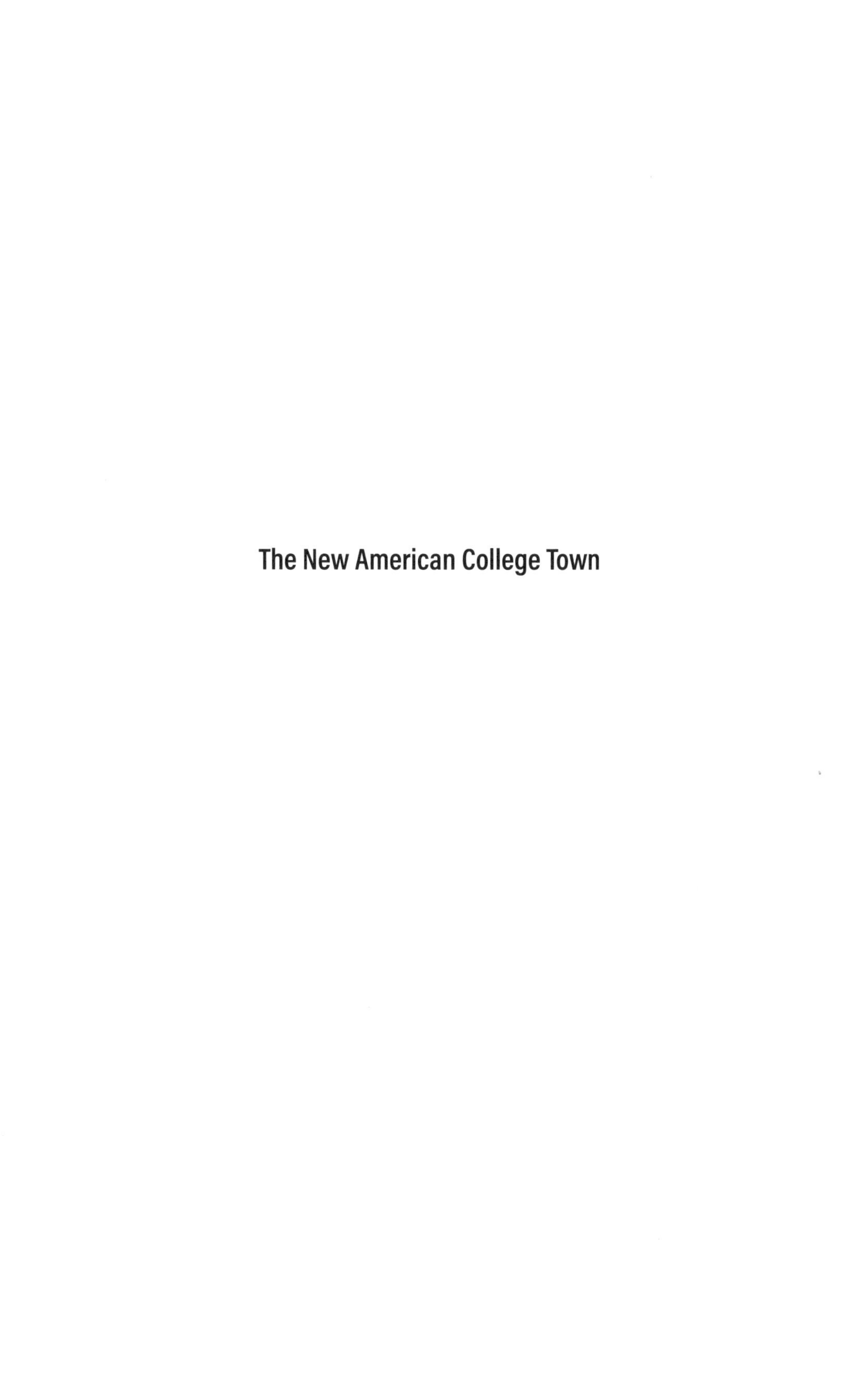

The New American College Town

THE NEW AMERICAN COLLEGE TOWN

Designing Effective Campus and Community Partnerships

JAMES MARTIN, JAMES E. SAMELS
& ASSOCIATES

JOHNS HOPKINS UNIVERSITY PRESS
Baltimore

Printed in the United States of America on acid-free paper
9 8 7 6 5 4 3 2 1

Johns Hopkins University Press
2715 North Charles Street
Baltimore, Maryland 21218-4363
www.press.jhu.edu

Library of Congress Cataloging-in-Publication Data

Names: Martin, James, 1948 January 14– editor. | Samels, James E., editor. | Samels Associates, editor.
Title: The new American college town : designing effective campus and community partnerships / James Martin and James E. Samels & Associates [editors].
Description: Baltimore : Johns Hopkins University Press, 2019. | Includes bibliographical references and index.
Identifiers: LCCN 2019001744 | ISBN 9781421432786 (hardcover : alk. paper) | 9781421432793 (electronic) | ISBN 1421432781 (hardcover : alk. paper) | ISBN 142143279X (electronic)
Subjects: LCSH: Community and college—United States. | University towns—United States. | Campus planning—United States.
Classification: LCC LC238 .N49 2019 | DDC 371.19—dc23
LC record available at https://lccn.loc.gov/2019001744

A catalog record for this book is available from the British Library.

Special discounts are available for bulk purchases of this book. For more information, please contact Special Sales at 410-516-6936 or specialsales@press.jhu.edu.

Johns Hopkins University Press uses environmentally friendly book materials, including recycled text paper that is composed of at least 30 percent post-consumer waste, whenever possible.

Contents

Preface

Although the number of books written about college towns prior to ours is strikingly small—that is, *one*—the idea of a college town with its leafy green associations nevertheless occupies a stereotypical place in American life. Almost every reader carries an image of what one should look like, even though the following chapters carefully illustrate how little that image now captures college towns across the United States from Unity, Maine, to Las Vegas, Nevada. This book does not attempt a history of the American college town; rather, contributors were asked to define the present-day college town and to present the best practices and lessons they have learned from their own experience—practices and lessons that presidents and provosts can use as they work creatively with civic leaders in their local and regional communities.

Research for our book *Consolidating Colleges and Merging Universities: New Strategies for Higher Education Leaders* (2017) focused on institutional mergers and strategic partnerships. In the course of that process, we interviewed several hundred campus planners, presidents, provosts, faculty leaders, chief financial officers, and advancement officers about how they were joining forces not simply with those at other colleges and universities but also with civic and business leaders in their local communities to leverage personnel resources, philanthropic opportunities, and infrastructure costs. After completing that project, it was clear that a practical guide and resource was needed for planning a new kind of American college town—a town or city that moves beyond stereotypes to achieve new objectives.

The authors of the following chapters form a wide spectrum of key players in the ongoing transformation of college towns. In part 2 of the book, on the president's role in town-gown relationships, eight presidents and their writing teams explain how they have created new college town identities and partnerships to leverage and extend their institutional resources. We also offer chapters and sidebars from other leaders, including seven current or former college town mayors, a strategic planner and chief financial officer, a senior student affairs officer, two higher-education attorneys, a national reporter for *Inside Higher Ed*, and the current or former executive directors of several national education associations, including the International Town & Gown Association, the Association for the Study of Higher Education, the Council of Christian Colleges and Universities, Student Affairs Administrators in Higher Education, and the editor-in-chief of the Princeton Review Guides series. Many chapters include photographs of significant buildings and infrastructure reflecting campus-community collaboration.

In addition, the authors provide the following original research:

- *Twenty characteristics* of new American college towns. Readers will note that some elements have been carried forward from traditional town-gown settings, but for the most part, they represent a new combination of attributes and opportunities illustrating effective campus-community relationships.

- *Eight leading practices* for fostering an effective town-gown relationship, presented by the executive director and several board members of the International Town & Gown Association (ITGA). This chapter distills the action steps that ITGA members have employed over the past decade to build new kinds of productive relationships between a college or university and the surrounding local and regional communities.

- New recommendations by Wim Wiewel, coauthor of *Global Universities and Urban Development* and *Partnerships for Smart Growth* and former president of Portland State University, for designing the most productive *urban-serving universities* of the future.

- Five recommendations from the president of Lehigh University for ways that presidents and campus planners can expand their focus beyond the "town" in town-gown thinking to *regional development*, as Lehigh has in the Bethlehem Valley.

- In response to the persistent stereotype that *nationally ranked, elite liberal arts colleges* are islands of self-sufficiency no matter where they are located, the presidents of Connecticut College and Colby College, both members of the New England Small College Athletic Conference, discuss the long-term benefits in collaborating to redevelop their downtown communities in New London, Connecticut, and Waterville, Maine.

- *Community colleges* are often recognized for sustained local engagement, and SUNY Broome Community College in Binghamton, New York, provides a good example of many elements of this commitment. In chapter 9, "Community College Towns," SUNY Broome president Kevin Drumm details five action steps for presidents to take in developing more meaningful relationships with civic leaders.

- The inside story of how *Las Vegas higher education leaders* worked intentionally to steer the city's internationally recognized brand away from simple entertainment toward greater cultural significance has value for presidents and provosts beyond Nevada. Some may ask us why a book about new American college towns would include a chapter singularly about Las Vegas. The author of chapter 16, Kim Nehls—a former executive director of the Association for the Study of Higher Education and a visiting professor at the University of Nevada, Las Vegas—shares lessons applicable to major universities across the country. Her narrative concludes with an on-site assessment of how the city and its collective higher education institutions partnered immediately and productively to address the traumas caused by the mass shooting at the music festival outside the Mandalay Bay Hotel in October 2017.

- The leaders of *an international architectural and design firm* illustrate, particularly for presidents, provosts, and chief finance officers new to their posts, eight best practices for engaging outside design consultants.
- A roundtable conversation focuses on what *town and city mayors* are seeking in their partnerships with higher education administrators. The current or former mayors of seven college towns offer candid observations and recommendations for presidents, trustees, and institutional planners.
- Sidebars distributed throughout the book offer insights by, among others, Stephanie Gordon, vice president for professional development at Student Affairs Administrators in Higher Education; Rob Franek, editor-in-chief of the Princeton Review Guides series; and Kathleen Hatch, former president of NIRSA (National Intramural and Recreational Sports Association): Leaders in Collegiate Recreation, concerning what they believe currently constitutes effective town-gown relationships.
- HigherEdJobs.com is the largest resource for career information in higher education with over 1.5 million visits per month, and, for the first time, its editorial leadership team provides a ten-year summary, backed by its own original data, of how college towns are impacting their local workforces.
- A national reporter from *Inside Higher Ed* presents a set of guidelines he compiled for trustees and presidents to use when developing property and construction agreements with members of the external community.

- A *legal primer* for both town and gown leaders answers the most frequently asked questions that planners must address.
- The final chapter *predicts what college towns will look like in twenty-five years.*

The book's chapters are grouped into three sections. Part 1, "Developing a New Definition of College Towns," opens with a chapter by Martin and Samels that presents the twenty characteristics that define the new American college town. In chapter 2, Beth Bagwell, executive director of the ITGA, and a colleague from its board of directors summarize for the first time the eight most important lessons drawn from several hundred initiatives the association has facilitated to create effective relationships between campuses and their communities.

Part 2, "Effective Campus-Community Relationships Start with the President," opens with a chapter by Wim Wiewel, a national authority on successful campus-community relationships, who takes a fresh look at the elements of a modern college town after having served for a decade at a university viewed as one of the most influential in shaping this new model.

Chapter 4, by John Simon, president of Lehigh University, provides the most intentionally regional focus of any of the chapters by presidents. Simon profiles a number of projects that Lehigh has sponsored beyond its city limits in the Bethlehem Valley, illustrating how college towns can carry a regional impact.

In chapter 5, Katherine Bergeron, president of Connecticut College, along with the dean of the college and a former director of community partnerships, acknowledges the need that even elite liberal arts colleges now have to collaborate with local civic leaders in order to achieve their missions. David Greene, president of Colby College, contributes additional perspectives in a chapter sidebar on the $65 million urban redevelopment project his college has undertaken with downtown Waterville, Maine.

Leaving the world of elite liberal arts colleges, Mauri Ditzler, president of Albion College, and Lorin Ditzler describe in chapter 6 how his institution helped to transform its namesake city, with a declining population of 8,200 and a median income of $28,500, while reinvigorating the college's mission in the process. In the following chapter, Miguel Martinez-Saenz, president of St. Francis College in Brooklyn, New York, illustrates how much a new, less experienced president can still accomplish in town-gown relationships during his or her first twelve months of leadership.

Continuing the focus on new college town identities emerging within the New York–New Jersey metropolitan area, Susan Henderson, president of New Jersey City University, adds a chapter on how important it is for a president, whether more experienced or less experienced, to work effectively with city and state political leaders to accomplish town-gown objectives. The section on presidential vision concludes with a conversation about "community college towns" confirming why this category of institutions is recognized as among the most effective partners with their external communities. Kevin Drumm, president of SUNY Broome Community College, outlines five key strategies for community college presidents to use in leveraging their resources through simple yet innovative collaborations.

Part 3, "Beyond the President's Office: Expanding Missions and Leveraging Resources," moves beyond presidential vision and leadership to the many offices and administrators on and off campus who are integral to achieving success in a campus–local community initiative. Chapters in this section have been written by a team of architects and designers, a senior student affairs officer, a national higher education reporter, two higher education attorneys, eight town or city mayors, the cofounder of HigherEdJobs.com, and the former executive director of the Association for the Study of Higher Education, among others. Part 3 begins with a chapter by a former vice president for finance and planning who focuses on "how planners think" about new forms of town-gown partnerships and what both sides should expect in terms of effective planning.

Building on this concept of planning, we observe that architects and designers are often the earliest sounding boards to a president's or board chair's plans for collaboration on campus infrastructure. In chapter 11, Stuart Rothenberger, global head of higher education, and colleagues from DLR Group Integrated Design share eight best practices for college and university leaders planning to retain an architecture, design, and engineering firm.

So that readers might learn what elected officials seek from their side of a town-gown initiative, Beth Bagwell, executive director of the ITGA, and Kate Rousmaniere, mayor of Oxford, Ohio, assembled for chapter 12 a roundtable of six mayors from almost every sector of the country to offer advice and lessons learned that can be used when working on a shared-resources project with a university or college leadership team. Following this conversation, in chapter 13, Rick Seltzer, a national reporter on higher education infrastructure development and other topics for *Inside Higher Ed*, presents guidelines and best practices requested by several presidents and trustees to use when negotiating land and property agreements with state and local officials.

Many of these same presidents, provosts, and board members asked us during our research how college towns directly impact their local job markets. In chapter 14, one of the cofounders of HigherEdJobs.com and his director of editorial strategy provide a first look at the original data the website has been collecting since 1996 on how college towns affect the labor markets in which they are situated. This information is published for the first time in this book.

Students are not always in the forefront of college town planning projects. To ensure that student expectations are met and that student voices are heard, Eugene Zdziarski, vice president for student affairs at DePaul University in Chicago, outlines in chapter 15 five ways of approaching student leaders in order to include them in collaborations with the external community.

The city of Las Vegas has worked diligently and relatively quietly over the past decade to transform elements of its worldwide reputation into one that more visibly values academic degrees, career training, and higher education. For readers who may still harbor suspicions about the legitimacy of this plan, Kim Nehls, former executive of the Association for the Study of Higher Education and a visiting professor at the University of Nevada, Las Vegas, offers a sustained inside look at how her university and other Nevada higher education institutions actively collaborate with the political and entertainment establishments to enhance their educational missions. As noted above, her chapter concludes with a detailed examination of how the city and its collective higher education institutions partnered to respond strategically to the mass shooting at the music festival outside the Mandalay Bay Hotel in October 2017.

Of course, not all college towns are located in urban or suburban areas. To illustrate how institutions, many of them faith-based, with enrollments of six hundred to eight hundred students or fewer, located in rural or remote areas partner with others to leverage resources, Robert Andringa, past president of the Council of Christian Colleges and Universities, offers several creative strategies employed during his leadership, sometimes between colleges and organizations outside higher education, that produced new models of town-gown collaboration.

Phillip DiChiara is the former managing director of the Boston Consortium, perhaps the nation's best-known organization for nonacademic, auxiliary operations, with members including MIT, Boston University, and Harvard. In chapter 18, DiChiara presents five principles that consortium members have followed in their work together forging town-gown partnerships on a broader scale.

Like all of our previous books, this one includes a chapter on legal issues. James E. Samels, a veteran higher education attorney, and attorney Arlene Lieberman of Samels & Associates, Attorneys at Law, provide answers to the dozen most frequently asked legal questions regarding plans and projects that involve the external community.

The volume's final chapter offers readers the opportunity to look twenty-five years into the future at how even the most innovative college towns today will continue to change in essential ways.

The authors would like to thank a number of individuals who made significant contributions to the planning and execution of this book. Beth Bagwell, executive director of the International Town & Gown Association, is a network unto herself and provided advice and contacts across the country. Wim Wiewel, one of the few American higher education leaders who has served as president of both a university and a college and who has written two books on urban-serving universities, shared wisdom while the book was still in its idea stage. Stuart Rothenberger and Krisan Osterby of DLR Group Integrated Design grasped from their first conversation with us how the volume would benefit from a conversation about how presidents and provosts can most effectively communicate with architects. And Andy Hibel and Kelly Cherwin of HigherEdJobs.com saw the value in sharing a summary of the workforce data that their organization has been collecting for more than a decade about how new college towns influence their local and regional job markets. We believe that the research shared in the chapters by Wiewel and by Hibel and Cherwin; the insights detailed in the work by Beth Bagwell; and the perspectives offered in our own opening chapter can provide useful background on these issues for PhD students and their program curricula.

In closing, we would like to thank two persons in particular: Liam Lair, our editorial assistant for this project, and Greg Britton, editorial director at Johns Hopkins University Press and our own editor. Liam once again managed the preparation and production of our manuscript with patience and creativity, and Greg continues to envision possibilities in our work before we see them and provides us with the kind of higher ed GPS that brings out the best in our writing. Having been privileged to have seven prior titles published by Johns Hopkins, we think we have completed one this time that even our late parents would have enjoyed, and thus we dedicate the book to Reverend Morrill and Jennyvee Martin and Gertrude and Murry Samels with all the love and respect that children can offer.

The New American College Town

PART I

DEVELOPING A NEW DEFINITION OF COLLEGE TOWNS

CHAPTER 1

The New American College Town

Twenty Characteristics

JAMES MARTIN AND JAMES E. SAMELS

More than being a study of particular college towns, this is a book about the ideas that are shaping and driving those places. Contributors have been asked to define what an American "college town" currently is and what it will become a generation from now when many current students will be leading its higher education institutions. In conducting our research, we found few books on college towns past or present, and nothing with the goals of this volume. As we completed the book prior to this one, *Consolidating Colleges and Merging Universities: New Strategies for Higher Education Leaders*, we noted how often college and university consolidations, mergers, and partnerships implicated local communities.

Gradually, we began to question what a college town is now in America, in what ways it has moved on from prior stereotypes, and how current university and college leaders are reshaping local relationships to accomplish expanded missions and market shares. Rather than focus on the traditional models of Ann Arbor, Palo Alto, and Cambridge, we spent a good portion of the past three years in conversations with leaders in places as disparate as Las Vegas, Jersey City, and Albion, Michigan, to record what the new American college town is becoming.

Traditionally, Americans have viewed college towns as one of three principal kinds or a combination of the three. The first is a campus closely connected to a city or town and within its boundaries. In the second, the campus "is located next to a city or town but remains somewhat separate from it."[1] In the view of architect William Rawn, Yale would be an example of the first type, and the University of Virginia, on the edge of Charlottesville, of the second. Finally, perhaps the most common type of college town is one in which the college or university may be near a locality yet essentially unconnected to it. Duke and Rice Universities are offered by Rawn as examples of this model.[2] This book will comment on all three types, but its focus will be on cities and towns not traditionally viewed as college towns but which incorporate many of the recent characteristics outlined in this chapter. We detail in the following section five drivers now shaping new college town identities, whether from the perspective of a current student, a recent graduate, or a long-term local employer. We will consider the views and expectations of presidents, mayors, city planners, state legislators, and scores of alumni, along with current or former leaders of the International Town & Gown Association, the Association for the Study of Higher Education, the Council of Christian Colleges and Universities, and NASPA: Student Affairs Professionals in Higher Education, among others, regarding new definitions of the familiar phrase, "college town."

FIVE DRIVERS SHAPING THE NEW AMERICAN COLLEGE TOWN

1. New college towns stimulate continuous innovation throughout their communities.

In their book *The Smartest Places on Earth: Why Rustbelts Are the Emerging Hotspots of Global Innovation*, Antoine van Agtmael and Fred Bakker explain that more innovation in society today is bottom-up than is top-down, and it occurs in "proliferating brainbelts where academia and business share brainpower and are hard at work to invent and design the smart products that address the challenges of the twenty-first century." In the authors' view, brainbelt initiatives that "support the continuous process of innovation" through grants, new technologies, teamwork, and collaboration are the most effective.[3] When translated into a college town context, continuous innovation thus becomes a driver that attracts new students and their parents, young faculty starting their careers, and employers seeking a strategically competitive territory in which to expand.

Similarly, the *Wall Street Journal* observed that college towns can provide a "steady source of employment, improved nimbleness of the local workforce, and [help] attract new businesses."[4] This point is confirmed by a Brookings Institution urban specialist who notes that "better educated places with colleges tend to be more productive and more able to shift out of declining industries and into growing ones. Ultimately, cities survive by continually adapting their economies to new technologies, and colleges are central to that."[5] Continuous local innovation, and skillful public interest campaigns advertising it, acts as a lever in both attracting new students and retaining recent graduates with enhanced career opportunities and quality of life.

Susan Henderson, president of New Jersey City University (NJCU), comments specifically on the benefits of continuous innovation for her university in its Jersey City setting (see chapter 8). "The minute NJCU slows its rate of innovation across the curriculum," she says, "it loses ground nationally, regionally, and even among the seven higher education institutions in its own Jersey City."[6]

2. New college towns intentionally redesign and advertise themselves as education networks.

Driven perhaps most of all by the iPhone, with its combination of mobility, power, and personalization as well as a ceaselessly growing number of apps, campus and civic leaders are beginning to treat their towns as flexible, evolving networks of educational resources in which faculty, administrators, students, alumni, and employers work together in conducting both daily business and long-term planning.[7]

As a result, as new graduates form the core of the workforce, many of them are finding it easier to remain in the local community, discovering a steady stream of education, civic, and lifestyle benefits in their college towns and regions as they transition from undergraduates to young professionals. For example, 93 percent of Millennials seek lifelong learning and are willing to spend their own time and resources on it, and 50 percent of them search for positions near their current geographic location.[8] In turn, the higher education and civic leaders of college towns are learning it is in their interest to seek to retain as many of these new workers as they can through low-cost continuing education programs and ongoing career advising. Reid Hoffman, cofounder of LinkedIn, believes that these new graduates are entering what he describes as the "Networked Age," an

Five Drivers Shaping New College Towns

1. New college towns stimulate continuous innovation throughout their communities.
2. New college towns intentionally redesign and advertise themselves as education networks.
3. New college towns establish, maintain, and enhance a distinct *brand*.
4. New college towns engage in collaborative, systematic, continuous planning cycles.
5. New college towns view themselves as powerful ideas and experiences as well as physical places.

era when "*what* you know—information—is framed by *who* you know—relationships." Thus, these networks "surface and accelerate what's most relevant to know."[9]

Eugene Zdziarski, vice president of student affairs at DePaul University in Chicago and author of chapter 15, notes the various ways that DePaul now more intentionally presents itself as a social media hub and network of connections within an expanded college town identity: "Today's generation of students is intricately connected to social media for news and events both inside our campus environment and its surrounding community. This connection, a kind of mobile college town, if you will, continues after they finish their degrees with us."[10] Phillip DiChiara, author of chapter 18 and for two decades the managing director of the Boston Consortium, adds, "Social media encourages virtual linkages for students, and faculty, that transcend geography, yet there clearly remains both an emotional and psychic necessity for face-to-face contact on a reasonable and regular basis."[11]

These new education networks are not limited to a single locality. In South Florida, city planners and higher education leaders have joined forces in what is now called the Consortium of Colleges on the Creative Coast. Located in Manatee and Sarasota Counties, six institutions, including the State College of Florida, the New College of Florida, and Eckerd College, have committed to "turn the area into a destination for higher education, facilitate collaboration among roughly 520 full-time faculty . . . and connect students to more employers." This initiative is viewed as a "collective branding" of that sector of Florida in which faculty work together on research, employers post jobs on a common portal, and students can participate in activities on all campuses in a "multi-versity environment with over 18,000 students."[12]

3. New college towns establish, maintain, and enhance a distinct *brand*. In 2017, the *Wall Street Journal* reported a 6 percent increase in in the number of college closures from 2015–16 to 2016–17 with the percentage threatening to accelerate rather than plateau or decline. As the reporter observed, "The broad decline lends credence to those who have long argued that higher education is ripe for a period of intense change."[13] Against this backdrop of potential decline, higher education administrators and strategic planners are realizing the value in forming lifelong education networks and brain hubs. One of the most effective vehicles for accomplishing this goal is the development of a trusted college town *brand*. As noted previously, this brand may be developed by multiple colleges and universities with a common goal to create a newly defined "destination" for higher education that goes well beyond classroom instruction and student activities.

Brands can powerfully attract new students and new businesses, and creating one now informs many campus-community relationships. As one observer notes, "The *theme* has become the central motif of contemporary town planning. To attract people to live in a new town there has to be a big idea, a brand, something that makes that city different, better, from everywhere else. . . . The last big push to redefine the city came after the Second World War. Britain had Milton Keynes . . . the U.S. had Las Vegas."[14] In chapter 16 of this book the head of the Association for the Study of Higher Education (ASHE) examines the relationship between Las Vegas and its higher education institutions over the past twenty years and explores the power of a fresh brand to transform lingering perceptions.

When it comes to developing a brand, college towns have natural advantages in terms of salary levels, continuing-education opportunities, career development pathways, and lifestyle choices, yet the brand still needs to be authentic in order to survive. Petter Nylander, CEO of Universum Communications, which describes itself as "the global leader in employer branding," observes, "The brand needs to be real and firmly established throughout the organization: current employees need to believe in its authenticity because even a few negative comments . . . can quickly spread and destroy years of persistent brand-building."[15]

The importance of a clearly defined, yet flexible brand has become another student and faculty recruitment tool for many college and university presidents. Before Kevin Drumm became president of SUNY (State University of New York) Broome Community College, he served as president of the Northern Wyoming Community College District. At both locations, he has experienced the power of brand development in his college towns. Drumm believes the best way a president can employ this tool is through sustained economic development projects. "The concept of branding a college town for economic development purposes," he argues, "has assumed greater value in recent years as community colleges in struggling regions focus more pointedly on economic development. For towns hosting community colleges in Wyoming, for instance, with no other higher education institution for 150 miles in any direction, it is the community college that builds the brand while helping to facilitate economic development. The state of New York, however, has more colleges and universities than any other state. In Binghamton, it is thus wiser for our community college to partner with multiple universities and colleges to achieve educational and economic priorities. The key in both states is to build the brand strategically."[16]

4. New college towns engage in collaborative, systematic, continuous planning cycles.

Wim Wiewel, author of chapter 3 in this volume and of *The University as Urban Developer: Case Studies and Analysis*, notes, "The nature of university-community relations appears to have improved over the past fifty years in terms of ethical criteria and principles of fairness and transparency. But . . . [r]elations between universities and city governments tend to be project- or task-oriented, episodic, and subject to political and personal vagaries. Given the importance of universities to their cities, and the importance of local government to university projects, it would make sense for both to engage in more systematic, continuous, and comprehensive joint-planning."[17]

Whether they are large or small, however, as Wiewel notes, college and university planning projects often take "considerably" longer to complete than private commercial projects because of the "multiple stakeholders involved, their high expectations of the university, and the longer time line for arranging financing."[18] As higher education becomes more "financialized"—that is, as "financial institutions and markets gain influence" over campus operations—and as students "are encouraged to think more like consumers, demanding returns on their investment," it is increasingly wise to reserve spaces for both undergraduates and faculty members on planning teams that engage the external community and to diligently focus, to the degree feasible, on joint planning for academic quality and student success.[19]

Tracee Reiser, former associate dean of community learning and partnerships at Connecticut College and a twenty-year veteran of town-gown planning projects with the city of New London, acknowledges the benefits in maintaining planning exercises as a multiyear commitment: "In my years at the College, continuous planning has allowed our leadership team to demonstrate that the institution is a committed partner and an 'anchor' for the city. Over time, it became clear to both sides that the relationship was not simply about one or two educational initiatives but rather was grounded more deeply in an intentional joint mission to strengthen New London, which, in turn, advanced Connecticut College."[20]

5. New college towns view themselves as powerful ideas and experiences as well as physical places.

In identifying a final driver, we observe that the idea of a college town has grown in sophistication over the past generation so that it no longer depends solely on a college or university within its city limits. With the emergence of concepts such as education networks, brain hubs, lifestyle

What is one way that college towns have changed over the past twenty-five years?
Mayors and civic leaders have become more creative and assertive in reaching out to college and university presidents for services, support, and engagement. Savvy presidents prepare for this appeal from town leaders and respond in ways that benefit both sides.

destinations, and brand identities, a growing number of college towns are defining themselves not only as physical localities and their academic infrastructures but also as *experiences*. As Michael Winstanley, principal of Michael Winstanley Architects and Planners in Alexandria, Virginia, explains, college towns are becoming something intentionally more complex and more influential than a traditional town-gown relationship usually allows for. "Academic deans and provosts," he told us, "are generally bred in cloistered campuses and when working with them on the new American campus we must drag them outside the campus walls into the sunlight to see the benefits of learning in an unstructured world."[21]

Looking to the future, more college towns will develop and maintain an evolving profile via technology combined with expanded opportunities for professional growth and development on site. Over time, this new college town *experience* will increasingly shape its buildings and infrastructure. In what follows, we identify twenty characteristics of a new model for American college towns.

THE NEW AMERICAN COLLEGE TOWN

We now present what the interviews, conversations, and other research we conducted reveal as the main features of new college towns in America. Not all twenty of these elements are found in every town or on every campus profile, nor are they entirely new attributes. Rather, they reflect new ways to think about places and spaces by leaders who seek to leverage their resources and capitalize on each form of collaboration. Described here are the cities and towns, for example, that have earned innovative grants in partnership with their college or university, or that have earned recognition from the International Town & Gown Association for bringing undergraduates into civic leadership roles via community service, or that have earned praise from the Society of College and University

Planners for their success in completing a major civic master plan. While not all college towns will reflect all of these characteristics, the strongest college towns will exhibit the most.

1. A walkable downtown presence. College town leaders now pay attention to their downtown presence the way prospective students, their parents, and business leaders scouting for new branch sites do. A walkable downtown focuses not simply on youth-focused retail options and boutique restaurants but also on more transformative elements such as mixed-rate housing opportunities and the scope of public transportation. While Saratoga, New York, is noted for having achieved a diverse, engaging downtown presence for Skidmore students, we offer Duluth, Minnesota, and Sacramento, California, as additional examples of cities that host colleges and universities—Lake Superior College and University of the Pacific, Sacramento Campus—and that have developed identities embracing higher education without becoming stereotyped or confined by it.

2. Ongoing capitalization. We have learned to follow the money and identify towns and cities that go beyond traditional levels of shared resources and collaboration with local universities and colleges. Some noteworthy cases are found far from urban centers and in states not always recognized for capitalization. In 2014 Fort Kent, Maine, home to a campus of the University of Maine, a place just about as far north as one can travel in New England without crossing into Canada, was certified as a "Business-Friendly Community" due to its commitment to "building and maintaining a strong economic base" by taking "proactive steps" with "streamlined regulations" to become a better partner with private industry and higher education.[22]

3. Commitment to codevelopment. Colby College, several hours south of Fort Kent in central Maine, purchased five downtown Waterville properties and began developing "a Main Street hotel and mixed use development, including student apartments," as well as a regional center for CGI, a Montreal-based technology company that promised 200 new jobs to the town of 16,000 residents. As one native exclaimed, "It's like Waterville hit the lottery." In an innovative, strategic codevelopment initiative, the college and the Alfond Foundation have pledged $10 million each toward the project to date. The project will also incorporate a downtown gallery of the Colby College Museum of Art, a public restaurant, and a bar. The concept reflects the belief of Colby president David Greene and other leaders that Waterville was a small but tremendously underleveraged city with "three colleges, two hospitals, terrific community arts programming, the world-class Colby College Museum of Art, and an active and determined business community." This initiative acknowledges both that Waterville needed an "economic jumpstart" and that the college would be solidifying a long and prosperous future by codeveloping significant improvements to its own college town.[23]

In a second example of innovative codevelopment, SUNY Morrisville worked with two business partners, Empire Farmstead Brewery and K16 Corporation, to launch SUNY Tax-Free Areas to Revitalize and Transform Upstate New York (START-UP NY). "As the college implements its plans for a new brewing studies program," a college press release announced, it "will work directly with Empire to manage the facility and educate students with first-hand practical business experience in production brewing." In addition, "K16 will provide educational technology innovations based on the needs of schools using Morrisville's computer technology and marketing students to help write the codes for the products and then marketing the products."[24]

4. Public infrastructure investment. The Science and Resilience Institute at Jamaica Bay, a research consortium led by the City University of New York, was awarded a $3.6 million grant in 2014 "to support research projects that will advance knowledge of resilience in urban coastal ecosystems" following the devastation of Hurricane Sandy. This is a nationally recognized example of town-gown infrastructure investment, but other, smaller-scale examples in many states abound that are just as noteworthy.

Twenty Characteristics of New Colleges Towns

1. A walkable downtown presence
2. Ongoing capitalization
3. Commitment to codevelopment
4. Public infrastructure investment
5. Cultural diversity
6. Hospitals and health care access
7. Technology and wireless infrastructure
8. Access to rivers and renewable energy
9. Public transportation and rail linkage
10. Mill redevelopment and reuse
11. Local newspaper
12. Resource-sharing consortia
13. Campus curb appeal
14. Youth fitness programs and athletic leagues
15. Major and minor league professional sports teams
16. Proximate military base
17. Access to golf and other leisure activities
18. Academic superstore
19. Hotel codevelopment and branding
20. Craft and microbreweries

In 2014 Northern Essex Community College opened the Allied Health and Technology Center in Lawrence, Massachusetts, supported by $24 million from a state higher education bond, $1 million from the Technical Training Foundation (founded by Ibrahim El-Hefni, for whom the center is named), $100,000 from Trinity Emergency Medical Services, and contributions from other individuals, companies, and foundations.[25] In 2016 a $900,000 city center and sidewalk enhancement project was completed that, as Northern Essex president Lane Glenn observed, "helps to create a safe and attractive connection between the college campus and the shops and businesses on Essex Street," forming "another important step in the ongoing effort to improve both the student and the consumer experience in downtown Lawrence."[26]

5. Cultural diversity. Cultural inclusivity is an increasing marker of new college towns as evidenced by the interest that the Princeton Review's guide *The 382 Best Colleges* now takes in both effective town-gown relationships and their cultural aspects.[27] In 2018, the Princeton Review ranked Loyola University New Orleans as the number-one higher education institution in the nation for "Town-Gown Relations," and one of the reasons was Loyola's appearance on "the nation's Top 20 Lists for cultural inclusivity, best college newspaper, and best quality of life." As Princeton Review's editor-in-chief, Rob Franek, explains, "We picked 384 'best' colleges for our book primarily for their outstanding academics . . . however, we know applicants need far more than academic rating or ranking to find the college that will be best for them."[28] A Loyola student added, "We all come from different backgrounds, different economic upbringings, different cultures, but yet we all come together at Loyola in unity and harmony. Everyone at Loyola has their own story, and my university gives many chances for us to share them."[29]

Houston, Texas, is a multicultural city and home to the Lone Star Community College System, which at various points in its history has claimed to be, with 95,000 total students, the fastest-growing community college system in the United States. This has placed both the city and the college on the front edge of addressing issues raised by diverse populations. To demonstrate its awareness of Houston's growing identity as a college town, in 2015 Lone Star hosted the Diversity Leadership Conference for high school students across Greater Houston. The conference's aim was to provide attendees with a "better understanding of what cultural competency means" and "the issues we [face] as a nation" as students "navigate through the college process." Sessions included topics such as "How to Be a Leader, Healthy Relationships, Mass Media and Culture, [and] Cultural Identity."[30]

6. Hospitals and health care access. As more colleges are coming to view themselves as hubs of lifelong learning and as attentive to quality of life concerns across the spectrum, it is natural for rising numbers of citizens at the end of their careers to choose these same towns as destinations because of their proximity to hospitals and varieties of health care support. When *Forbes* magazine asked in 2014, "Should you retire to a college town?" the answer was simple for many readers. In Asheville, North Carolina, as one example cited in the article, "college towns typically offer other important advantages besides access to classes and cultural events. For one, many have world-class teaching hospitals that draw top medical talent." This was combined with the fact that "housing prices in some college towns like Asheville can be surprisingly affordable."[31] Wherever the town is located, hospitals and other health care facilities provide the major share of the clinical education for medical students and serve as anchors for new models of college towns.

7. Technology and wireless infrastructure. Today, students often do not take their laptops to class, much less to the campus library, to complete term papers or other homework because of the availability of mobile apps. New wireless technologies and their ceaselessly expanding connectivity are changing campus life and, in fact, causing planners to reimagine what a "campus" is becoming. Similarly, this kind of thinking is influencing what students and young professionals believe a "college town" should be. As one social media journalist recently wrote, "There's a new wireless standard in town, and it is set to revolutionize what colleges can do with their networks and the speed at which students can burn through online media."[32] The writer was describing the fifth generation of wireless networking standards that Cisco and others have been preparing for campuses to adopt in order to utilize the entire Wi-Fi spectrum more efficiently when, in the future, connected devices will dominate networks.

It remains safe to assume that the greatest wireless connectivity occurs on and around campuses in densely populated urban areas, yet this also is a lingering stereotype about both college towns and small towns in general. As one Illinois reporter described it, "Small towns move at the rate of horse and buggy rather than high speed internet, and therefore tend to reside on the wrong side of the digital divide. However, digital divides are not fixed or homogeneous, and small towns can surprise you." He describes Greenville, Illinois, with barely seven thousand citizens, as the kind of town in which one simply goes "to the bathroom on the way from St. Louis toward Indianapolis." Yet, in the late 1990s, Greenville College, a small, local Christian liberal arts school, skipped building heavy technology infrastructure altogether at a time when other colleges were doing so—Greenville did not come close to having the financial resources—and instead "jumped right to wireless." In doing so, Greenville College was, according to the *St. Louis Post Dispatch*, the first campus in the nation to install wireless internet. In the view of the college's IT director, Greenville installed wireless across the entire campus for the cost of placing a port in every room.[33] From its town-gown perspective, the college led the way, given that the technology infrastructure of the town of Greenville was years behind it and without a master plan.

8. Access to rivers and renewable energy. River access for a college town is a typically overlooked advantage. River proximity provides college towns like Binghamton, New York, and Lowell, Massachusetts, with three-season ecotourism opportunities, and even more important, their rivers offer renewable energy sources. The ability to place a turbine in a river basin can produce large-scale renewable energy in places where it might easily link with the region's power grid.

Although this technology is still comparatively untested, there were more than 120 applicants to implement such projects in 2011. Turbines do not need dams and do not present many of the challenges that accompany one, yet because water possesses much "greater density than air and [its] flows are more constant than wind, underwater turbines can deliver much more energy than wind turbines."[34] It seems only a matter of time before one or more joint exploration committees from other universities near fast-flowing rivers and their local civic leadership seriously explore this energy-producing—and -saving—option.

9. Public transportation and rail linkage. While this factor may mean little to some traditional, campus-based undergraduates, there are new generations of undergraduate and graduate students for whom public transportation and rail access make a critical difference in completing their degree programs and then remaining local to pursue professional opportunities. Urban planner Shlomo Angel, in his book *Planet of Cities*, shows that cities and towns of the future are more likely to require "the development of transport networks that increase the connectivity of the city as a whole rather than the connectivity of the city [simply] to its center." Interestingly, Angel also notes that the density of cities, perhaps surprisingly to some town-gown planners, has "been in persistent decline for a century or more, and we can expect [it] to continue to decline as long as incomes increase and transport remains relatively inexpensive."[35]

As *Washington Post* columnist George Will observed in a forum titled "Responding to the Change in How Infrastructure Is Developed": "Most of America's commutes are not from the suburbs into . . . cities; they are from one suburb to another, changing all of our infrastructure assumptions."[36]

With the density of many aging cities decreasing and with more current students calling for affordable public transportation options, college town planners will need to engage with city transport administrators more systematically over time to devise sustainable models of success.

10. Mill redevelopment and reuse. Similar to river and rail access, mill development is an overlooked, sometimes initially unattractive option for college town planners, even though grants and state and federal funding continue to be available for innovative reuse. Compared to other regions, New England has a major share of unused mill properties. A cursory look across the region's six states reveals properties available for college or university development in almost every one, including the Great Northern Paper Mill in Millinocket, Maine, the Amoskeag Mill in Manchester, New Hampshire, the Lorraine Mills in Pawtucket, Rhode Island, and the Fairfield Hills Psychiatric Hospital in Newtown, Connecticut. All four of these are currently being redeveloped, and some are already hosting college programs. In fact, in Lawrence and Lowell, Massachusetts, Norther Essex Community College has established the Mill Cities Leadership Institute to "boost entrepreneurship" and build a network of socially responsible leaders.[37]

In Easton, Pennsylvania, Lafayette College is implementing its "College Travelways Improvement Plan" to ensure pedestrian safety and streamline transportation from the campus to downtown. In 2017 the college was awarded a $1.1 million grant from Pennsylvania's Commonwealth Financing Authority for the first phase of the project. In addition, the city of Easton received $250,000 from the state's Greenways, Trails, and Recreation Program to erect "a pedestrian bridge connecting Lafayette's Karl Stirner Arts Trail to the Simon Silk Mill."[38]

11. Local newspaper. Newspapers are not a new college town indicator because they are read faithfully, or even periodically, by current students. Mobile phones and their apps provide news to students today. Rather, newspapers constitute one of the foundational characteristics of a new college town for two reasons. First, a local or even regional newspaper provides a historical record of the town, its population, and its prior collaboration with its resident university or college. Second, the paper provides a key voice in shaping the community's self-image and interest in future town-gown partnerships.

Thus, whether it is the *Las Vegas Sun* acknowledging, "UNLV has designs on a more collegiate feel," or the *Grafton News* in Massachusetts—population 17,700—proclaiming, "Grafton hopes to become a College-town," newspapers reflect and shape public opinion regarding town-gown initiatives more effectively than almost any other vehicle.[39]

The Ten Highest-Ranked College Towns by Analysts at *WalletHub*, 2018

To produce the following ranking, analysts compared 415 small, medium, and large U.S. cities with college student populations of 7,500 or more. Then, they evaluated each city based on twenty-eight factors across three categories: "wallet friendliness," "social environment," and "academic and economic opportunities." To evaluate each factor, analysts used a range of data, including those from such federal sources as the U.S. Census Bureau and Bureau of Labor Statistics as well as travel websites like TripAdvisor and Yelp.

1. Ann Arbor, Michigan
2. Orlando, Florida
3. Rexburg, Idaho
4. Provo, Utah
5. Austin, Texas
6. Las Vegas, Nevada
7. Scottsdale, Arizona
8. West Lafayette, Indiana
9. Tampa, Florida
10. San Diego, California

Source: Bernardo, "2018's Best College Towns & Cities in America."

12. Resource-sharing consortia. The concept of a consortium, discussed in more detail in several other chapters, is cited here simply to emphasize the benefits of partnerships for both town and campus planners. In 2013, for example, SUNY Canton and SUNY Potsdam, two colleges located in remote northern regions of New York State, completed a memorandum of understanding (MOU) that that defined "the scope of collaborative ventures in three key areas: shared services, shared purchases, and shared academic programs." The MOU's goal is to make both campuses function more efficiently while reducing overall costs. Accordingly, several positions would be shared between the two campuses, including human resources officer, vice president of business affairs, chief of police, and director of environmental health and safety. Several of these positions, including policy, environmental health and safety, and business affairs would have direct influence on relations with the campuses' external communities.[40]

In a Michigan-based example of resource sharing with direct impact on town-gown relationships, Macomb Community College and Wayne State University, with funding from the National Science Foundation, created in 2014 the Center for Advanced Automotive Technology to provide educational opportunities "to meet the expanding workforce needs of the automotive industry in advanced automotive technology including materials lightweighting, automated and connected vehicles, and vehicle electrification."[41]

13. Campus curb appeal. As distinct from a walkable downtown presence, curb appeal reflects the impact a campus makes visually during both first and return visits. An entire cohort of campuses with classic natural settings come to mind when curb appeal is mentioned, such as Santa Clara University, the University of the Pacific's main campus in Stockton, and Middlebury College in Vermont. But the number of visually gifted campuses of this kind is small out of the four thousand higher education institutions across the nation. The new kind of curb appeal we are citing here can be viewed on those campuses that were not given the natural resources or financial endowments to achieve memorable photo opportunities. Two examples can be found in rural Nevada and an industrial section of California.

Nevada's Great Basin College enrolls 3,800 students on campuses that stretch across 86,500 square miles, two time zones, and ten counties. The college's recruitment area encompasses parts of Arizona, Oregon, Idaho, Utah, and California, while its main campus in Elko was "transformed into a high desert oasis" between 2008 and 2018 with construction of a "landmark bell tower, pristine waterway, outdoor amphitheater, [and] glass solarium," all completed through a $4.5 million grant awarded from the Donald W. Reynolds Foundation.[42]

In Cupertino, California, De Anza College was founded in 1967 on the site of a former winery and since then has "contributed significantly to the growth of Cupertino from a small town to an industrial city."[43] Besides maintaining a museum of art and a visual and performing arts center, De Anza also holds a monthly flea market in its parking lot. These two institutions reflect a flexible approach to traditional concepts of curb appeal, as they work creatively with the physical and financial resources they have to define the visual aspects of the campus experience.

14. Youth fitness programs and athletic leagues. Sports leagues and recreational facilities open to the youth of the entire community signal parental and civic commitments that form another new college town characteristic. The "50 Fittest College Towns in America" and the more specialized "Best Minor League Baseball Towns" (discussed more fully in the following entry) are well-known annual rankings. Blacksburg, Virginia—home of Virginia Polytechnic Institute (VPI) and ranked the third fittest college town in the country in 2016—listed "personal training, dance and gymnastics lessons, a wellness program, and [youth] fitness classes" as available through VPI's Department of Recreational Sports.

On the other coast, the University of California at Davis offered "a climbing wall, intramural sports, aquatics, club sports, and youth programs," and Coral Gables, Florida, home to the University of Miami and several other colleges, advertised "a unique set of fitness activities for the whole family," including kite surfing, hiking, and wellness education.[44]

15. Major and minor league professional sports teams. College towns that host a major or minor league sports team gain multiple long-term advantages, including expanded opportunities to secure philanthropic support, greater numbers of internship opportunities, and heightened community engagement. In Charlotte, North Carolina, the Charlotte Checkers, a minor league hockey team, provide annual internships in community relations, corporate partnerships, marketing, and game operations.[45] Johnson & Wales University, with a campus located in Charlotte, actively promotes these opportunities to students in its Sports Entertainment and Event Management program.

In 2016 Round Rock, Texas, home of the Round Rock Express minor league baseball team (which achieved fewer wins than losses that year) was ranked for the second year in a row as the nation's best minor league baseball town when judged by measures such as average discretionary income, violent crime rate, unemployment rate, and general "game day experience."[46] Perhaps unsurprisingly, there are five colleges and universities within nine miles of Round Rock's center and five more within an additional five-mile radius.[47] Round Rock benefits from this cluster of higher education institutions, and over time its civic leaders have increasingly begun to leverage these local resources.

16. Proximate military base. As the federal government reduces the size of the nation's force of active-duty soldiers, military bases are becoming a new and affordable housing choice for the general public. Formerly open only to military retirees, reservists, or federal civilian employees, bases in Delaware, Maryland, Kansas, Louisiana, Arizona, and Washington are now being occupied by families who seek safety, security, and recreational facilities for their children.[48] An increasing number of colleges and universities are advertising the benefits of proximity to a military site.

A 2014 article entitled "Best Military Bases to Retire Near" mentioned four bases: Tinker Air Force Base in Oklahoma, Fort Carson and Peterson Air Force Base in Colorado, Fort Hood in Texas, and the Norfolk Naval Station in Virginia. In every instance, the military base was marketed as being near a college or university. For those at Tinker Air Force Base "interested in furthering their education, there's the local University of Oklahoma," and for those who might be interested at Norfolk Naval Station,

The Ten Lowest-Ranked College Towns by Analysts at *WalletHub*, 2018

To produce the ranking, analysts compared 415 small, medium, and large U.S. cities with college student populations of 7,500 or more. Then, they evaluated each city based on twenty-eight factors across three categories: "wallet friendliness," "social environment," and "academic and economic opportunities." To evaluate each factor, analysts used a range of data, including from such federal sources as the U.S. Census Bureau and Bureau of Labor Statistics as well as travel websites like TripAdvisor and Yelp.

406. New Rochelle, New York
407. East Los Angeles, California
408. Brookline, Massachusetts
409. Shreveport, Louisiana
410. Kendall, Florida
411. Bridgeport, Connecticut
412. Newton, Massachusetts
413. Arlington, Virginia
414. Silver Spring, Maryland
415. Germantown, Maryland

Source: Bernardo, "2018's Best College Towns & Cities in America."

"the College of William and Mary, Old Dominion University, and Hampton University are nearby."[49] In light of the potential contributions to a college town's financial stability and population base, it seems more than likely over the next decade that more universities and colleges will begin advertising the advantages of a branch campus on a military base.

17. Access to golf and other leisure activities. As the author of "Golf College Towns" notes about North and South Carolina, as examples, "Many retirees are giving in to the pull of the college campus, mindful that these institutions are magnets for concerts . . . top sporting contests, [and] comprehensive libraries. . . . Luckily for golfers, some of the most highly rated golf communities in the Carolinas are located just a few miles from campus."[50] And, as the publisher of *Golf Course Home* observes in his article "Get Smart! College Towns near Amenity Communities": "We present communities in Florida and North and South Carolina that are close to college towns. Here you can regain that excitement for learning and be close to future leaders and ideas that will shape the world."[51]

As with a nearby military base, a local golf course, even one of renown, has not yet moved to the front of college town strategic planning and marketing, in part because it is of far greater importance to grandparents than undergraduates, but this is again not so much the point as is the reality that golf courses and other leisure activities have become elements of the broader conversation for all planners about what makes a college town meaningful and worth returning to and calling home.

18. Academic superstore. Over the past two decades, college and university bookstores have been transformed into heavily accessed cultural centers, in some instances arguably as important to a small or medium-sized town as the institution itself. They have become sites not only for literary readings but also for recitals, colloquia, committee meetings, and, of course, book clubs. Used and rare book stores have long been associated with college towns, but it seems unlikely that future town-gown relationships will draw the bulk of their cultural capital simply from a single independent bookshop, though stores such as these maintain local followings and enrich their local environment.

Rather, college towns of the future will also invest in the destination "academic superstores" designed by Barnes & Noble. Bookstores of this scope focus not simply on being an individual campus vendor but also on serving as a partner to local enterprises in order to "drive student success and deliver unmatched experience that supports strong revenue growth and continuous innovation."[52] Barnes & Noble wants each of its stores to serve as "the center of the community and appeal to other consumers, not just the students," by offering such options as larger cafés, clothing sections, and cosmetics counters.[53] Barnes & Noble believes that as it transitions on a major scale from being a bookstore to offering a lifestyle brand, customers will follow and towns (and cities) will benefit.

19. Hotel codevelopment and branding. *The Wall Street Journal* reported in the summer of 2018 that one of the fastest-growing trends in the lodging industry was the development of hotels on or near college and university campuses. As an adjunct professor at New York University's Hospitality and Tourism Center observed, "It used to be universities sending out customer proposals, but that's almost disappeared as a phenomenon. Now it's real estate developers and hotel brands seeking out universities."[54] Besides connecting, not surprisingly, with major universities like Michigan and Clemson, new corporate-college partnerships have also spread to boutique locations like Hamilton, New York, and Sewanee, Tennessee, where Colgate University and the University of the South, respectively, have opened hotels with the Charlestowne Hotels Corporation and have even taken ownership of the Colgate Inn and the Sewanee Inn.

Graduate Hotels, another boutique lodging company, has raised $1.5 billion since 2014 for its "college hotels" and now operates twelve across the country. The company is already planning to open eight more of this type by the end of 2020 and to be in "100 markets in the next 10 years."[55] Clearly, town-gown planners on both sides have noted that the college hotel market is less vulnerable to fluctuations in the nation's economy, and as Michael Tall, president and CEO of Charlestowne acknowledges, "there's always going to be visitation to the markets. You might as well even use [a stay at a hotel] as a sales pitch for the university."[56]

20. Craft and microbreweries. Although craft breweries and microbreweries may have different definitions in terms of annual brewing capacities and production techniques, to the population of a college town they are synonymous and rapidly growing in popularity, number, and economic impact. According to the Brewers Association, the craft brewing industry contributed "$55.7 billion to the U.S. economy" in 2014 and "provided more than 424,000 jobs."[57] Many of these breweries are purposefully located in or near a college town and have themselves become brand destinations for noncollege consumers.[58] In New York State alone, there are more than eight hundred breweries, and colleges like SUNY Cobleskill, SUNY Morrisville, and Schenectady County Community College are developing or now offering programs in brewing and fermentation.

A single internet search reveals a lengthy list of articles with titles like "Ten Awesome Breweries in College Towns" and "The 11 Best Breweries in College Towns across America." Examples range geographically from Crow Peak Brewing near Black Hills State University in Spearfish, South Dakota, to BLDG8 Brewing down the street from Smith College in Northampton, Massachusetts.[59] Across the country, it has become a fact of life for town-gown planners that breweries, bookstores, and pop-up shops and restaurants are helping to shape the college towns' brand for both incoming students and returning alumni.

CONCLUSION: WHAT MAKES A COLLEGE TOWN *NEW*?

In this chapter, we have described the "new" American college town both as a traditional place and as a set of emerging ideas and concepts not bound by campus infrastructure or undergraduate activities. Increasingly, college town leaders, on and off campus, plan for lifelong experiences that respect campus life and traditions while also moving beyond them. A college town is deemed new because it maintains a focus not simply on providing four quality years for each matriculant but also on keeping talented students engaged in its local life as young professionals after graduation. A reflection of this commitment is found in articles like "The 50 Best College Towns to Live in Forever," the author of which opens candidly: "College towns are great for more than just the time while you are in school. Many of them have a thriving economy and culture that make them perfect for a long-term commitment to the area. . . . There are many cities and towns across the country that [now] strive to retain their alumni."[60] Also mentioned are factors such as neighborhood solidarity, school excellence, and overall quality of life.

The chapters that follow highlight the capacity of civic and campus administrators to connect continuously and innovatively through social media with alumni, neighbors, and local business leaders. We point out in closing, however, that for all of their technological and social-media savvy, leaders on both sides will need to provide more than a stylish online identity and enhanced interactivity. This is because today's students are "digital content connoisseurs [and] mobile natives. They aren't loyal to the big technology giants such as Facebook or Microsoft . . . [and] are the harshest critics and earliest adopters of new consumer apps."[61] These students already spend up to *nine* hours per day using media, according to Common Sense Media, and this heavy use is also gradually producing, across an entire generation, heightened levels of anxiety, depression, and sleep deprivation.[62] Thus, it is important for those building healthy, broad-based, town-gown partnerships to remember that within this great digital migration "face-to-face contact in education, medicine, and child care has become a luxury commodity. As a fundamental human need, it should remain accessible to all."[63] Going forward, new American college towns will effectively balance their mobile, media-driven identities with authentic reasons to return, remain, and thrive—in person—as contributors to a model of lifelong community.

CHAPTER 2

Fostering an Effective Town-Gown Relationship

Eight Leading Practices from the International Town & Gown Association

MICHAEL FOX AND BETH BAGWELL

The town and gown concept remains an ideal model for identifying and addressing the span of community issues associated with the annual influx of students to our college town communities. The town-gown relationship is certainly not new, as higher education and the gathering of larger and larger numbers of 18- to 25-year-old students have existed since the creation of the university centuries ago. Given such a long history of the relationship between students and the communities where they gather to live, learn, and mature, one might think that college and civic leaders would have recognized the realities of the situation and that much attention and deliberative planning and governance would have been put in place to avoid conflicts while maintaining a balance between traditional residents and the newly arrived students. Sadly, the historical record shows that many university and community leaders have traditionally waited until there was a crisis and significant media and public attention before addressing, or "solving" the problem, often with draconian local ordinances and increased police enforcement. In some cases, the "solution" reflects a direct conflict between representatives of the "town" and those of the "gown," the local university administration and its student population.[1]

The main objective of this chapter is to provide college, university, and community leaders with the resources they need to create a successful blueprint for the new American college town-gown relationship. Leaders of the International Town & Gown Association (ITGA) have identified four critical questions over the past decade that constitute a starting point for effective campus-community collaboration: (1) How engaged is your community with the relationship between the municipal government leaders and the leadership of the university and its students, staff, and faculty? (2) How important is the relationship between the town and the university in terms of economic impact, housing issues, and police and fire services, as well as the economic, cultural, and educational opportunities available across the community? (3) How consistently does your town-gown relationship address issues of noise, unsightly properties, large concentrations of rental housing, near-campus expansion, and unlawful gatherings? (4) How do you measure both the positive and the negative impacts of these issues and plan for long-term cooperation between your institution and the local town or city?

These four questions, and shared responses to them, have brought members of the ITGA together regularly to help university, college, and municipal leaders in forming an effective professional organization dedicated to enhancing the quality of life in campus-community relations. Established in 2008, the ITGA provides a network of resources to assist campus communities as they address issues and collaborate on projects of mutual benefit. The ITGA's nearly 400 members consist of colleges and universities, towns and cities, and individuals (including academic researchers and students), and corporate partners from the United States and across the globe. Over the past decade, ITGA has taken on the critical leadership role of acting as *the* central resource for positive relationships between communities and the universities and colleges located therein.

Each year, the ITGA hosts a conference at a different university and its home community across the country, offering hundreds of leading-practice sessions for university officials, municipalities, students and faculty, neighborhood associations, and a wide range of other concerned community members. Notable about these annual gatherings is the significant shift in focus over the years, from dealing with "students as problems" and the conflicts they might create in the near-campus and downtown neighborhoods through noise, parties, and housing issues, to dealing with "students as partners" by focusing on the strategic benefits of creating ongoing partnerships, research, leadership and planning teams, economic and social impacts, and ways of enhancing respect and productive relationships among these groups.

We asked ITGA members from all of the country's regions the following question: *Which two or three key factors or recommendations would you offer a university president and local mayor for developing an effective relationship between the university and the local community?* Their responses and examples of leading practices will assist you in taking on a leadership role in town-gown relations. The overarching advice from all of our members starts and ends with the need for ongoing strategic leadership in creating and maintaining a balance in the relationship between the university and its civic partners.

KEY FACTORS IN CREATING AND MAINTAINING A BLUEPRINT FOR TOWN-GOWN RELATIONS

Factor 1

Leadership, in good times and bad. Whether provided by the president of the university, the mayor of the city or town, an influential faculty member, a neighborhood association representative, or a member of student government, *leadership*, both on campus and in the community, is the universal theme in the responses we received from ITGA members. Strong leadership is supported in combination with the other proposed principles and practices of university-community partnership listed below, yet this synergy is facilitated and strengthened through deliberate, consistent, and collaborative organizational leadership. Leadership is an essential element of successful university-community partnerships.[2] It is also an important component of a community's capacity for change.[3] Stephen M. Gavazzi calls for "intentional leadership" on the part of the university president and municipal leaders; David Nichols suggests that "aggressive leadership" on the part of the university president and civic leaders is needed in order to set the tone for the importance of the overall relationship. ITGA members speak of the most enduring mechanisms that come from strong leadership, including the creation and maintenance of a university-community liaison office and commitments to staffing, funding, and strategic planning in town-gown relations. While executive-level meetings might happen only a few times a year, effective leaders know the value of this high level of support for regular meetings and consultations between key city and university departments, such as the city manager, police, communications, planning, and zoning, as well as a range of university personnel from the president's office to the dean of students and administrators in charge of government relations, student services, off-campus housing, student conduct, and the like. A sustained town-gown relationship ensures that regular contact and relationship building, so that problems and issues are dealt with as part of the larger, more positive set of connections that have been established. Like any relationship, the good times allow partners to build trust and a habit of dialogue in order to deal with the more challenging times that may come along. Thriving relationships, trust, and cohesion should be institutionalized consciously in the respective community and university. Of course, many communities are home to more than one university or college, and these places offer an added set of relationships and partnership possibilities in having multiple leaders and related institutions. While this chapter tends to focus on the one-to-one relationship that exists in the traditional college town, we need to acknowledge the multiple post-secondary educational leaders and constituencies that dot the landscape of larger municipalities and regions. This certainly adds to the dynamic and challenge of creating a sustained set of town-gown relations in multicampus communities.

Factor 2

Recognize relationships and build comprehensive partnerships. ITGA members report that the most visible indicator of the importance of positive town-gown relations is the result of *location, location, location.* Because colleges and neighborhoods are place-bound and virtually immovable, the relationship between them is of utmost importance. Gavazzi and Michael Fox offer a metaphor that illustrates this point:

> What if you have a marriage that was arranged by others, that could not be ended, but that you had to make work regardless of how you felt about your partner? That, in a nutshell, is the relationship between campus and the community that surrounds it.[4]

Through the analysis of member responses and leading practices that have emerged over the years, we have identified the strengths and weaknesses of the relationship between town and gown as the central theme in addressing the new college town. Gavazzi, Fox, and James Martin have created a typology of town-gown relations based on marital relationships, with each type defined by the level of comfort and effort required and the resulting level of satisfaction within the relationship. Town-gown

Maintaining Effective Town-Gown Relations

- Provide leadership, in good times and in bad
- Recognize relationships and build comprehensive partnerships
- Recognize that the ebb and flow of students coming into the community and leaving upon graduation is a continuous process of social, physical, cultural, and economic change that must be continuously monitored, managed, and planned

relationships are similar to marriages in that they are formed between two independent entities with the potential for shared activities and interests; yet they differ from a marriage in that the entities are not able to leave the relationship because of their spatial location and physical connection. The authors propose that we strive for stronger, more stable, healthier, and more satisfying relationships; these qualities exist in relationships with constant attention to building partnerships for mutual benefit and to strengthening the relationship. While a shared vision for the relationship may never be realized, especially when there are multiple colleges in one community, ITGA members have demonstrated that a long-term commitment to university-community partnerships through shared activities and leading practices are at least of mutual benefit and certainly deepen the relationships that are created.

Factor 3

Recognize that the ebb and flow of students coming into the community and leaving upon graduation is a continuous process of social, physical, cultural, and economic change that must be continuously monitored, managed, and planned. The term *studentification* was coined by Darren Smith to describe the processes of urban change tied to growing residential concentrations of students in the localities of higher education institutions.[5] University and community officials need to continuously devote resources to monitoring, managing, and planning these changes, reflected in the movement, concentration, and resultant negative and positive aspects of having large numbers of students living in the community. There are four coexisting dimensions to the process:

- Social: the replacement and/or displacement of a group of settled residents, leading to new patterns of social concentration and segregation
- Cultural: the growth of concentrations of young people with shared cultures, lifestyles, and consumption practices that in turn results in the growth of certain types of retail and service infrastructure
- Physical: the upgrading or downgrading of the physical environment, depending on the local context
- Economic: the inflation of property prices and a change in the balance of the housing stock, resulting in neighborhoods becoming dominated by private rented and shared housing in a wide variety of structural types and densities

EIGHT LEADING PRACTICES FOR FOSTERING AN EFFECTIVE TOWN-GOWN RELATIONSHIP

A great benefit of a professional group such as the International Town & Gown Association is that no college, university, or community needs to deal with the issues associated with studentification all on its own. Listed below are just some of the leading practices shared among members of ITGA. Rather than a quick fix that can simply be replicated, each of these practices and strategies can be adapted to the unique needs of your own campus or community, with the appropriate commitment from leaders, staff, and students.

Leading Practice 1

Clemson, South Carolina—a founding member of ITGA with a long-term, integrated approach to town and gown issues. Within the world of university-community relations, and as one of the North American communities originally identified with the physical, social, and economic processes involved in these complex relationships, ITGA members consistently look to Clemson University and the city of Clemson as offering a model of an overall long-term investment in town-gown relations. This commitment involves strong leadership from the mayor and the university president, formation of the Joint City-University Advisory Board in 1985, and becoming a founding member of ITGA in 2008. Current leading practices include an alcohol and drug strategic plan that targets high-risk drinking and illegal drug use through prevention, protection, intervention, treatment, and environmental management. Clemson has developed its Community Coalition, made up of community and university students and administrators, to promote cultural change by engaging in education, coalition building, environmental management, and other activities to reduce high-risk behavior, such as alcohol and drug use among college students in the community.

Clemson's well-established Party Registration System aims to reduce the negative consequences of excessive noise and other nuisance incidents associated with parties in residential neighborhoods. This has been added to with the development of the Environmental Context for Safety, with water risk and safety plans, integrated campus-community fire response, and law enforcement agreements and shared activities, such as downtown street cameras, improved street lighting, and critical-event scenario planning, including bar crawls.

A major difference between Clemson, South Carolina, and other international communities with a university is the significant attention to sporting events, particularly Clemson's city-university football planning scenarios and preparation. Every fall season, this town of 15,000 residents hosts 100,000 visitors on seven or eight weekends.

Clemson also has an integrated public transit and parking system shared between town and gown. Bus transit is free of charge for all and 25 percent of students are regular riders. Part of an integrated planning approach, this significant leadership and outreach makes sustainability education an integral part of the curriculum, civic service learning, and civic engagement practice.

Clemson also demonstrates that no president, mayor, or community can rest on its laurels, as the pressures of the university-community relationship are always present and may flare up at any time. Clemson is currently addressing a significant number of land use issues, as both on-campus and off-campus housing developments continue to impinge on town-gown relationships. Having a long-standing relationship and solid partnership, in good times and bad, will surely prevail in this latest test.[6]

Leading Practice 2

The University of Colorado and the city of Boulder—leadership in building a strong city-university partnership. Any discussion of leading practices for addressing the social, cultural, economic, and physical dimensions of the town and gown process in North America must acknowledge the longtime leadership of institutional and civic representatives at the University of Colorado (CU) and the city of Boulder. Various direct and meaningful relations have existed between university and civic personnel and their offices since 1988. Over the years, individual and institutional leadership has been nurtured and supported, with a deep commitment to enhancing the overall quality of life for everyone in this community. Issues have included groundbreaking practices in areas ranging from parties, noise, overoccupancy, parking, and excessive littering to the complex relationship and societal issues surrounding alcohol and drug use, sexual assault, and the educational aspects of legal and judicial systems, landlord-tenant issues, and personal codes of conduct and responsible behavior. As founding members of the International Town & Gown Association, CU and Boulder have developed and shared joint city-university programs that provide students with a better understanding of their rights and responsibilities regarding living off-campus and becoming positive members of the community. A wide number of leading practices have been developed here, including programs involving rental housing services, restorative justice, community living classes, party registration programs, move-in workshops, neighborhood walkabouts, lease disclosure and review processes, student honor codes, and sexual assault awareness. A strong relationship between the university and the city of Boulder's university liaison has been able enhanced strategic partnerships among CU, city agencies, and neighborhood groups in managing joint university-city, interagency, and community work teams that address common goals, including assisting students in becoming good neighbors and contributing to the community.

One of the most important features of the leadership and impact of this relationship is the early adoption of representatives and functional offices from the city and the university, both of which have been long-time employees and champions of town-gown relations. The University of Colorado has had a director of off-campus housing and neighborhood relations for thirty years. The city of Boulder's university liaison has been in place for fifteen years. Together, the city-university commitment has created one of the leading organizational approaches to the college town management model that we have seen in the North American context.[7]

Leading Practice 3

Blurring borders between town and gown: Amherst and the University of Massachusetts create a strategic approach to a long-term, sustainable community through enhanced communications and partnerships. "Physically disconnected and disengaged over time" was a recent summary observation made on the relationship between the town of Amherst and its university. How does a community that has been home to a state university campus for over 150 years find itself at this point of benign neglect, where the presence of the university is often identified with the physical, social, cultural, and economic issues at the root of the university-community dynamic? In terms of a real or perceived gap in

Eight Leading Practices

- A long-term integrated approach to issues
- Demonstrate leadership in building a strong city-university partnership
- Sustain community through enhanced communications and partnerships
- Take a research-based approach to common sources of conflict
- Employ a community liaison officer
- Map and share student data while maintaining confidentiality
- Collaborate on economic development
- Create a blueprint via the ITGA certificate program

university-community relations, Amherst is certainly not alone, yet its recognition of the need to identify and take action on the issues associated with sensitive and complex relationship is noteworthy.

In 2013 the university chancellor and the town of Amherst committed to a long-term analysis of the key issues associated with the relationship and the creation of a "University/Town Collaborative." Beyond dealing with the daily, more immediate issues of large, unruly gatherings, student behavioral issues, noise and parking infractions, a consulting firm was engaged to work with the collaborative in addressing short- and long-term strategic issues by examining planning documents, transportation plans, housing market supply and demand data, and economic development goals and innovation plans as the key to finding and addressing the underlying causes of the episodic problems of students attending university and living in the community with their neighbors.

The University/Town of Amherst Collaborative, supported by strong civic and university leadership, has discovered some significant ways forward by addressing the recommendations for change, including a focus on mixed-use housing and planning for land use compatibility, as well as fostering local innovation, assisting start-ups, and creating an entrepreneurial community. Recognizing a shared responsibility for town-gown relations, the collaborative has now taken the lead on creating an "innovation ecosystem" that recognizes the high value of research activities, creative fields and activities, and entrepreneurship and startup activities, as well as advanced manufacturing. Including the innovation and economic drivers within the university is a key change, as is sharing the university's housing and services needs with the larger community.

In the months since its inception, the collaborative has now created subcommittees, with cochairs drawn from the town and university, in order to identify key goals and undertake initiatives and interventions within the community. In particular, the subcommittees have addressed three key areas: (1) housing (including student housing, housing for faculty and staff, and affordable housing); (2) economic development (including university partnerships, entrepreneurship and start-ups, food retail, and amenities); and (3) quality of life (including public safety and student behavior). All of these developments represent a significant cultural shift in university-community relations in Amherst, and this approach represents a leading practice in addressing the root issues associated with the town and gown dynamic. Both town and university partners are confident that they have transformed the culture in a way that engages old and new stakeholders in shaping their long-term town-gown success.[8]

Leading Practice 4

Achieving Community Together—San Marcos and Texas State University take a research-based approach to common sources of conflict in a university town. Many university towns place enormous amounts of funding into fighting the usual outcomes of town and gown conflict, rather than the core issues. The City of San Marcos was dealing with large numbers of students living in the community through an over-reliance on police enforcement, especially patrolling, investigating, arresting, and prosecuting without detailed understanding of the specific social, economic, and physical nature of the student-based housing and social conflict processes. In 2008, realizing that noise complaints were the number-one call type for police officers, the city decided to deal with the core issues of the problems through a detailed understanding of the research and planning required in dealing with these complex problems. ACT has been developed as a collaborative effort between the City of San Marcos and Texas State University to reduce common sources of conflict in the community: noise, parking, trash, and the upkeep of rental property.

ACT is overseen by the ACT Committee, comprised of representatives from the university, city, and community. The Committee includes the Vice President for Student Affairs, Dean of Students, Director of Housing and Residential Life, offices of Off Campus Living, Attorney for Students, Student Health Center, University Police Department, Student Diversity and Inclusion, and Parent and Family Relations. Representatives also include the City of San Marcos Assistant Chief of Police, Community Liaison, offices of Code Enforcement/Neighborhood Services, the Central Texas Dispute Resolution Center plus members of the Council of Neighborhood Associations and community-at-large. ACT represents a significant change in the way in which communities deal with the impacts of student housing and entertainment concentrations by integrating research, planning, education, innovation, and relationship building between the key actors across the community. The symptoms of the problems are now dealt with by understanding the core characteristics of the dimensions of the process, with a focus on the occupants and the places they occupy—noise and housing have become the focus.

In terms of dealing with housing, "ACT Ally" is a program of ACT in collaboration with the Department of Housing and Residential Life at Texas State. Through ACT Ally, innovative approaches are used to address quality of life issues for a successful off campus living experience. Resources are available to assist with roommate disputes, landlord disputes, maintenance concerns, and leasing issues to help resolve conflicts. ACT Ally connects students to the rental housing industry through ACT members and affiliates, who promote a healthy living environment plus demonstrate a pattern of fair and equitable business practices in the delivery of related services and products. As a participant in ACT Ally, an apartment complex, rental property, product, or service provider is included in a select group to help students and parents make more informed decisions when choosing off campus housing.

A key issue in dealing with the effects of having large concentrations of students in a community is truly understanding the complexities of housing and student behavior in those off-campus structures and neighborhoods where students choose to live. By dealing with those directly responsible for the ownership, planning, occupation, and behavior of student occupied structures, San Marcos has been able to establish expectations on the overall quality of life of these areas through a model for both students and businesses that are engaged with students living in the community. Through ACT, the university administration works directly with San Marcos police and code enforcement officers on issues with students living off-campus, including follow-up with student noise violations and housing property maintenance standards. They work with housing providers and other businesses to create a balance of power between landlords and tenants, as well as event management that does not market using excessive alcohol consumption, as well as planning, zoning, and inspection of rental properties.

The results of the ACT program have been impressive, with a 34 percent reduction in noise complaints from 2008–2015 and noise complaints no longer the most frequent police call type, dropping from 6.1 percent of total calls to just 3.4 percent. Arrests and citations have been reduced by a staggering 63.4 percent, allowing police resources to be devoted to other issues and areas of the city. San Marcos has shifted the allocation of resources from dealing with the symptoms of the problems to delving into the core issues behind these patterns and processes. Through a shared response, both city and university have made an enormous improvement in the overall quality of life, created positive off-campus living arrangements, reduced citizen complaints, and created patterns of fair and equitable housing and business practices as the core issues.[9]

Leading Practice 5

Building strong town-gown relations—the community liaison officer at Colorado State University and the city of Fort Collins. Created in late 2001, the community liaison position was the result of a university-community committee's study of student life in neighborhoods surrounding Colorado State University's campus. The city ultimately created a public nuisance ordinance and identified the need for increased university-community communications in dealing with the negative aspects associated with high numbers of students and the physical and social issues associated with their off-campus land use and behavioral patterns. This jointly funded position had a mandate to promote "positive relationships between students and long-term residents through education, outreach, partnerships and connections."[10] This type of position represents a leading practice in that it distributes responsibility equally on the city and the university, with an open and flexible approach to the issues that are root causes to town-gown conflict. The positive and sustained presence of this office has a highly successful fifteen-year record. The community liaison addresses the communications required between the various boards and committees, deals with structural intricacies, attends meetings and public sessions, and forms a real presence at the table for critical issues in planning and land-use issues, neighborhood issues and task forces, student governance and university educational efforts, and housing and student party policies and advisory services. Having the right people in place has proven to be key to this position, including those in leadership positions, as well as the high-energy, high-touch, and highly visible role of the liaison officer. ITGA members have looked to Colorado State and the city of Fort Collins in modeling this leading practice in their own town-gown relations.[11]

Leading Practice 6

Michigan State University advances community relations and planning by mapping and sharing student data. One of the most dramatic changes in the relationship between universities, their students, and the larger community where they are located has been the transition to the internet and the growing awareness of students' privacy rights regarding personal data and locational information. Most university-community relationships have to operate in an atmosphere of technological anonymity that often requires guesswork as to who and where students live once they move off campus. Even when the university has the information, it is typically not shared with others, due to perceived confidentiality regulations and policies. In identifying the need to extend their community relations efforts with the greater Lansing community, Michigan State University (MSU) officials developed a leading practice in sharing some of this vital information while maintaining confidentiality of student personal information. In developing a highly innovative student data mapping program, MSU has been able to collect data on year of study, gender, ethnicity, international student numbers, on-campus and off-campus numbers, and local and permanent addresses. Using a mapping program, the university has created a series of spatial distribution maps that indicate numbers and densities of off-campus student housing across the greater Lansing area for any particular term. These distributions are shared with the wider community so that planners and other officials can slice and dice the data in the tables and maps and thereby glean detailed information on student housing, including neighborhood ratios of permanent residents to students, year of study distributions, graduate student locations, and international student distributions.

Providing this data has given an enormous boost to understanding the college town dynamic, enabling planners to drill down to the individual apartment complex, neighborhood, and municipal region and determine percentages of housing occupied by MSU students, all while protecting personal data. The university's willingness to require data-driven solutions to municipal housing represents a dramatic shift, whereby university officials are now sharing the data with civic officials, neighborhood groups and real estate developers, and any others interested in discussing the issues around students living in the community. The data provide clear spatial indicators on the actual student housing landscape, rather than relying on the rental markets or anecdotal evidence.

The university's decision to share information with the larger community has significant implications for the relationship with that community in terms of local and regional planning, housing development, and the provision of amenities and public safety, as well as transportation planning, fire and police services, and business development. As student enrollments continue to increase, these data are also helpful as part of the Michigan State University Housing Policy, which requires that a balance be coordinated between on-campus and off-campus housing options. In terms of the spatial implications of off-campus housing and the use of data in planning and decision making, we believe this approach is truly a leading practice with wide implications for the North American context.[12]

Leading Practice 7

Economic development through town-gown collaboration in Amherst, Massachusetts. The University of Massachusetts–Amherst (UMass-Amherst) and its home community have already been identified as one of the North American college towns that have responded to the impact of high concentrations of students through a complete overhaul in the relationship between town and gown actors. By recognizing the value of establishing and nurturing an ongoing relationship, UMass and Amherst have moved from episodic friction between students and off-campus neighborhoods to a blurring of the borders between campus and community by the creation of a collaborative committee that includes economic development through a neighborhood land use "anchor strategy" that works with students, faculty, university administrators, and municipal planners and economic development officers. Collaborative subcommittees focus on three key areas: housing (for students and for faculty and staff, and affordable units), economic development (university partnerships, entrepreneurship and start-ups, food and retail, and the promotion of amenities), and quality of life (public safety and student behavior). By recognizing the social, economic, physical, and cultural aspects of the town and gown dynamic, officials at UMass-Amherst are confident that they have created a shift in the culture that engages old and new stakeholders in shaping their long-term university-community relationship.[13]

Leading Practice 8

Creating a blueprint—the ITGA certificate program in town-gown relations. A collaborative relationship between the community and the local college or university contributes to the overall quality of life for everyone involved. However, issues such as local budget cuts, off-campus student conduct, and campus expansions too often cause strained town-gown relations. Initiating a dialogue and opening up the lines of communication

---

International Town & Gown Association (ITGA)

ITGA Vision Statement
The International Town & Gown Association is the premier resource for addressing challenges, emerging issues and opportunities between and amongst institutions of higher education and the communities in which they reside.

ITGA Mission Statement
The International Town & Gown Association strengthens town/gown partnerships by providing a network of professionals and resources, identifying and sharing promising practices, innovative solutions and professional development opportunities for municipal and university communities.

ITGA Values
Facilitate, communicate, foster, assist, create, design, lead, guide, promote, nurture, and support.

Source: "About," International Town & Gown Association, accessed October 20, 2018, https://www.itga.org/about/mission.

---

between the campus and its neighbors can foster a positive relationship based on a common understanding of the role that each plays—or can play—to promote a healthy and thriving community.

In offering the new, comprehensive Certificate in Town-Gown Relations at its annual conference, the International Town & Gown Association brings to bear its industry experience in the world of town-gown relations. Designed for busy university professionals, community leaders, city officials and their staff, and students, this program uses real-world experiences to inform practical solutions. The modules are led by professionals who have specialized for decades in addressing the social, cultural, physical, and economic situations unique to communities that are home to college and university campuses.

The purpose of this program is twofold: (1) To help all stakeholders understand and address complex challenges and processes associated with city-university relationships; and (2) to identify, foster, and promote the skills necessary for the effective development of collaborative partnerships and alliances throughout college towns. The program is designed for university or college professionals, city and county officials and staff, community leaders, and undergraduate and graduate students interested in town-gown relations, public service, political science, and other fields.

> **Benefits:** Participants can (1) develop a deeper understanding of the issues that strain town-gown relationships so they can be resolved; (2) learn to identify collaborative partnerships and practical solutions that benefit all "sides" in town-gown issues; (3) network with and learn from counterparts in other communities around the country who are working to improve town-gown relations; (4) cultivate professional excellence and opportunities for career advancement.
>
> **Program structure for levels 1 and 2:** The professional expertise of instructors and students from across the country and the globe ensures an interactive exchange of ideas, solutions, and challenging topics. Participants are awarded their Certificates of Completion at the conference in a special ceremony.
>
> **Strategic proposal:** The strategic proposal is a formative assessment that demonstrates the knowledge and skills of students completing the certificate program. Two months after the conference, participants are required to submit a community-based, collaborative strategic plan that meaningfully synthesizes, evaluates, analyzes, and applies knowledge gleaned from the modules.[14]

Over the past decade, the annual ITGA conferences have consistently served to demonstrate how and why some North American towns and cities have been transformed by processes tied to growing student populations and the expansion of universities in off-campus locations.[15] Similar patterns may be seen in towns and cities across the globe despite different systems of higher education and widely diverse student lifestyles across different national contexts. Reviewing just some of the leading practices that have emerged in the new American college town provides a valuable framework that university and civic leaders and other stakeholders across the country can use in finding more effective ways to integrate students into the physical and social fabric of the college town community. At the same time, following these leading practices has fostered more harmonious town-gown relations, as well as more fully unlocking the proven benefits of universities and students for regional and local economies, societies, cultures, and overall quality of life.

The eight leading practices highlighted here are drawn from member presentations at International Town & Gown Association conferences. Although there is a rapidly increasing uptake of the overall university-community relationship by North American researchers, a broader overview of the American context is lacking, particularly regarding a deliberate and ongoing blueprint to guide municipal and college leaders in building and maintaining meaningful town and gown relations.[16] Evidence from the recent annual ITGA conferences reveals that there are marked differences in expressions of leadership and planning in these college towns. Clearly, the effects of the mix of people, policies, and related activities are place-specific and reflect the peculiarities of universities, housing and labor markets, local cultures, and leadership styles. As a result, constant care and attention to the relationship, as demonstrated through the ITGA, speak to the need for partnerships, relationships, and strategies tailored to local contexts, between university administrations, faculty and staff, student governments, local government, local communities, and other stakeholders over the long term, rather than traditional episodic moments in the wake of an issue or crisis.[17]

LOOKING FORWARD: PUTTING THE "NEW" IN THE NEW AMERICAN COLLEGE TOWN

The United States is home to thousands of colleges and universities that are dotted across every state and region. The goal of American higher education has been critical to the social, economic, and political relationship between those places of teaching, learning, and research and the places where they take place—the thousands of communities that act as home for students, faculty, and staff, and the billions of dollars of research and teaching infrastructure that allow it all to happen. What has been underresearched and sometimes forgotten are the people and the associated land uses that take shape in those college towns, including on- and off-campus housing for students and staff; businesses, entertainment venues, and recreational facilities and their related employment function; and the range of municipal services and staff that serve this exceptional and cyclical population dynamic within the community. The key to the new college-town relationship is the recognition that most of the problems—and solutions to the problems—concerning university-community relations are addressed through effective communication and strong leadership.

Ongoing research and the development of leading practices revealed through the work of ITGA have shown that the traditional college towns have historically had weak and inconsistent records in working cooperatively to solve the issues and problems associated with the presence of students.[18] The new American college town blueprint reveals that communication and leadership are essential to the overall mission and strategic planning of both the college and the community. Rather than dwelling on past problems, town-gown frictions, episodic events, and stereotypical us-versus-them attitudes, adopting leading practices, like those outlined here, certainly will help in addressing campus and community issues wherever you are. It is only through continuous planning and engagement that there will be long-term, shared, and meaningful results. The relationship is just too important to do otherwise.

PART II

EFFECTIVE CAMPUS-COMMUNITY RELATIONSHIPS START WITH THE PRESIDENT

CHAPTER 3

Urban-Serving Universities

Rethinking the College Town for the Twenty-First Century

WIM WIEWEL AND ERIN FLYNN

INTRODUCTION

The term *college town* often conjures up pastoral images of a large state university or a private liberal arts college serving as the economic and cultural centerpiece of a small municipality. Today's higher education reality is, in fact, quite different. In the twenty-first-century United States, "college towns" are, by and large, cities. Institutions of higher education located in major cities represent 68 percent of all colleges and universities in the country and they serve some 20 million students.[1] These institutions range in scale and scope from elite private schools to flagship public research universities. Yet the largest class of universities located in US cities are regional, public-access institutions commonly referred to as urban-serving universities, or USUs. These institutions serve as the gateway to the middle class for millions of first-generation college students and enroll more minority, low-income, and nonresidential students than traditional colleges and universities. Many students enrolled in urban-serving universities have transferred from the local community college and work full- or part-time. These students are usually older than traditional college students, and many have children of their own and families to support. A distinguishing feature of urban-serving universities is that their identities and programming are highly place-based. These schools draw primarily from a regional student population, and alumni are much more likely to live and work in the metropolitan region following graduation. They play a significant role in supplying the local labor force and often align curriculum and programming—both undergraduate and graduate—with the needs of regional employers, government agencies, and civic organizations.

Urban-serving universities have gained national attention in recent years due to their high level of community engagement as well as their role as "anchor institutions" in metropolitan regions. In an era of corporate mergers and acquisitions and globalization, the staying power and place-based nature of USUs have facilitated long-term and deep engagement with their host cities. Urban-serving universities are usually among the largest employers in the metro region and play a significant role in cocreating public policy, developing urban real estate, devising economic and workforce development strategies, incubating companies, and designing and implementing community revitalization initiatives. Woven into the social and economic fabric of their cities, these institutions are usually located in the urban core in close proximity to major employers and civic institutions. Examples from across the country include San Diego State University, the University of Colorado–Denver, Indiana University–Purdue University Indianapolis, the University of Illinois at Chicago, Cleveland State University, Wayne State University, and Florida International University.[2]

This chapter explores how Portland State University (PSU) and other urban-serving universities have begun to institutionalize and professionalize their community engagement agendas over the past decade. As with many other urban-serving universities, PSU's engagement and partnership activity has grown organically over more than two decades. The effort to coordinate, communicate, and centralize this work has provided valuable lessons that may help new university presidents more quickly move toward effective strategies. In addition to PSU, the chapter draws examples from urban-serving universities with expertise and experience in community engagement.

URBAN-SERVING UNIVERSITIES: BACK TO THE FUTURE

Nationally, the focus on urban-serving universities has intensified over the past decade as the need to educate a greater share of the population has become evident. Increased skills requirements across all sectors of the economy and the decline in the number of middle-wage jobs that require no college degree (e.g., manufacturing) have placed a premium on higher education. Because many first-generation and low-income students cannot afford to attend a residential college or university away from home, the local community college and urban-serving university emerge as a logical choice. While there is renewed public policy interest in these place-based institutions of higher education, they have a long history and tradition of serving less privileged students. As Steven Diner documents in *Universities and Their Cities*, urban universities have been a mainstay of higher education since the turn of the twentieth century. In contrast to rural universities and gated ivory towers set apart from cities, city universities took root and grew in the early twentieth century to educate immigrant and working-class "day students" and adult "night students." They also established professional programs in public administration, education, and law to serve the growing needs of city governments, public schools, and the judicial system stemming from mass urbanization.[3] From their inception, these institutions of higher education have been deeply engaged with the urban environment and have played a critical role in the democratization of higher education.[4]

Today, urban-serving universities are the norm for a majority of American college students.[5] Their urban location, once viewed as a shortcoming, is now viewed as an advantage as students seek to gain experiential and applied learning as well as paid work experience while they pursue their degree.[6] In the past two decades, urban-serving universities have benefited from economic and demographic trends that now favor cities. Following decades of suburbanization and urban decline in post–World War II America, cities have made a dramatic comeback. Cities and their surrounding metropolitan regions drive the nation's economic growth and give rise to specialized industry clusters that fuel global trade and the US gross domestic product. The return to cities as the primary unit of economic and social life is particularly evident among millennials—those born between 1980 and 2000. Educated millennials, like the "yuppies" who came before them, have now flipped the postwar urban development paradigm. Economic growth cities offering good jobs and a high quality of life have become the destination of choice for a generation seeking an urban lifestyle that includes close-in, walkable neighborhoods, a range of public transit options, and abundant amenities ranging from brew pubs, restaurants, and cafés to music venues and bike paths. An unintended consequence of this trend is that many cities (e.g., San Francisco, Portland, Seattle, Brooklyn, and Boston) have experienced the near complete gentrification of their cores, driving lower-income residents to the urban periphery where housing is more affordable.

With more and more economic, social, and cultural activity rooted in cities, urban-serving universities have deepened their community engagement, experiential learning, and partnership activities, utilizing the urban environment as a living laboratory for faculty and students interested in applied research and problem solving. Myriad engagement and partnership focus areas have sprung up on urban campuses, ranging from partnerships with public schools, nonprofits, and state agencies, to workforce development, technology transfer, and entrepreneurship, to real estate, public safety, and transit. Many USUs have taken advantage of the engagement opportunities made possible by geographic proximity to differentiate themselves from flagship and land grant institutions, many of them located hours from the urban core. In fact, the "community engagement" agenda of urban-serving universities is so widespread at this point that it has given rise to a multitude of conferences and academic membership organizations designed to facilitate the sharing of best practices and encourage the "scholarship of engagement."[7]

Professionalizing Community Engagement

If we assume that urban context and active engagement confer benefits on students, faculty, and community partners alike, how are urban-serving universities building, measuring, and communicating the burgeoning community engagement agenda? The answer to this question is as varied as the cities in which the universities reside. Today, many urban-serving universities are working to organize, coordinate, and institutionalize their engagement and partnership work at an institutional level. This work poses significant challenges, however, as engagement and partnership work is often highly decentralized and relationship dependent. A recent survey of twenty-three institutions conducted by the Coalition of Urban Serving Universities (CUSU) found that USUs are deepening their integration into the community through university policies and processes that codify and create accountability for the engagement mission.[8] Specifically, the survey found that an increasing number of USUs

- Require community-engaged coursework to matriculate and graduate.
- Consider community-engaged research in promotion and tenure decisions.
- Have hired or appointed a senior administrator to lead the engagement agenda.
- Have established an office to centralize the engagement agenda.
- Include engagement and partnership as a priority in the campus's strategic plan.
- Are developing consistent impact metrics and issuing impact reports.
- Are creating searchable, visual databases to connect faculty, staff, students, and the community.

Admittedly, there is little consistency in practices across institutions. The CUSU survey describes "a hodgepodge of quantitative and qualitative project data, department data, foundation and federal tracking requirements and other external or fragmented influences." Nevertheless, the survey reveals "a nascent administrative infrastructure" emerging to coordinate, improve, and make visible the depth of community engagement work.[9]

Portland State University: Let Knowledge Serve the City

Portland State University is an urban-serving university located in the heart of Portland, Oregon—a thriving city in the Pacific Northwest with a rapidly growing economy and population. Over the course of several decades PSU has evolved from a teaching college (Vanport College, established in 1946 as part of the GI Bill) to a full-service research university offering a broad range of undergraduate and graduate degrees. Today PSU enrolls 28,000 students and graduates 6,000 annually. Occupying fifty acres of prime downtown real estate, PSU is a dense, urban campus within walking distance from City Hall and most major downtown employers and within a short bike, bus, or car ride from multiple government agencies, businesses, and nonprofit organizations. The most diverse university in Oregon, PSU is considered one of the "big three" along with the University of Oregon (flagship) and Oregon State University (land grant).

Portland State University's motto, "Let Knowledge Serve the City," exemplifies its commitment to community engagement and partnership. For over two decades, community engagement and partnership have been distinguishing features of PSU's mission, strategies, and operations at every level.

Colleges and Universities in Portland, Oregon

- American College of Healthcare Sciences
- Carrington College
- Concorde Career College
- Concordia University
- Lewis & Clark College
- Linfield College, Portland Campus
- Multnomah University
- Oregon College of Oriental Medicine
- Pacific Northwest College of Art
- Portland Community College
- Portland State University
- Reed College
- Sumner College
- University of Portland
- University of Western States
- Warner Pacific University

Historically, the clearest manifestation of this commitment has been the senior Capstone requirement, established in 1992. The Capstone is the culminating, senior-level course in PSU's University Studies general education program, and consists of teams of students from different majors who work together and collaborate with one or more community partners to complete a project addressing a real-world problem in the Portland metro region.

Community engagement and partnership emerged as a centerpiece of the PSU faculty and student experience in part because of the university's central urban location. But proximity was not the sole factor driving community engagement. By the mid-1990s, engagement and partnership, grounded in the Capstone requirement, were celebrated and highlighted as a strategic advantage by senior administrators who sought to forge a distinct identity for PSU as an urban-serving research university.

Since the early 1990s, when the Capstone requirement was established, many other forms of community engagement and partnership work have taken root across the university. Examples include a large body of professional service and sponsored research delivered by various colleges and institutes across campus to a range of local, county, and state government agencies in the health, education, and social service fields; a wide range of partnerships with local businesses and industry related to workforce development through internships and employment; an active

Karl Miller Center (the new business school), 2017. Office of the Associate Vice President, Portland State University

business accelerator deeply embedded in the city's entrepreneurial ecosystem; a significant body of engagement and partnership work related to city and regional planning and environmental sustainability; and ongoing professional application opportunities for fine and performing arts students in the city's nonprofit arts organizations.[10]

LESSONS LEARNED: INSTITUTIONALIZING THE ENGAGEMENT AND PARTNERSHIP AGENDA

Universities are by nature highly decentralized institutions. Organized into various schools, departments, units, institutes, and centers, they can make it extremely difficult to track activity of any sort, let alone partnerships that are often initiated by individual faculty. One of the challenges facing urban-serving universities with respect to engagement and partnerships is the seeming proliferation of activity and the correspondingly limited, central infrastructure available to better coordinate, document, and measure the impact of this activity.

In establishing engagement and partnership as a top priority, the presidents of many institutions of higher education have sought to codify the agenda in order to improve service to partners and demonstrate impact. This leadership commitment is essential to lifting engagement and partnership to a higher and more visible level within both the university and the community. It is also necessary to fulfill the rigors of the Carnegie Foundation's Classification for Community Engagement—a status that many universities seek to demonstrate and validate their commitment and capacity for engagement and partnership work.[11]

The remainder of this article provides lessons learned and best practices from PSU and other USUs that seek to institutionalize and professionalize their community engagement and partnership agenda.

Best Practices for Building Partnerships

- Presidential vision and leadership
- An institution-wide view of engagement
- Organizational structure and funding
- Partnerships utilized to highlight strengths and institutional priorities
- Advanced engagement agenda: multi-institutional collaborations
- Quality control

Presidential Vision and Leadership

Many urban-serving universities have been involved in community engagement and partnership for decades. However, only recently have university leaders sought to create central administrative infrastructure to coordinate, improve, and make visible the depth of community engagement work. Several motivating factors are at work: (1) the need to demonstrate to key stakeholders—trustees, the state legislature, employers, taxpayers, students, parents—that the university is serving a public purpose and advancing social and economic goals through hands-on, engaged teaching, learning, research, and work experience; (2) the oft-expressed frustration of partners at how difficult it is to navigate the university and find what they are looking for; (3) the need for professional management of complex, long-term, institutional partnerships involving multiple schools, departments, units, and the like. Responding to these pressures, many presidents have prioritized engagement and partnership and made it a key plank of their leadership platform.

For the past twenty-five years, the vast majority of PSU's engagement and partnership work was initiated by individual faculty members, staff, or administrators who had personal relationships with nonprofit, business, and government leaders. Historically, the engagement and partnership agenda at PSU relied on *individual* rather than *institutional* relationships. In 2008, when Wim Wiewel became the eighth president of PSU, he established five guiding themes for the university, one of which is to "provide civic leadership through partnerships." As a scholar of city-university relations, Wiewel was well versed in the concept of universities as "anchor institutions." Upon arrival at PSU, he charged the university to (1) lead as a civic partner, (2) deepen engagement as a critical community asset (3) demonstrate leadership in regional innovation, and (4) serve as an anchor institution in the metropolitan region. To deliver on these goals, Wiewel established the executive-level Office of Strategic Partnerships in 2010, organizationally situated within Research and Strategic Partnerships (RSP). In addition to raising the university's research profile, RSP was created to develop and advance "strategic partnerships" and serve as a front door for community engagement.[12] In 2011 PSU appointed its first-ever associate vice president for strategic partnerships to build out this function and deliver on presidential goals related to engagement and partnership.

Other presidents have also made engagement central to their leadership and have established structures to support the commitment. Under the leadership of Ron Berkman, for example, Cleveland State University (CSU) made a significant commitment to "engaged learning," establishing its Office of Civic Engagement within the Division of University Engagement, led by the vice president for engagement, diversity, and inclusion. At CSU, the Office of Civic Engagement provides support to faculty, students, staff, and administrators that allows them to develop, expand, and sustain collaborative, mutually beneficial partnerships with community residents, organizations, and institutions. In addition, as part of its engagement agenda CSU has made a substantial commitment to internships and co-ops, providing three thousand opportunities for student work experience annually.

In some instances, entire university systems are pledging their commitment to partnership and engagement in order to improve their communities. In 2017, for example, nineteen of New Jersey's colleges and universities formed the New Jersey Coalition of Anchor Institutions and pledged to help revitalize the five cities of Atlantic City, Camden, Newark, Paterson, and Trenton. Nancy Cantor, the chancellor of Rutgers University–Newark, and other education leaders in the state publicly recognized the need to reinforce the public mission of New Jersey's college and universities and enhance the quality of life for its citizens.[13] The coalition seeks to design and implement scalable and systematic changes to communities, including workforce development agreements with corporate partners.

Rob Franek on What Makes a New American College Town

ROB FRANEK is the editor in chief of the Princeton Review guides, which total almost 150 separate publications annually headlined by *The Best 384 Colleges* (2019). Franek provides his perspective on how American college towns are evolving and how The Princeton Review team arrives at its annual rankings.

The Princeton Review ranked Loyola University, New Orleans, number 1 in town-gown relations in 2018. What set that university apart from all others when you considered town-gown issues nationally this year?

To determine our rankings, we polled more than 138,000 students and asked them a simple question: "Do students at your institution get along well with members of the local community?" When we tallied the results, Loyola, New Orleans, was a standout number 1. With number 1 rankings also for "Best College Newspaper" and "Best Quality of Life," it was relatively easy to see how the university earned, and deserved, the highest grade for town-gown relations.

(*continued*)

In your view, what is the best first step for a college or university president to take in building a successful college town partnership with a mayor or local civic leader?

It is simple: invite local citizens to campus and actively welcome them into the life of the college or university. Advertise art exhibits, athletic contests, and student and faculty performances in the external community, and allow members of the community to audit any course on a space-available basis. By doing these things, the institution clarifies and strengthens its connections to the external community while also addressing the needs of both alumni and current students. This characterizes the best new college towns.

Looking toward the future, as other contributors to this book have done, what is one difference that you believe will characterize college towns in 2025?

The AARP. By this I mean, with the aging of the baby boomer generation, I believe that over the next ten to twenty years a growing number of colleges and universities will partner more fully with the American Association of Retired Persons to lessen the distance between town and gown. They will do this not only through familiar education programs for seniors but also via newly designed services and support to preserve the seniors' engagement in their communities through enhanced quality of life.

An Institution-Wide View of Engagement

For university leaders contemplating a more centralized approach to engagement, an initial barrier is simply getting a handle on what constitutes engagement and partnership and getting faculty, staff, and administrators on the same page. As noted earlier, the highly decentralized nature of engagement work poses challenges with respect to establishing an institution-wide view and building central capacity.

As PSU began to build its Strategic Partnership Office in 2011, it became clear that the university had little institution-wide understanding of its partnership landscape. Two decades of active partnership development had led to a tremendous amount of engagement and activity, but there had been little sustained effort to catalog, document, or measure the quantity, quality, or impact of this activity. Structured interviews with representatives from all seven of PSU's colleges revealed that the word *partnership* was being used to describe everything ranging from one-day student volunteer projects to multiyear research projects with state agencies. Through campus interviews and extensive review of existing partnerships, patterns emerged that led to the development of a partnership typology that would clarify the major categories of engagement and partnership work at PSU and build an institutional view of activity.

The Engagement and Partnership Spectrum, along with clear definitions for each category contained within it, provided an organizing vehicle that enabled faculty, staff, and administrators to view themselves as part of a shared engagement agenda. It also enabled the Office of Strategic Partnership to better categorize work and develop quantitative measures. For example, PSU now tracks student service hours and is able to report on sponsored research serving local and state agencies and nonprofit organizations.

Building on the Engagement and Partnership Spectrum, PSU launched the Partnership Council in the fall of 2014. The overarching goal of the Partnership Council is defined as follows:

> PSU seeks to be at the cutting edge of "community-university" engagement and partnership work nationally. While honoring the personal relationships upon which many partnerships are built, PSU seeks to build campus infrastructure and support systems that lead to greater standardization and an ability to more readily assess and communicate the impact and value of this work. The end goal is to provide more consistent and better engagement and partnership opportunities to more faculty, staff, students and stakeholders.[14]

The Partnership Council—composed of some twenty faculty and staff representing PSU's seven colleges, as well as key institute and center directors

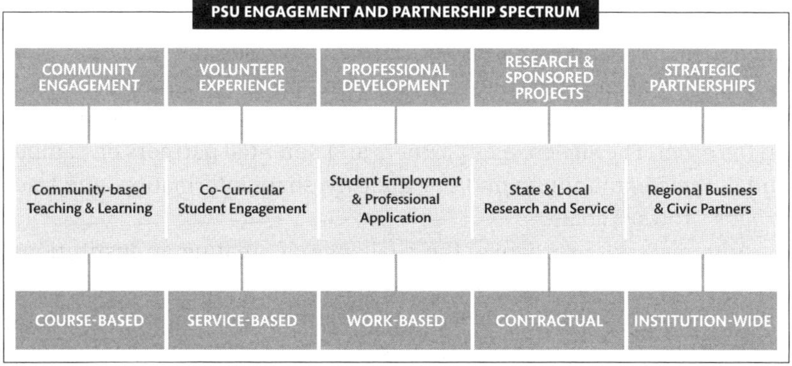

Office of the Associate Vice President, Portland State University

and staff—meets quarterly to drive PSU's engagement and partnership agenda forward. Today, the Partnership Council serves as the implementation body for PSU's Strategic Plan Goal 3: *"Extend our Leadership in Community Engagement."*[15]

The University of Minnesota, Twin Cities, has established a similar Public Engagement Council (PEC). The PEC, situated within the university's Office of Public Engagement, serves as the consultative body on issues pertaining to the university's public engagement agenda. Much as at Portland State, University of Minnesota's PEC focuses on "improving the University structures, policies, procedures, and programs in ways that further the institutionalization of all forms of public engagement and the alignment of the public engagement agenda to the University's key strategic priorities."[16]

A relatively new way that USUs are developing an institution-wide view of engagement is through searchable, electronic portals that enable internal and external stakeholders to identify engagement and partnership work by topic area, faculty member, college, and partner. These "partnership portals" can be designed to simultaneously collect data (on, e.g., student learning hours, community-based courses, sponsored research projects) and reduce the information costs associated with navigating multiple colleges and university administrative units. The University of North Carolina at Greensboro (UNCG), for example, has piloted the "Community Engagement Collaboratory," designed to track partnership and public service activities between universities and communities.[17] According to UNCG's Institute for Community and Economic Engagement, the Collaboratory will "facilitate measurement of activities, identify patterns of engagement, and provide ongoing data collection to convene people and resources around important community priorities." Cleveland State University has also created a web-based portal called the Cleveland Engagement Project. Managed by the Office of Civic Engagement, the Cleveland Engagement Project showcases and facilitates partnerships between community organizations, institutions, and businesses on one hand and Cleveland State University faculty, staff, and students on the other. The site enables partners and potential partners on campus and in the community to find one another, share information, and track progress toward goals.

Administrators recognize the challenge of creating an institutional view of engagement and partnership. Whether it is an administrative office, a campus-wide council, or an electronic portal that is contemplated, consensus appears to be emerging that some type of intentional central mechanism is required to effectively build the engagement and

Architects and Engagement: Achieving Positive Change

MICHAEL WINSTANLEY, AIA AICP, is the founding principal of Winstanley Architects & Planners, begun in 2004. Prior to that he was the design director for Leo A. Daly. Two notable, recent college town projects that Winstanley has undertaken are the University of New Hampshire hotel and mixed-use development in Durham, and the Catholic University redevelopment in Washington, D.C.

What is the single most important piece of advice you would offer to a college or university president who is starting work with an architect and design team to accomplish a college town or town-gown project?
Campus and student life does not end at the campus gates. The quality of the environment that *surrounds* the campus is perhaps more important than the environment inside the campus. And a quality environment means not just green lawns and trees but vibrant retail, housing, and entertainment.

What is a key lesson learned regarding the importance of engagement that you have taken away from your work with mayors, civic leaders, and higher education administrators (i.e., both "sides") on town-gown projects?
Economic activity (i.e., retail and entertainment) is a foundation for creating vibrant college towns that are key ingredients to recruiting and retaining both students *and* faculty.

From your perspective and over the course of your career, how has the American college town changed or evolved?
Years ago, the college campus was predominantly a cloistered, gated environment. Today, the boundary of the college campus is blurred and the best college towns are both colleges and towns together.

partnership function. A recent case study of the University of Washington, Tacoma (UWT), by the Coalition of Urban Serving Universities, for example, praised UWT's active engagement in the community and the value it brings to public, private, and nonprofit partners. The case study highlighted more than a dozen projects the university is engaged in to stimulate urban regeneration. However, the study also noted that without a staffed community engagement office or a systematic or central data repository of engagement activities, the aggregate impact of the work could not be fully determined. The authors urged UWT to employ more systematic and purposeful data collection to communicate to internal and external stakeholders the depth and magnitude of the university's impact on the lives of students and the region.[18]

An additional challenge sited by many institutions is the extent to which engagement work is valued in the tenure process. Despite a declared commitment to community engagement and engaged scholarship, many universities have difficulty assessing this work in any standardized way in the tenure review process. An important goal of consultative bodies such as PSU's Partnership Council and the University of Minnesota's Public Engagement Council is to provide senior leadership with recommendations regarding how engaged scholarship should be evaluated for promotion and tenure.

Organizational Structure and Funding

As university leaders seek more systematic mechanisms for organizing, delivering, and documenting the engagement and partnership agenda, questions inevitably arise about where this function should reside institutionally. The reality is that partnership and engagement work cuts across every college and multiple campus administrative units, including the president's office, academic affairs, research, career services, and student affairs. Accordingly, it isn't always obvious where a central partnership function should be located. Each leader must determine the best organizational home for partnership and engagement based on the cultural and political context of their university.

Today there is tremendous variety in terms of where engagement and partnership offices reside, who they report to, and what they are called. What is perhaps more important is that each office serve a university-wide function for partnership management, data collection, and communications and is viewed as the authoritative, central mechanism for this agenda. Some institutions, such as Virginia Commonwealth University, have centralized all aspects of engagement in a single office; others, such as PSU, continue to have multiple nodes across campus that take responsibility for different aspect of engagement. A small sampling of universities with a strong engagement commitment demonstrates the range of centralized, organizational options, and administrative titles (see table 3.1).

Regardless of its location or title, leaders responsible for engagement and partnership work need to be consummate relationship builders and communicators able to work across administrative silos within the university and with external partners (public and private), all the while spotting mutually beneficial opportunities. These roles are sometimes filled by people from outside the university with deep networks in the community

Table 3.1. How Six Universities Centralize the Engagement and Partnership Function

	Senior administrator for engagement and partnership agenda	Name of division / office
Portland State University, Oregon	Associate Vice President	Office of Research and Strategic Partnerships
University of North Carolina, Greensboro	Vice Chancellor	Office of Research and Engagement
University of Minnesota, Twin Cities	Associate Vice President	Office of Public Engagement
Virginia Commonwealth University	Vice Provost	Division of Community Engagement
Florida International University	Vice President	Office of Engagement
Cleveland State University, Ohio	Vice President	Division of University Engagement

upon which they can draw. Senior administrators from outside the university benefit from being paired with internal university staff who have a deep working knowledge of community-based learning, engaged curriculum, internships, and other forms of engagement.

The costs associated with staffing a central engagement function are not insignificant. PSU, for example, has a small central office that consists of an associate vice president and two directors (the director of community research and partnerships and the director of the Center for Entrepreneurship). Some universities have created entire divisions for engagement, with up to a dozen or more staff. At the same time, engagement and partnership activities bring in a significant amount of funding through philanthropy, contracts, and sponsored projects. PSU's largest annual sponsored project is a partnership with the Oregon Health Authority that provides approximately $7 million a year to PSU to provide training and evaluation services through its Center for Improvement of Child and Family Services.

A tension inherent in any university's commitment to partnership and engagement work is that sponsored projects associated with community engagement typically bring in lower overhead than federally funded projects. At PSU, community-serving research projects and contracts usually bring in a 20 to 26 percent overhead rate, compared to nearly 44 percent for federally funded projects. Some legacy partnerships bring in even less. This can put faculty at odds with one another as federally funded researchers feel that they are subsidizing local, engagement, and partnership work. This is an area where presidential leadership and clarity regarding university mission and priorities are critical.

Partnerships Utilized to Highlight Strengths and Institutional Priorities

Establishing engagement and partnership as a top university priority creates expectations that the university will commit to partnerships that produce real, tangible results for students, faculty, and the community. It is critical, therefore, to invest resources in those partnerships where the university has existing expertise and where there is genuine demand from partners to engage. At PSU, a long-standing relationship with the city of Portland provides the backbone for the university's engagement and partnership agenda. PSU's nationally ranked School of Urban Studies and Planning, located within the College of Urban and Public Affairs, has over time established a strong partnership with the city of Portland's Bureau of Planning and Sustainability (BPS). BPS is the city agency responsible for comprehensive land use planning, energy and waste reduction, and policy actions to address climate change. The college and its centers and institutes serve the bureau in multiple capacities, including policy advisor, program evaluator, research partner, service provider, urban designer, and workforce provider. The partnership between PSU and Portland's BPS is deep and broad, revolving around three mutually beneficial goals: (1) co-creation of knowledge and solutions; (2) high-quality student learning and employment experiences; and (3) community impact.

A revealing illustration of the partnership is the Climate Action Collaborative (CAC), managed by PSU's Institute for Sustainable Solutions. BPS is responsible for the Portland region's Climate Action Plan. It establishes policy and supports actions that mitigate climate change. Through the CAC, PSU faculty and students provide research, data, analysis, and tools that enable the city to deliver on specific goals of the Climate Action Plan. PSU faculty have undertaken multiple research projects to support the Climate Action Plan, including mitigation strategies to address extreme heat events and a block-by-block tool that helps planners and policy makers address the problem of urban heat islands. This innovative partnership has garnered national recognition from funders. Underwritten by the Bullitt Foundation, the CAC is serving as a model for similar city-university partnership across the Pacific Northwest.[19]

Medical Schools and Their College Towns: New Opportunities for Leadership

BRIAN L. STROM, MD, MPH
Chancellor, Rutgers Biomedical and Health Sciences
Executive Vice President for Health Affairs, Rutgers University

Rutgers Biomedical and Health Sciences is the umbrella organization for the schools and assets acquired by Rutgers University after the July 2013 breakup of the former University of Medicine and Dentistry of New Jersey. While its various facilities are spread across several locations statewide, Rutgers Biomedical and Health Sciences is considered the university's fourth campus. In 2016 the university's Board of Governors approved Rutgers Health as the university's clinical arm, and Rutgers Health Group was additionally approved as a subsidiary nonprofit corporation that will function as an integrated faculty practice plan with more than one thousand Rutgers-based physicians, dentists, psychologists, nurses, pharmacists, and other clinicians.

What is the single most important piece of advice you might offer to the president of a university with a medical school about how to work creatively and productively with local civic and business leaders in order to accomplish one or more major objectives?
Our institutions bring not only economic opportunities with our large student and employee populations but also present challenges to local communities for municipal services. A major new clinical care facility can bring needed health care services to a community, but also disrupt local traffic patterns. Much more can be accomplished when there is a positive relationship with civic and community leaders.

What is a sometimes overlooked pitfall or challenge that presidents and deans of medical schools discover when collaborating with local leaders in a town-gown relationship?
Community engagement is essential for the success of the enterprise, especially in the delivery of health care where the population includes not only the neighbors of the institution but our patients. For members of the host community to embrace the institution, they must feel respected by institutional leaders and believe that their input is valued and their needs are recognized. Academic health centers are in a symbiotic relationship with the local community: our students depend on the patient base in the community to learn and practice their skills, and the often medically underserved community relies on us to provide health care.

(continued)

What is one observation you would make about how relations are changing between medical schools and their college towns?
Higher education and health care institutions are recognizing that they are "anchors" of the communities in which they reside. Institutions are becoming more aware of their responsibility to their host communities. We are embracing our roles as major transformational agents in the economic, cultural, and civic life of the college town.

Another example of an urban-serving university with long-standing ties to its city is the University of Illinois at Chicago. UIC developed the Great Cities Initiative back in 1993 as the umbrella for its commitment to its home metropolitan area. It pulled together multiple existing initiatives and also started several new ones, such as the College of Urban Planning and Public Affairs, the Great Cities Institute, and the UIC Neighborhoods Initiative. The last named of these consisted of multistrand programs between various UIC programs and schools, community organizations, and health organizations in a Latino and an African American neighborhood adjacent to the campus. The initiative was funded by state sources as well as the Community Outreach Partnership Center and other grants from the US Department of Housing and Urban Development. Over more than two decades, UIC faculty, students, and staff participated in dozens of research, education, service, and health care activities focused on these areas. While many other activities continued in other parts of the region, the UIC Neighborhoods Initiative brought much greater visibility to the institution, increased the impact on the community, and institutionalized knowledge and trust between the university and community institutions.

Advanced Engagement Agenda: Multi-institutional Collaborations

A key driver behind the professionalization of the engagement agenda at many colleges and universities is the growing complexity of partnership work. The pursuit of strategic institutional goals often requires a university to engage with multiple large organizations over extended periods of time. Holding together multiple-stakeholder partnerships requires increasingly sophisticated management, communication, and relationship skills.

Increasingly, Portland State University is engaging in multistakeholder collaborations to advance strategic regional goals. In 2015, for example, PSU committed to enter into a memorandum of understanding with three large anchor institutions to build joint programming and realize the po-

The Collaborative Life Sciences Building (opened in 2014)—a result of the partnership between Oregon Health and Sciences University, Oregon State University, and Portland State University to advance the life sciences. Office of the Associate Vice President, Portland State University

tential of Portland's emerging "Innovation Quadrant"—a geographic district within the city with existing and potential assets to foster innovation, entrepreneurship, and workforce pathways in the health and technology industries. In close collaboration with Oregon Health and Sciences University, Portland Community College, and the Oregon Museum of Science and Industry, PSU's Office of Strategic Partnerships has led a yearlong process of community engagement to provide early design parameters for the Innovation Quadrant (IQ). As momentum for the IQ has grown, the city of Portland, real estate developers, business incubators, corporate partners and other stakeholders have joined an emerging public-private consortium committed to building a globally competitive innovation district in Portland's South Waterfront and Central East Side. Now in year two of the planning phase, partners continue to look to PSU to hold the coalition together and move the IQ to a formal organizational structure incorporating a public-private board and an executive director.

Urban anchor institutions are increasingly playing a lead role in these multistakeholder partnerships. In Richmond, Virginia, for example, Virginia Commonwealth University (VCU) anchors the region's cradle-to-career partnership "Bridging Richmond." Bridging Richmond is a growing partnership of regional institutions from education, business, nonprofit, government, and philanthropic sectors that is establishing shared education and workforce priorities through a collective action framework that utilizes shared data to make real-time improvements in the education system. The VCU Division of Community Engagement provides the "backbone staff" for Bridging Richmond, including the partnership executive director and the network coordinator.

Quality Control

A key role for central engagement and partnership functions is quality control. Colleges and universities should be cautious and clear-eyed about who they enter into partnership with. Community partners often believe that colleges and universities can and will provide free services. Many partnerships begin with a time-limited grant or funding source, yet expectations regarding continued university engagement and services may remain even after funding runs out. Another challenge that can quickly upend a community partnership is leadership turnover. PSU, for example, entered into a strategic partnership with Portland Public Schools—the region's largest public school system—shortly before a scandal rocked the district and resulted in a near complete depletion of senior administrative leadership. For these reasons, it is important to establish ground rules or a formal partnership agreement or charter, or both, at the beginning of any significant undertaking.

On the university side, it is important to not overcommit to partners. Entering into partnership with community stakeholders is often exciting, and there is shared energy to identify mutually beneficial goals. However, unless the university is confident it can deliver, it is better to be conservative and hold back. Failed expectations can quickly erode trust, which is the foundation of all successful long-term partnership activities.

CONCLUSION

This chapter makes the case that the "new college town" is urban and that most students attend college in cities. Furthermore, it argues that a majority of city-based students attend urban, regional comprehensive universities, also called urban-serving universities. Over the past decade, USUs have leveraged their urban location and proximity to government, private industry, and the nonprofit sector to create myriad opportunities for students, faculty, and staff to engage with the community through hands-on learning, applied research, internships, and demonstration projects.

As USUs have embraced their status as anchor institutions, many have sought to professionalize community engagement and partnership activities. Over the past decade, USUs, along with other colleges and universities, have invested time and resources in professionalizing and centralizing key aspects of this agenda in order to improve services, document impact, and communicate results. While a high degree of variation remains across institutions in terms of organizational structure, central data collection, and standardized reporting, it appears a majority of urban-serving universities are now moving in this direction.

At Portland State, the institutionalization of the engagement agenda is illustrated through three major developments since 2010: (1) establishment of the Strategic Partnerships Office (2010); (2) formation of the Engagement and Partnership Spectrum and the campus-wide Partnership Council (2014); and (3) inclusion of "Engagement" as a key plank of the PSU Strategic Plan (2016–2020). A similar institutional pathway is evident at other engaged urban institutions, such as the University of Minnesota, Twin Cities; the University of North Carolina, Greensboro; Virginia Commonwealth University; and Cleveland State University, to mention just a few. Experimentation will no doubt continue in this realm as urban-serving universities seek to deliver even greater value to their internal and external stakeholders. Fortunately, there is already a significant body of best practices for new presidents to draw from as they consider how to best organize and execute this important agenda.

CHAPTER 4

How College Towns Have Become Regional Economic Drivers

JOHN SIMON, FRED MCGRAIL, AND ALLISON STARER

INTRODUCTION: CITY, REGION, AND BEYOND

How does a university balance its responsibilities to the city where it is located while still recognizing the need to have a regional impact? How does the university build support among its constituents—faculty, staff, students, trustees, neighbors, and community partners? How does it allocate limited resources to have an impact and effect change? These are some of the questions addressed here via the decisions Lehigh University has made over the past decade. Our responses highlight both successes and failures, and reveal several key lessons learned as the university attempts to make a difference both in the local community and in our expanding region.

Lehigh University is located in the Lehigh Valley, which is anchored by the cities of Allentown, Easton, and Bethlehem, Pennsylvania, and has a population of 650,000 people. It is the home of two Fortune 500 companies (industrial gas manufacturer Air Products and Chemicals, Inc., and utility company PPL Corp.) and five companies with revenue of more than $5.43 billion, and is one of the fastest-growing regions of the country. While there is certainly loyalty and affinity to the cities and municipalities in the region, most residents, industries, nonprofits, and other entities think of themselves as part of the Lehigh Valley and understand that the health of the region is critical to the health of the individual cities and towns.

This sentiment is reflected in Lehigh University's approach to its efforts to affect the region positively while recognizing that we also have a specific strategy to impact and support the city of Bethlehem.

Over the past twenty years, universities across the country have accepted and embraced their roles as "anchor institutions," entities that have been stable and have endured in their communities, even when many corporations were moving their offices and operations out of the region for various reasons. A particularly impactful corporate change occurred in Bethlehem and the Lehigh Valley when Bethlehem Steel Corporation, which was founded in 1904 and traced its roots back to 1857, declared bankruptcy in 2001.[1] With that bankruptcy, the character and economics of the Lehigh Valley changed dramatically. Bethlehem grappled with the challenges inherent in becoming a post-industrial city. What had once been a thriving operation running twenty-four hours a day and employing 31,000 workers at one site became the largest brownfield in the country. The neighborhoods that housed these workers were soon abandoned, and the goods and service businesses these workers used lost their customers.

In many ways, Bethlehem has made a remarkable recovery since then. The Bethlehem Steel site is being developed with a major arts center, industrial history museum, casino, and hotel. The reimagination of the former Bethlehem Steel brownfield into a thriving venue for the arts has been particularly successful, building on Lehigh's institutional commitment to the arts through the construction in 1996 of the Zoellner Arts Center, a state-of-the-art performance venue. The mixed-use district that comprises the 9.5-acre SteelStacks campus was inspired by repurposed industrial sites in Germany and grew out of a consortium led by the city of Bethlehem's Redevelopment Authority.[2] Anchored by the steel company's iconic blast furnaces, the complex includes an outdoor amphitheater, a visitor's center, a public television station headquarters, and the ArtsQuest art, culture, and educational center. Collectively, these attractions draw 1.5 million visitors to Bethlehem every year. In addition, Lehigh supports the creation of the South Side Arts District, which aims to build upon the community's innovative, artistic, cultural, and entrepreneurial heritage to enhance and support further economic development in South Bethlehem.

This entrepreneurial spirit, driven in part by Lehigh University's graduates in programs such as technical entrepreneurship and those at the Baker Center for Innovation, is creating fertile ground for entrepreneurs in the Lehigh Valley. Despite such progress, Bethlehem and the Lehigh Valley confront the challenges facing many American post-industrial cities in urban environments. As one example, poverty in South Bethlehem, comprising the neighborhoods that once housed the steelworkers, is far higher than the national average. More than 90 percent of students who attend elementary and middle schools in South Bethlehem qualify for subsidized lunch programs, and a high transient population means that one-third of students who begin the school year will move before the year is out. While much progress has been made, the challenges that

The SteelStacks Arts Venue was developed on the brownfield formerly occupied by Bethlehem Steel and is part of a revitalized arts district that draws roughly 1.5 million visitors a year to the city. Photo by Ryan Hulvat

remain in the Lehigh Valley are persistent and systemic and require strategic, long-term approaches. Two examples of the university's commitment to regional engagement include investment in the Rising Tide Fund, a pool of capital administered by a community organization that provides loans to businesses that cannot access capital through traditional banks, and support for a regional enterprise zone that provides funding for entrepreneurial ventures.

A promising initiative is the new College of Health, which will open doors to innovative partnerships with the two Lehigh Valley health care systems and another in Philadelphia, and which will address health care disparities in disadvantaged communities. An innovative leadership program for school principals has seeded Lehigh Valley public schools with

Partnership Development at Lehigh: Five Lessons Learned

- Engage the trustees
- Build relationships first, then act
- Leverage both intellectual and human capital
- Centralization versus decentralization: find the balance
- Capitalize on capital projects

energetic educators prepared to tackle the challenges of underperforming schools. As Lehigh University has made a commitment to its region, we have learned some hard-won lessons. We have come to recognize more than once that meaningful change takes more than good intentions, and mistakes along the way have accelerated our learning. Successful collaborations between our campus and the expanded local community require strategy, execution, resources, and sustained engagement.

LESSONS LEARNED IN THE PAST DECADE

Lesson 1: Engage the Trustees

Trustees of any institution of higher education are charged with charting the long-term strategy and establishing the institution's core values and principles. To be effective, community relations efforts need to rise to the strategic level so that they are on the agenda of the Board of Trustees. There are several reasons for this step. The first relates to resources. When we began a strategic community relations program at Lehigh University, we were faced with a fundamental question from trustees and from others on the campus: With limited resources and tremendous needs and opportunities, does an investment in the community come at the cost of academic programs?

This is a fair question, and it must be addressed before any progress can be made. Our answer is that community engagement can be part of the university's academic and service mission. There are opportunities for research, service, and the practical application of certain disciplines in a community setting. In addition, students benefit from programs in public schools, from work with nonprofits, and from academic work in the community. We believe that the health and vibrancy of the university are inextricably connected to those of the region. Finally, and importantly, the Board of Trustees can instill confidence that there will be continuity in the university's commitment. Community organizations and political leaders are understandably concerned that as presidents and administrations change, the priorities and commitment to the community can also change. Active and visible participation in the community efforts of the university provides tangible evidence of a sustained commitment. At almost every meeting of our trustees' Public Affairs Committee, at least one agenda item relates to community initiatives. In addition, our trustees devote an entire three-day meeting every two to three years to these initiatives. They meet with civic leaders, community activists, advocacy organizations, businesses, and nonprofit groups to discuss the issues we collectively face. Some of these conversations are difficult and sometimes criticism is aimed at the university, which is fine.

We realize that the active engagement of trustees is valued and appreciated. From the university's perspective, this level of active engagement builds a deep understanding of the challenges and accomplishments of our regional strategy.

Lesson 2: Build Relationships First, Then Act

Lehigh University's regional community relations strategy is grounded in relationships with organizations and other members of the community. To be effective, we need the trust of community partners who will work with us and guide our efforts. The point may seem obvious, but it is a lesson we learned the hard way. Universities can be seen as formidable, even forbidding, entities by members of the external community, yet we have found that sustained change can be accomplished only when those community partners are heard on multiple levels. Trusting relationships take time to build and can sound to some like a lot of talk and not enough action. Complicating this learning process is the fact that a university community is not a monolithic entity with a single voice and point of view. To the contrary, it can seem more like a cacophony where the loudest voices are not necessarily the wisest. All want to be heard, and it is incumbent upon the president, provost, and other senior administrators and faculty to enable this expression of views.

We have learned that the foundation for any meaningful change is formed by relationships between the university and community leaders throughout the region. Developing plans that truly include those leaders at the earliest stages, working with them through implementation, and honestly assessing results together is the only way to make progress. To that end, several university administrators and faculty serve on committees across the region that focus on economic development, historic preservation, community action, and resource development. This form of community involvement has facilitated a more nuanced understanding among university personnel of civic and political priorities, and it is through these commitments that meaningful partnerships have emerged via the following strategies:

1. *Collaboratively fund initiatives*. We do not always directly control what we fund. The university funds the Main Streets program of the city of Bethlehem. This program is overseen by a quasi-public city agency where the university has one of seven seats. This approach represents a bit of an adjustment. The agency board was at first unsure we were really willing to give up control—it was univer-

Colleges and Universities of the Lehigh Valley Area

- Alvernia University–Schuylkill Center
- Fortis College
- King's College
- Lackawanna College
- Lehigh Carbon Community College
- Lehigh University
- Luzerne County Community College
- Penn State, Lehigh Valley

sity money, after all. When it became clear that we wanted to empower the agency and would respect its decisions, there was a new level of trust between the university and Bethlehem leaders.[3]

2. *Cooperatively solve problems.* We work to ensure that anything we undertake includes partners from the community. Even if we have identified a problem as important, solving it by going it alone is viewed as a red flag. If we are unable to convince others that it is a priority, focusing elsewhere is probably the best course, at least for the time being.
3. *Agree to sometimes disagree.* We do not have to agree on every issue with our partners. Off-campus student behavior has been problematic at times for community residents. As a university, we have learned to acknowledge such problems, resist becoming resentful or feeling besieged, and work to resolve them. We do not let criticism prevent us from seeking opportunities to work together.
4. *Communicate with candor.* Frequent and candid communication with elected city and regional officials and those in government is essential. These officials have an imperative to understand the university's plans and actions. Recognizing that these officials maintain varied and complex relationships and constituencies is fundamental to forging a strong partnership. Not all parties will agree on all points, but there is much that all would agree on that can lead to progress for the city and its neighborhoods.
5. *Acknowledge missteps.* Miscommunications, confusion in planning, and lack of coordination in execution will all occur at some point in a complex initiative. The work we are doing in our region engages many constituencies. Misunderstandings occur, and addressing each one candidly, even when this is a challenge, builds credibility for later decision making.

Lesson 3: Leverage Both Intellectual and Human Capital

A financial commitment to the region has been essential to confirming that Lehigh is serious and dedicated to making long-term change. Yet a university's nonfinancial resources are enormous, and failure to bring these resources to the external community constitutes a huge missed opportunity. The drive and energy of undergraduate students, faculty research, and community expertise that reside on our campus can be valuable assets to the greater Lehigh Valley.

One of the greatest resources is our undergraduates' potential. Many students want to contribute to making the community better, and they fulfill this passion for service in a variety of ways. Students volunteer 60,000 hours in after-school programing and homework assistance provided by university undergraduates. Their work has led to measurable improvements in the academic performance of the local schoolchildren they serve. Entrepreneurial students have also started several companies in the Lehigh Valley, and employers in the region are taking increasing advantage of their talents. Lehigh has worked with the United Way and multiple corporate partners to establish a Community Schools model in a number of districts. College faculty have worked with the local schools to establish program parameters, hire an executive director, and evaluate effectiveness. Many of the school principals in our region are graduates of the university's graduate College of Education.[4]

Graduate students, many interested in nonprofit careers, work across the region as Community Fellows. These yearlong fellowships are jointly funded by the university and the hiring organization and provide talent and expertise to nonprofits and government agencies. Typically, the Community Fellows take on a project that the organization badly needs but is unable to address, and the experience the students gain is invaluable as their impact often exceeds the sponsoring organization's expectations. The university's involvement in the Rising Tide Fund, in fact, grew from a faculty member's service on the board of the nonprofit that administers it. The Lehigh leadership saw an opportunity to expand the program and provide additional funding for small businesses and entrepreneurs in the region. In addition, the original faculty member created an internship program where qualified finance students work with the fund to make loan decisions on applications and provide portfolio management, which enables the nonprofit to expand its loan portfolio. Lehigh also recently established the Center for Community Engagement, which helps coordinate such projects and provides service-learning opportunities to enable more such initiatives.[5]

Lesson 4: Centralization versus Decentralization—Find the Balance

At many higher education institutions, there is a constant tension between centralization and decentralization, and most, including Lehigh University, devise a hybrid model that works best for their circumstances. Our leadership team believes there needs to be a well-informed, experienced point person for community relations. Such a person can be especially effective in dealing with elected officials and governmental agencies that want and expect to contact someone who can speak with authority for the university. This single voice is critical when dealing with sensitive issues like permitting and public safety. Nongovernmental agencies also typically expect to be able to contact someone who can give them guidance and reliable advice.

Though having identified this need, the Lehigh leadership team has resisted the temptation to force all community connections and relationships through a single office, as key faculty often maintain existing relationships and a commitment to improving communities stemming from their sometimes long-standing research and scholarship. The Center for Community Engagement is charged with coordinating and supporting academic involvement in the region. Similar to the university's Community Affairs Office, the Center for Community Engagement often serves as a convener and facilitates connections for multiple campus–external community initiatives. Neither the center nor the Community Affairs Office attempts to control interactions; rather, their goals are to create the staging for successful collaborations across the region. Lehigh's Community Schools initiative offers a telling example of such facilitation and coordination. The Community Affairs Office worked with faculty and administrators in the College of Education to begin the discussion, and office personnel scheduled meetings among the college, the United Way, and the school district to plan how a Community Schools program could be implemented. Once the implementation phase began, the Community Affairs Office largely stepped out of the process. It had identified the opportunity, convened the right people to move it forward, provided some university funding to initiate the project, and then played a later role in its annual evaluation. Without a centralized function seeking such opportunities, bringing the right players together for a constructive dialogue would, in our view, have been more difficult.

At the same time, the president and provost recognize that faculty often have regional connections, research, and scholarly interests that do not require a centralized approach. As mentioned earlier, the Lehigh Valley is home to two prominent health care systems. Faculty continually make connections with both in ways that support their professional work, but there is no need for an administrative office to be involved, and the university resists the idea that administrative offices must be a part of every such contact. Finding the right balance between centralization and decentralization in town-gown planning is challenging. Regional organizations continue to assume that the university has a centralized model, which is common in a corporate environment, and expect a single office or function to coordinate all regional connections. Meanwhile, many on campus chafe at administrative offices becoming involved in ways they see as intruding or compromising their independence. It is a process of constant evaluation and negotiation, one that is well worth the effort given the contributions it can make to the region.

Lesson 5: Capitalize on Capital Projects

Integrating the university into the community has been a primary goal at Lehigh. For some time, however, there were few capital building projects under way, so there were limited opportunities to pursue this goal. With an ambitious plan for expansion having begun in 2016, the university routinely incorporates the impact on our community in all capital projects planning. As we have noted, Bethlehem is a post-industrial city that has made progress but is still recovering. Aside from the casino, there was, for years, a marked absence of development in the South Bethlehem business district that abuts the university. To help spur this much-needed development, Lehigh and the St. Luke's University Health Care system decided to become lead tenants in a vacant lot at one of the gateways to South Bethlehem. With leadership provided by the city's mayor, a new parking garage and office and retail complex were constructed. Lehigh's development and human resources offices, along with several other administrative functions, now occupy two floors of the five-story building. While both the university and St. Luke's had other options, they decided to make the investment they believed would best benefit the city, the university, and the region. Following development of this site, more than two hundred people will be newly located in the once-overlooked South Bethlehem business district.[6]

Lehigh is also developing a historic downtown structure once used for ice storage into thirty-two-unit apartment building with retail shops on its first floor. This development will bring additional residents to the downtown area and generate traffic beyond the workday, an important element in revitalizing the business district. The development was also conceptualized collaboratively with city and university planners to serve constituencies well beyond their town-gown footprints. Like Lehigh, many universities were originally built to stand apart from the cities and towns

A Lehigh University orientation leader conducts new students on a tour through South Bethlehem's revitalized business district at the start of the academic year. Photo by Ryan Hulvat

in which they were located. We have observed that a growing number of these institutions are beginning to reverse that dynamic—and building projects are a primary means to achieve this. Clearly, such projects involve major costs, and there are numerous other community implications. Yet creating these physical and human connections can lead to substantial benefits for both the university and the community.

THE WAY FORWARD

It is now accepted wisdom that universities have an important role to play in the regions where they are located. Increasingly, anchor institutions such as a university or medical system rooted in the region recognize their potential to be a force for positive and enduring impact and consider this reality in their strategic planning. Yet each university has its own complex set of institutional priorities, historical realities, regional and community relationships, infrastructure, and aspirations. It is a fair question for trustees and others to ask: Could the money we invest in the community be better spent on academic programs and more university-centric initiatives? At Lehigh University, we believe that investments in the region—investments leveraged with intellectual and human capital—directly benefit our students, and the students at colleague institutions as well, by providing opportunities for a richer educational experience. We also believe that the university's long-term health is tied to the region, and we accept the challenge of making prudent investments and capitalizing on opportunities to contribute.

At Lehigh our commitment to the region is a strategic priority. Our community and region are both changing rapidly, as is the university. In this dynamic environment, we have made mistakes and we have had significant successes as we have continued to assess what we are doing, whether it is working, and what needs to be improved in the future. While uncertainty remains about many outcomes, our commitment to engaging with regional needs and priorities is critical and constant.

CHAPTER 5

The Public Purpose of Higher Education

Building Innovative College-Community Partnerships

KATHERINE BERGERON, TRACEE REISER, AND JEFFERSON A. SINGER

Since its founding over a century ago, Connecticut College has enjoyed a relationship with the city of New London that demonstrates the powerful role that a private educational institution can play in a local democracy. This chapter details how Connecticut College and the broader New London community have collaborated to expand educational opportunities for both local citizens and students at the college while addressing known challenges, bolstering social systems, and strengthening the economy.

Student engagement with New London is at the heart of this collaboration. Connecticut College and New London share resources, facilities, and personnel to foster connection and advance the public good. Students interact in a wide range of environments where they develop nuanced skills in communication, collaborative problem solving, and leadership while also building their understanding of intercultural and intergenerational communities. They activate their education by acquiring valuable career and business experience in local public schools, health centers, hospitals, museums, and offices associated with economic development, public policy, research, and the environment—experiences that, in turn, prepare them for fellowships, graduate and professional school, and other national and international programs. In short, through these engagements, graduates leave Connecticut College with a wide repertory of experiences to pursue lives of meaning and purpose as citizens committed to the social, civil, and educational rights of all people.

The origins of Connecticut College serve to underscore this commitment to equity-minded education. The school was founded in response to an injustice—when in 1909 the only men's college in the state, one that had briefly accepted female applicants, abruptly closed its doors to women. Advocates for women's education immediately formed a committee, visited cities and towns across Connecticut, and began designing a new college. They reviewed different properties and settled on one they deemed "the finest site in the world," offered by the citizens of New London, which sits atop a picturesque hill overlooking Long Island Sound. The city was asked to raise $100,000. It raised $135,000 and won the bid. The state issued a charter in 1911. Buildings were designed and erected, a curriculum was prepared, faculty were hired, and the first students arrived in 1915. The partnership between school and community was born, creating the unique ethos of the liberal arts at Connecticut College. That same partnership eventually helped to define an educational concept that embraces off-campus learning as the centerpiece for engaged citizenship through which students learn to respond to challenges together with local citizens. This reciprocal relationship has created award-winning and mutually beneficial initiatives for both the community and the college. In short, the future of Connecticut College and the city of New London are linked in a vision of higher learning committed to educating students to put the liberal arts into action.

New London is located on the Connecticut shoreline two hours from Boston and New York City. It is six square miles and densely populated, with 26,000 residents who represent a wide range of racial, ethnic, and international backgrounds. Originally a land occupied by the Pequot, Mashantucket, and Mohegan peoples, it was transformed into a center for shipping and trade by English colonists in the seventeenth and eighteenth centuries; into a whaling capital in the nineteenth; and into an educational hub in the twentieth, with the arrival of three institutions of higher education: Connecticut College, the U.S. Coast Guard Academy, and Mitchell College. Today, New London is characterized by a historic waterfront with some architecturally distinctive neighborhoods, a downtown with a grand movie palace–turned–performing arts center, unique art gallery spaces, record and antique sellers, restaurants and coffee shops, florists and wine merchants, a food co-op, and fair-trade shopping. It supports local maritime and historical societies, a vigorous arts community, a symphony orchestra, and many talented artists, musicians, and writers. Ocean Beach Park is a vibrant public waterfront with amusements, a municipal pool, a boardwalk, and a natural wildlife preserve. Many faith communities welcome the college's students to churches, synagogues, and mosques.

New London is also a regional transportation center with bus terminals, ferries, and the longest continuously operating train station in the

Northeast Corridor. It is a medical hub with a major hospital and many regional health centers; it is the county seat with district and superior court houses; and it is a nexus of human and social services with a wide range of facilities for those facing domestic violence, addictions, food insecurity, and homelessness, and is the only area municipality with viable public housing. In short, New London is a small city with many fine assets and some of the same pressing challenges found in larger urban centers. And yet, as this chapter shows, its relatively small scale and long-standing relationships with the college and other community partners have made it possible for the city to establish systems to help address its challenges.

Connecticut College's mission is to educate students to put the liberal arts into action as citizens of a global society. It fulfills this mission in the full range of work it supports; in compelling faculty research; in distinctive academic programs; in the campus's diversity, equity, and shared governance; in the adherence to common ethical and moral standards; in the efforts to educate the whole person; in the commitments to community service and global citizenship; and in the ongoing stewardship of the environment. In all of these endeavors and priorities, Connecticut College offers a holistic education that challenges students to become integrative thinkers, collaborative leaders, and engaged citizens who can excel in chosen professions and skillfully contribute to building a healthier and more just world. The entire college organizational structure supports the mission and values, from academics to student life and athletics, from career, to equity and inclusion, to community partnerships. The college's graduates are leaders in science, technology, media, the health professions, law, government, public policy, and the arts. They are also peacemakers, community builders, politicians, and social entrepreneurs. They succeed in their chosen careers by working to build communities that effect change.

The Colby College–Downtown Waterville Project

Marking an important moment in the history of Colby College and its home city of Waterville, Maine, the Bill & Joan Alfond Main Street Commons, housing two hundred students, faculty, and staff, opened in August 2018 in downtown Waterville. Part of a $65 million revitalization effort undertaken by college and city leaders, as well as local businesspeople and community organizations, the complex has spurred private investment in real estate as Colby has renovated a historic bank building downtown into a technology center housing CGI Group, Inc., which hopes to create up to two hundred

(*continued*)

additional jobs in the Waterville area, a business incubator space, and restaurants on its ground floor. The project intends to bring new energy and engagement to the downtown area and to serve as a model for other private colleges by deepening the connections between the Colby community and the broader Waterville community.

Several months after the opening, **DAVID GREENE**, Colby's president since 2014, who has made it a priority to connect Colby's liberal arts curriculum more fully with the world beyond its campus, responded to three central questions about the Downtown Waterville Project:

What is the single most important piece of advice you would offer to a college or university president now undertaking a major collaboration with members of its external community?
Take the idea of a *partnership* seriously. We spent nearly nine months planning the collaboration and redevelopment with a group of twenty-five civic and business leaders. We had to break through stereotypes and distrust and ultimately forge a true, mutually beneficial partnership with shared goals and purposes. This carefully designed approach has served us well in the intervening years.

Although the Downtown Project is still in various stages of development, what is one key lesson that you have already learned by participating in this town-gown collaboration?
Persistence and adaptability are key in any type of town-gown collaboration. Undertaking major projects on campus is hard enough, but it becomes all the more challenging when the number of constituent groups expands and when they have relationships to the efforts very different from those of campus groups. There will be many obstacles—some anticipated and others completely out of the blue—and working through them in a systematic and dogged way is key. At the same time, being humble enough to recognize that early plans might not be entirely right or that compromise is the best course of action is also important. Finally, there is no such thing as communicating too much.

From your presidential perspective, what are the most important ways that the downtown project will transform Waterville as a college town?
Our efforts are designed first and foremost to create jobs, stimulate commercial activity, and help the city and its inhabitants prosper. A thriving city is good for everyone. We want to see growth in the population and tax base, stronger schools and services, and the kind of vibrant downtown that enriches the quality of life for all those living and visiting here.

THE CONNECTICUT COLLEGE MODEL OF ENGAGEMENT

The Connecticut College model of engagement is effective because it includes the broadest range of partners across campus, in the New London community, and on a national level. At the college, the president articulates the vision and provides leadership in the spirit of Campus Compact, a national coalition of college and university presidents committed to fulfilling the public purposes of higher education. The dean of the college and the dean of the faculty work to realize this vision by expanding classroom and out-of-classroom learning into local, national, and international contexts.

Through our Office of Community Partnerships, the Holleran Center for Community Action and Public Policy, and the new Walter Commons for Global Study and Engagement, a campus-wide culture of engagement is fostered, inviting collaboration among our local partners and every division on campus. The faculty are engaged through opportunities to develop new courses, community-based learning, and action-oriented research. Many staff make the partnerships successful. The Financial Aid Office, for example, enables our students to participate in community service by providing substantial work-study funding and special engagement scholarships. The Division of College Advancement, and in particular the Office of Corporate and Foundation Relations, works to find donors who can provide financial support for initiatives. When grants are secured, Finance and Accounting insures compliance with all policies, regulations, and reporting requirements. The extensive campus programming that takes place annually requires the services of Events and Catering, Facilities Management, and Dining. The Athletic Center opens its facilities to allow swimming, wall climbing, skating, basketball, and other physical activities year-round for local students, while Library and Information Services teaches the basics of information and computer literacy. Our print shop provides flyers, posters, and handbooks to support these activities. Finally, the Office of Communications works to tell the story through articles, pictures, video, and social media. Without the assistance of all these offices, it would not be possible to host the hundreds of workshops, conferences, and fund-raising events that take place every year, events that raise thousands of dollars for local scholarships, refugee relief, cancer research, affordable housing, and services for the homeless.

At the national level, Campus Compact, the Corporation for National and Community Service, and AmeriCorps VISTA enhance the capacity of Connecticut College and New London to address pressing social issues. The college's Community Partnerships Office secures grants to enable two

AmeriCorps staff members to join the college each year. These young professionals, usually recent college graduates, demonstrate a commitment to community engagement and bring relevant skills from their prior internship and academic experiences.

More locally, the college has built relationships with the municipal government, the New London public schools, and a range of businesses and nonprofits. College staff belong to local task forces, advisory boards, and school improvement teams, and offer expertise on established committees and institutes in the areas of community health improvement, police and community relations, parent leadership training, and the United Way. The college has worked to secure both large and small collaborative grants for which we act as fiduciary, and we have also supported the acquisition of grants on behalf of our many partners by helping to write proposals, create budgets, and provide matching contributions and in-kind resources. Some projects cover just a semester's efforts, while others provide significant multiyear funding. These are some of the ways that we extend opportunities for education, skill development, community building, and knowledge creation. The following examples demonstrate these relationships in practice.

New London Public Schools and Connecticut College

A dynamic partnership has grown from a commitment to reciprocity and collective action in advancing educational excellence at both the New London Public Schools and Connecticut College. The partnership leverages intellectual and practical resources from across the organizations, involving stakeholders at multiple levels and locations. Goals established for each program are constantly evolving. To handle the dynamic nature of this partnership, it is essential to have not just individual leaders but also a permanent administrative structure to support its development. The college's Office of Community Partnerships, working with the Education Department, plays the key role on campus, while several staff in the New London Public Schools, including the director of partnerships, the chief academic officer, and individual school principals, provide school leadership.

The wide range of projects, programs, and shared resources fall within the following broad categories:

- *Facilities and resource acquisition.* We share facilities and support services for meetings, classes, conferences, and fund raisers. We also support one another in completing grant applications and securing external resources, particularly in areas of mutual benefit. We have secured grants from multiple government agencies, private and public foundations, individual donors, and corporate entities.

Five College-Town Projects with New London Public Schools

- Facilities and resource acquisition
- Reciprocal student learning and academic support
- Professional development
- Capacity building
- Unique programs

- *Reciprocal student learning and academic support.* We collaborate to raise educational attainment levels in New London by ensuring access and opportunity for reciprocal pre-K–12 and college student learning experiences. We have created and implemented a wide range of projects including College Access and Success; Women in Sciences; Kids, Books & Athletics; SISTER; My Brother; ENRICH; Camp Rotary; and the Advocating for Brighter Choices Mentor Program. In addition to specific programs, we work together to train and place college students in classrooms as mentors and tutors, including those offering instruction in Chinese, Arabic, Russian, and other less commonly taught languages. During the past two years, Connecticut College students who speak Arabic and Turkish have also assisted Syrian refugees in local classrooms and within the larger network that provides services to the newest members of our community. Further, we have a vibrant teacher preparation program through our Education Department with whom we partner on field placements, including student teaching assignments.
- *Professional development.* We work together to provide opportunities that respond to the needs of local educators and community members. Teachers and high school students from the region are able to take tuition-free courses at the college through our New London Scholars Program.
- *Capacity building.* College faculty and staff collaborate with New London on school improvement, governance councils, and hiring committees, while New London teachers and staff offer courses and guest lectures at the college. The set of collaborative activities is concretized in a memorandum of understanding that recognizes the ongoing partnership between Connecticut College and the New London Public Schools.
- *Unique programs.* Local, state, and national agencies have recognized these collaborations for their impact. Campus Compact recently honored the college with its Campus Community Partnership Award

for the excellence of ENRICH, one of the most distinguished programs we've developed in the past decade. ENRICH is an extended-learning-time initiative that provides middle-school students with a range of dynamic teaching and learning activities on the Connecticut College campus. Local middle-school students travel to the college twice a week after school to work with their student teacher-mentors. They study piano and music theory; learn about images and messages in the media; practice film making, editing, and production; and create projects that blend scientific inquiry with art. They also swim in the college pool, skate on the ice rink, and engage in dance and athletics that promote physical fitness and well-being. Through their participation, Connecticut College students acquire vital experience in mentoring and workshop development while building strong positive relationships with the youth. Many of the participating Connecticut College students are themselves first-generation students who have a passion for education and want the middle-school students from New London to understand exactly what it takes to get into and succeed in college and other post-secondary school endeavors.

How Colleges and Universities Enhance College Towns through Sports and Recreation

KATHLEEN HATCH currently serves as the executive director of recreational sports at the Ohio State University. She is recognized as an international healthy-campus specialist who pursues opportunities that enhance the overall well-being of students and the larger university community. Kathleen served as president of NIRSA (National Intramural and Recreational Sports Association): Leaders in Collegiate Recreation from 2013 to 2014 and speaks and consults for several higher education associations. Prior to joining Ohio State, Kathleen spent twenty-five years at Washington State University as executive director of university recreation and assistant vice president for campus life.

Healthy campuses are built, in part, through recreational programs that support curriculum and the university's mission. Increasingly, however, the cities and towns surrounding these campuses are being enhanced by opportunities to participate in these same recreational programs and activities.

At their core, these strategies attempt to disperse and diversify responsibility for healthy students across the campus and, where feasible, into local communities, creating a holistic systems approach. This broader, socio-ecological approach recognizes the interdependent elements that contribute to a healthier individual, community, and society and that promoting healthy people in healthy communities is a collective responsibility.

The Okanagan Charter: An International Charter for Health Promoting Universities & Colleges (2015) is one example of a framework for supporting a common vision to enhance the success of our institutions in this regard. Combining what are often viewed as competing or divergent priorities, the Okanagan Charter's fundamental call to action is to *"create a campus culture of compassion, well-being, equity, and social justice; improve the health of the people who live, learn, work, play, and love on our campuses; and strengthen the ecological, social, and economic sustainability of our communities and the wider society."** A growing number of universities and higher education associations, including NIRSA, are adopting and endorsing the charter or similar models as part of a commitment to shift from individual efforts, including at an association level, to a cross-sector collaborative or collective endeavor.

One area positioned to make a significant contribution to a healthy campus of the future is campus recreation. No other entity on campus offers the same opportunity, or has the same daily responsibility, to mobilize and influence a large, inclusive community electing healthy behavior. A growing body of research provides evidence of the effects of collegiate recreation on individual student success, putting the potential to impact larger communities within reach, on and off campus. Many universities are taking seriously the correlation between movement and a healthy brain and are rethinking the paradigm of simply making options available and instead intentionally designing movement-conducive environments.

Just a few examples that highlight this shift include Let's Move at the University of Toronto, which infuses exercise breaks into longer classes and lectures; outdoor adventure and nature retreats at the University of Wisconsin–Oshkosh, which targets communities such as first-generation students and those working through grief and anxiety; PLAY 30 Minutes a Day at Portland State University, which makes it easy for participants to see improvement in general health, including a reduction in depression; and RECESS, a campus-wide event that focuses on the importance of taking a break at the Ohio State University and highlights the connection between physical activity and overall well-being.

Access to these services and facilities also creates stronger communities surrounding these campuses. Campus recreation environments—including

(continued)

programs, services, and facilities—that interface with the college towns in which they are situated provide some of the most promising practices and opportunities for collaboration focused on health and well-being. Examples include shared bike programs with stations on and off campus; coordinated land use and facility master plans; professional certification programs such as fitness and mental health first aid; youth camps and programs; welcome festivities and celebrations; and collaborative recreational and sporting events.

*Okanagan Charter: An International Charter for Health Promoting Universities and Colleges, International Healthy Campuses, 2, accessed February 21, 2019, https://internationalhealthycampuses2015.sites.olt.ubc.ca/files/2016/01/Okanagan-Charter-January13v2.pdf.

One Book, One Region

Those who promote regionalism tend to focus on shared resources, integrated transportation systems, or economic development strategies. The partnership One Book, One Region is a different type of regional initiative that brings people together to read about and discuss critical issues of our time.

One Book, One Region (OBOR) began in 2002 led by a group of local public library personnel. The aim was to create opportunities for people from all walks of life to have a shared reading experience and to come together for discussions around a chosen book, including an author visit. People in the greater New London region convened, for example, to read *Across a Hundred Mountains*, to discuss the question "What would constitute fair and equitable immigration policies?" and then meet the author, Reyna Grande, to discuss possible answers. They tried to understand the horrors of the Holocaust by reading *The True Story of Hansel and Gretel* and talking with the author, Louise Murphy. They examined issues of health care in Haiti and dialogued with author Tracy Kidder. They struggled with concepts of redemption and abuses of power while reading *The Kite Runner* and conversing with its author, Khaled Husseini. And they discussed the trauma and healing of those affected by 9-11 by reading *Extremely Loud and Incredibly Close* and speaking with author Jonathan Safran Foer.

In 2016 OBOR invited Connecticut College to collaborate and expand the program's impact. We secured major funding from local and family foundations to develop a series of community- and campus-based programs, thereby building relationships across a more diverse range of perspectives and identities. The expanded vision brought the region together in new and compelling ways to bear witness to the human experience and to find our common humanity—a crucial outcome in this time of political and social turmoil.

The book selected for the 2016 OBOR program was *Just Mercy* by Bryan Stevenson, one of the most influential public advocates of our time. In the same year, President Katherine Bergeron launched the President's Distinguished Lecture Series at Connecticut College, bringing Stevenson to campus for the series' inaugural lecture and the culminating event for OBOR. In anticipation of the lecture, we implemented a series of free, public events and reading groups that explored the book's critiques of the US justice system, community-police relations, the tenacity of racism, human rights activism, and the power of compassion. We encouraged faculty to include the book and related teachings in their courses and to let students know about the public events as additional learning opportunities, and we integrated the initiative into our Winter Read program and gave copies of the book to Connecticut College students. Following this, we provided local high schools with copies of the book as well, and they integrated it into various diversity initiatives. High school and college students thus wrestled together with the far-reaching questions posed by the author, strategizing about methods and actions they might take to promote justice and equity. Finally, Bryan Stevenson came to Palmer Auditorium on the Connecticut College campus and gave a talk that mesmerized an audience of more than a thousand people, after which the college bestowed on him an honorary degree. The event inspired college and community members alike to become the active citizens we need to make our region more just and merciful.

Building on that success, in 2017 we continued the partnership, bringing together people of all ages and socioeconomic circumstances to discuss issues of race, identity, slavery, and freedom. Working with OBOR, we selected the book *Homegoing*, by the young Ghanaian author Yaa Gyasi. Gyasi's debut novel, *Homegoing* earned the National Book Critics Circle John Leonard Award for best first book and the PEN/Hemingway Award for a first book of fiction. It is a sweeping multigenerational novel set in Ghana and the United States about the legacy of slavery across the centuries.

The book explores vital contemporary issues regarding identity, immigration, and the far-reaching impact of human trafficking. The college connected the OBOR program to its summer reading initiative for incoming students and sent copies of the book to all first-year and transfer students as well as faculty and staff advisors. Books were once again provided to area high-schoolers and their advisors and teachers. Community members, professors, and staff led a range of campus- and community-based programing for several months and integrated the book into courses and activities with students from the New London schools. At the end of September, Yaa Gyasi traveled to Connecticut College, met with a select group of students and community members, and then engaged in a riveting dialogue before a capacity crowd—gathered again in Palmer Auditorium on the Connecticut College campus. The audience included students, teachers, and neighbors from schools as far away as Hartford, showing that the One Book, One Region partnership has begun to foster a broad, intergenerational conversation to build understanding and create change. The college plans to continue the partnership in fall 2018, when Mohsin Hamid, author of *Exit West*, a National Book Award finalist, is scheduled to appear as the third major guest in this ongoing collaboration.

Thames River Innovation

Thames River Innovation is a coalition of higher education institutions, start-ups, local business incubators, and government agencies. Among these are Connecticut College, SparkMaker Space, BioCT, the city of New London, the town and city of Groton, and the Chamber of Commerce of Eastern Connecticut. The group conducted preliminary research, raised matching funds, and applied for and received a $50,000 planning grant from CTNext and the Connecticut Department of Economic Development in 2016 to create the plan for transforming our area into a center for entrepreneurism and innovation, a magnet for talent, and a launching point for early-growth companies.

To develop the full proposal, the coalition completed extensive planning assisted at every phase by Connecticut College student interns. In addition, a special course in design and public practice, taught by Professor Andrea Wollensak of Connecticut College, sought to work with community partners to create a geographic information display of local assets. In June 2017 CTNext and the Connecticut Department of Economic Development selected the proposal as one of only four Innovation Places in Connecticut and allocated up to $900,000 for the first year of implementation. The designation includes the possibility of three years of extended funding. This is a significant opportunity for the college and local communities to work together to strengthen and grow the local economy. Included among the catalytic projects are the following startups:

- *Cultivator Kitchen* is establishing a large-scale experimental kitchen to serve as an employee-and-entrepreneur education and business development vehicle designed to create new restaurants that will enliven vacant spaces in parts of New London and Groton. Project participants are also discussing ways to connect dining services at Connecticut College to the Cultivator Kitchen.

- *Ignite* is a creative initiative to promote education, events, and business development that will connect people, spark new ideas, and embrace ingenuity. For example, community members and students from local colleges and schools participated in a hackathon designed to spark innovative responses to regional transit problems.
- *Community Concierge* provides a comprehensive program to assist employers in the recruitment, relocation, and retention of employees by making meaningful connections to local arts, culture, history, shopping, restaurant, school, service, and community involvement opportunities.

Building on emerging economic developments and partnerships, Thames River Innovation developed these components based on the unique identity of the community: alternative, diverse, and intelligent.

The research and planning process for the CTNext grant generated five design principles for Thames River Innovation to guide assessment and improvement:

1. Aim high and grow into the project by design
2. Hold true to who we are and what we have the potential to be
3. Create unlikely partnerships to produce outsized impacts
4. Pursue success through reciprocity
5. Foster enlightened agency

The selection committee saw the great potential of Thames River Innovation to help our region become a hub for innovation, entrepreneurship, and growth. The greatest "innovation," of course, will be getting more and more people engaged in improving our cities through collective enterprise.

LESSONS LEARNED AND PITFALLS TO AVOID

Numerous lessons have emerged from this rich range of partnerships. The first and most obvious is this: town-gown relations cannot be seen as a special project to be completed. Rather, it is an evolving ecosystem based on the mutually beneficial exchange of knowledge and resources. Just as the college participates in major discussions within the community, the community contributes to a range of campus dialogues. Structured communication is established through the process of planning, implementing, and assessing shared enterprise. Many departments, offices, faculty, staff, and students engage in different initiatives, but it is the institution, Connecticut College, that maintains the overall commitment to the community. While the college's mission, values, and learning outcomes articulate that commitment in various ways, ensuring the success and coherence of campus- and community-wide efforts requires dedicated and centralized coordination and planning. Our recent Civic Action Plan, part of the national Campus Compact initiative, exemplifies the engagement of all sectors of our campus in community partnerships.[1]

Second, the college must prepare students, staff, and faculty to engage in intentional and ethical ways. This includes developing a greater awareness of self in relation to the history and demographics of local, regional, national, and international communities. We have a range of forums for practicing essential skills—critical thinking, collaborative problem solving, and creativity in communication and intercultural awareness—that enable meaningful off-campus experiences. We organize a range of dialogues about public responsibility in a global context and the ethics of engagement in real-world contexts. We provide classes and workshops for the guided exploration of structural inequality. We develop opportunities for people to reflect on their experience and to integrate new perspectives, insights, and knowledge into their lives and work. All of this skill building and leadership development is woven into our new, four-year program of integrative education called Connections.[2]

Finally, the college must enable students to acquire business, foreign language, and citizenship skills in all kinds of community settings both near and far. The work to be explored can range from teaching to administration and designing public policy and from producing pamphlets and communications to writing research and grant applications and creating murals, gardens, and performances. Students need to learn firsthand the value of such field experience for their careers, fellowships, work in graduate and professional, and other national and international opportunities. This educational mission is at the core of the Holleran Center for Community Action and Public Policy, the Community Partnerships office, and our new Otto and Fran Walter Commons for the Study of Global Study and Engagement, whose purpose is to advance dialogue and justice across disciplines, borders, and boundaries.[3] The director of the Commons, in fact, oversees the Global Engagement Council, composed of representatives from Community Partnerships, the Holleran Center, the Toor-Cummings Center for International Study in the Liberal Arts, the Office of Career and Professional Development, and the Office of Study Away. This council works to build culturally informed and ethical practices into all off-campus activities undertaken by our students, with the goal that these values become habits that persist in their lives and engagements beyond college.

In every project detailed above, the college has also learned that there are hazards to avoid. Chief among them is adopting the wrong attitude. We are not saviors and our mission is not charity. Our focus is teaching and learning. Keeping this in view deemphasizes individual and community deficits and produces active learners and willing participants. Partnerships should be directed toward reciprocity and mutuality, where deeply respected community partners work with our students as adjunct faculty and guides. Students should expand this perspective through opportunities to reflect on the role of class, race, and gender in society in multiple settings, including community-learning courses, advising sessions, attendance at lectures and events, and their own research. Students may be exploring their own passion for social change; however, this exploration should lean toward community priorities while emphasizing the cocreation of knowledge in advancing common goals.

Another circumstance to avoid is becoming overextended. The list of potential partnerships is endless, and requests will come from everywhere. Finding the right engagements means defining priorities for both the college and the community, priorities that, in turn, guide the selection of programs and initiatives. New possibilities, while enticing, should not disrupt effective long-standing relationships. Trust and commitment are earned, not given. Although emerging trends and innovation are important, certain associations need to be sustained in order for trust to endure. Of the many examples described above, some have been decades in the making.

We often say to our students that we want them to be transformed by their Connecticut College experience, and this includes their experience within the New London community. As this chapter seeks to show, Connecticut College and the city of New London are jointly committed to this kind of educational transformation. Together, we encourage students to find their way across different worlds of experience with open minds and hearts, by leaning into difficulty, and by learning to feel comfortable with the uncomfortable. Together, we change for the better by learning to see ourselves and others from different vantage points and appreciating the intersections of our different value systems. Together, we are developing people, joined in collective action, who possess the intellectual and emotional capacities necessary to contribute to the advancement of sustainable, thriving communities. This is how we produce true citizens. And this work has never been more urgent.

CHAPTER 6

Starting from Scratch

How Albion Reinvented Its Town—and Its College in the Process

MAURI A. DITZLER AND LORIN DITZLER

If you are searching for a successful liberal arts college, head to a small town. Forty percent of the institutions in *US News and World Report*'s list of the top 100 national liberal arts colleges are located in towns with populations of 16,000 or fewer, and 31 percent are in towns with fewer than 10,000. Meanwhile, our major cities host almost none of these top schools. Of the top one hundred schools, New York City has only one, Los Angeles has another, and Boston and Chicago have none.[1] It is difficult to imagine any other "industry" that is so disproportionately represented in small towns. No one would expect to find a majority of the nation's top one hundred hospitals, law firms, or high-tech companies located in small-town America. Clearly, something about these small communities makes them ideal hosts for residential liberal arts colleges. A large part of that competitive advantage may reside in the bonds among the college, its students, and its civic partners.

A survey of graduates of residential liberal arts colleges identifies student-faculty conversations outside the classroom as the best predictor of the students' lifetime success.[2] Graduates cited unstructured learning, often serendipitous, as the defining feature of their education. Given this advantage, it is not surprising that these colleges have historically flourished in small towns. When faculty live within walking distance of campus, as they do in so many small towns, they are likely to encounter students while walking a dog or taking an early-evening stroll. When the campus provides the best athletics, music, or theater in town, the probability of impromptu meetings during intermission is high. Life in small towns reinforces the educational practices that strengthen the colleges they host. Regrettably, this small-town advantage now faces a formidable threat. Many small towns, particularly those in the Northeast and the Midwest, are struggling economically in post-industrial America. Professional employees, including college professors, are not inclined to establish homes in towns where the public schools are underfunded, hospitals are closing, and downtown districts are disappearing. Regardless of whether students live on campus or off, it is hard for a residential college to function without residential faculty members. As more faculty become commuters, some of our finest small colleges are in danger of losing their historic advantage.

Our schools, our students, and our towns alike will suffer unless something is done to turn around this trajectory. Luckily, the colleges that call these places home have the ability to make a profound impact on their town's health, and a compelling self-interest to do so. Albion College is one institution that has opened a path by which a college can leverage its many local community and civic resources to guarantee an enriching and inspiring place to call home. Albion, Michigan, was a booming industrial town during much of the nineteenth and twentieth centuries. Foundry workers poured in from southern states and European countries to pour the molten iron that formed parts for Detroit's automobile factories. When those gritty plants closed two and three decades ago, and even backup industries like black-and-white television picture tubes left town, the local economy collapsed. National retail stores, local shops, and the hometown movie theater all shut down. Franchise restaurants were shuttered, the hospital closed, and eventually the public schools were annexed by a neighboring community. New-home construction disappeared and the tax base fell. Jobs were scarce and the city struggled to support a citizenry whose population dropped from 13,000 to about 8,500. For several decades, Albion College stood out as a healthy institution in a struggling city. In 2004, enrollment was at an all-time high of 1,950 students for this private residential liberal arts college with a national reputation, but gradually the deteriorating infrastructure of the town became increasingly problematic for prospective students and their families. Enrollment over the next decade dropped to 1,250 students with no sign of rebounding. Longtime faculty and staff continued to live in the neighborhoods surrounding campus, but newer hires were more likely to commute from far-removed communities like Ann Arbor and East Lansing.

By 2013 the town of Albion, like many other small industrial towns, was facing an existential crisis. Albion College, like many other small residential liberal arts colleges, had to acknowledge that its future was linked to the health of its host community. Yet some wondered if this realization was already too late. After a visit to Albion, Richard Longworth of the Chicago Council of Global Affairs speculated in print about whether the community and town were too far gone for a linked recovery.[3] Add to this assessment, a *Wall Street Journal* article on the linkages between the plight of colleges and their host communities focused on Albion as a worrisome case study.[4] However, the past five years of strategic, coordinated efforts by the college and the town are producing results which suggest that the historic synergy between small colleges and their host communities is still viable. The college has worked with the community to attract over $20 million in investments in the downtown district. Those investments are coming to fruition as the college's enrollment is bouncing back, from 1,250 to 1,550 in three years. Confidence is growing; the local paper's 2018 headline "Albion Businesses Look to 2018 with Renewed Hope" would have been hard to imagine just a few years ago.[5] For other small colleges in small towns seeking to replicate this process, a few themes are particularly relevant: taking action in the face of uncertainty, reframing local quality of life as a college priority, and applying the diverse talents of alumni, faculty, and students to local improvement, even among individuals who seem unlikely players in such a role. In the following sections, we provide examples and discuss these strategies in more detail.

STRATEGY 1: TAKE ACTION IN THE FACE OF UNCERTAINTY

"Plan if you must, but we really need to get some things done." That sentiment was shared often as the work to renew Albion gained momentum. The intent was not to criticize planning or the numerous master plans that already existed but instead to encourage activation of those plans. As is often the case, there was no shortage of individuals willing to debate the right course of action, but prolonged discussion presented the real danger that the college would get caught up in "paralysis by analysis." This is not an unusual situation for small towns that host colleges. In fact, the author of *Boomtown USA* identifies the presence of a college as one of the factors that, statistically, mitigate against the success of small towns.[6] Presumably, this correlation reflects the challenge of agreeing on a path forward when there are so many opinions held by those who can persuasively articulate their point of view. Fortunately, in Albion, a collection of individuals were ready and willing to take action in the face of a crisis, and they started down the path before all elements of the path were defined.

Renovation of the downtown Bohm Theater was one of the first benefits of the "act-now" attitude. The Bohm was built with all the glamour of the 1920s—high ceilings, ornate walls, majestic balcony, and plush seating—and designed to accommodate over five hundred patrons watch-

Albion's Five Best Practices to Strengthen Town-Gown Relationships

- Take action in the face of uncertainty
- Align the needs of college and community while improving quality of life
- Leverage alumni talent
- Expand campus support by including unlikely players
- Move beyond historical barriers

ing silent movies on a single screen. Having fallen on hard times, the theater closed for what seemed the final time in 2008. While many small towns desire theater renovations, the sometimes million-dollar-plus cost estimates can simply overwhelm local fund-raising strategies. Fortunately, the head of the Albion Community Foundation had the passion and perseverance to raise nearly $4 million at a time when the blocks surrounding the theater were also dark. When the rehabilitated theater's marquee lit up for the first time, a large crowd came to celebrate, even though it was a lone beacon on a dark street. The community had taken a chance and invested in the Bohm with no certainty of what was coming next or when it might happen.

At about the same time that the Community Foundation championed the reopening of the theater, a group of Albion College trustees recognized that the historic buildings that lined the brick-clad main street were on the verge of slipping beyond repair. Many of the storefronts were vacant, and others housed small businesses that were not generating enough revenue to fix their leaky roofs and crumbling walls. Those board members worked, in the face of great skepticism, to pull together a handful of partners willing to purchase and stabilize many of the town's historic buildings. As one result, many of the original investors in properties soon realized that the town was in such deep economic difficulty that their initial expenditures and investments of time would need to become donations rather than economic investments. Albion Redevelopment Corporation, a 501(c)(3), was created to accept donations of property and oversee their development. In most cases, it was not clear what would become of the buildings, yet those involved realized that the time for action was short.

With help from a collaborative effort that increasingly grasped the benefits of a "college town" approach, the purpose for the buildings soon became clear. An experienced developer with ties to the college donated his time and sold properties at cost for the creation of an upscale hotel in the midst of the town's deteriorating infrastructure. Simultaneously, the college purchased a string of renovated buildings in order to create a presence on Main Street before there was evidence that its multiyear enrollment decline was turning around. Much of this critical work was driven by faith that the college could and would bounce back, coupled with an understanding that the reinvigoration of Albion as a new model of the American college town could help achieve this goal. Still, while there was ample skepticism locally, Albion College's Board of Trustees gambled on a struggling town at a time when the college was looking for a reason to believe in its future. This gamble became justified by the clear and advertised linkage between rebuilding the host community and enhancing the college's mission.

STRATEGY 2: ALIGN THE NEEDS OF COLLEGE AND COMMUNITY WHILE IMPROVING QUALITY OF LIFE

Colleges have an ethical responsibility to support their host communities and the quality of life in the surrounding region. Just as it is unethical to ignore the intent of a donor, no matter what the size of the gift, it is also inappropriate to ignore the needs of the local community. In addition, colleges that foster a quality residential experience have a pragmatic reason for focusing on the local environment. As mentioned above, the serendipitous learning that often occurs when students and faculty run into each other at a soccer game or in a grocery store happens only when faculty live in the town, yet keeping both senior and newly hired professors close by becomes a struggle in small towns with a declining quality of life. Recognizing and articulating an educational benefit to economic revitalization generated a decisive consensus on the Albion campus as to the importance of allocating resources to its town. It was clear in 2015 that in order to attract faculty and staff, the college needed better faculty housing options, after-hours health care, more robust public education, and cultural opportunities in all four seasons. These are some of the key actions the college took to rebuild its college town identity and relationships.

- *Housing opportunities*: The college invested in the purchase of abandoned or distressed houses in the neighborhood between campus and the downtown. An alumni couple established a fund that was used to assist faculty and staff in purchasing and renovating these houses. In return, the purchasers agreed to live adjacent to campus for at least five years. This project is transforming the neighborhood that students must traverse to access the new downtown

The interior of the Career and Internship Center, a project by Albion College that converted five old storefronts into a site that supports collaboration between the city and the college. Albion College

shops, hotel, restaurants, theater, and coffee shops. It is rebuilding a tax base and providing customers for local businesses. And, most important, it is increasing the amount of time faculty and staff spend on campus.

- *Health care improvements*: Albion lost its local hospital shortly after the last foundry closed. Several medical groups established clinics in town, but after-hours care was not available to community residents. The same was true for college students, as the campus health care services were open only during normal business hours. The need for more comprehensive health care to attract faculty and staff to the town, the needs of local residents, and the needs of the college's students provided strong justification for the college to negotiate with a regional health care provider to open an after-hours clinic near campus. The combined populations of local residents and students, along with a state allocation, established the basis for an upgrade to local health care.
- *Local school enrichment*: Public education in Albion was a casualty of Michigan's school-of-choice program. As an eroding tax base undermined the quality of local schools, families sent their students, and their tax revenue, to schools in surrounding communities. This

created a self-perpetuating budget crisis that led first to the closing of the local high school, then the middle school, and finally the elementary school. Albion College partnered with a neighboring school district to rebuild the town's public education options. This support included providing a scholarship program for high-performing, low-income students from the Albion district. For each entering class, up to ten local students receive room, board, and tuition at the college in return for volunteer service in programs designed to benefit the community. College students from underrepresented populations can apply for a no-cost post-baccalaureate program in teacher education in return for teaching in the local public schools. As of this writing, the ratio of college-student tutors to elementary students is nearly one-to-one at the neighborhood school.

- *New cultural attractions*: As described above, residents raised nearly $4 million to renovate the abandoned Bohm movie theater. The college provided support by underwriting free tickets for students at all showings. Several faculty members, working on their own initiative, promoted live music in the venue, and the resulting monthly schedule of concerts inspired more residents to believe that the downtown was coming back to life.[7] This led to foundation funding to create a facility in an adjacent building for local and college theater groups.

All of these projects address critical needs for the town of Albion, and, equally important, they support the college's mission and approach to undergraduate education by inviting and encouraging faculty and staff members to live in the neighborhoods of the revitalized college town.

STRATEGY 3: LEVERAGE ALUMNI TALENT

As small towns fall on difficult economic times, there is a natural exodus of those with the expertise to lead a turnaround. A college town, however, has an advantage: a national network of alumni with a range of valuable expertise. The challenge, of course, is getting them to return to a place they loved as a student and provide the expertise they have acquired as an adult. As the town of Albion struggled to find its way in the post-industrial Midwest, the college's alumni were often unable to articulate their vague unease with the collapse of a town that had been, at best, tangential to their college experience. The town they remembered was not a place where they ever considered staying, and while they may have admired the grit of residents, Albion was a town to be respected from a distance.

For those graduates who remained, it became clear that the collapse of the local economy was pulling down their college. Some were troubled by what they saw but also overwhelmed by the task of rebuilding what was already being called a ghost town. Other alumni were convinced that they had outgrown the small college of their youth and were ready to accept its seemingly inevitable decline as simply another assault on nostalgia. Fortunately, there was a small group of graduates with the inclination and the ability to spark a transformation. They believed in their college and understood that its future was linked to the economic health of its host city. Sam Shaheen was part of that small group; he had graduated from Albion College in 1988 and gone on to become a surgeon and faculty member at Central Michigan Medical School. Along the way, he acquired an interest in urban development, and by the time he joined the Albion College Board of Trustees, he had extensive experience navigating the government programs and private financing necessary for urban renewal. He recognized Albion's need for a high-quality hotel and had financed and built similar facilities in other depressed cities. Shaheen found just the right partner in Bob Mahaney, a 1980 graduate who had established a business that manages luxury hotels in secondary markets. The alignment of these two alumni resulted in the construction of an $11 million Courtyard by Marriott hotel that now anchors the downtown district.

Jeff Petherick, another trustee and Albion graduate, had experience with an angel investment fund for Detroit. He applied that know-how to creating the New Albion Impact Group (NAIG) to support start-up businesses in town, and this group immediately aligned with the Albion

A Marriott hotel serves an anchor facility near the Albion College campus. It was built and is managed by alumni. Albion College

Redevelopment Corporation, a public charity that focuses on providing space to start-ups. The initial project drawing on NAIG resources is a microbrewery, established by a team including a faculty member and a recent graduate of the college. Alumni Bill and Karen Dobbins, local citizens who run a manufacturing plant on the edge of town, have grasped the benefits of the college town momentum and are renovating a series of buildings to provide apartments, a bakery, and a retail store. As these initiatives gathered strength, individuals with no prior affiliation with the town of Albion or the college recognized the opportunities and began buying properties to develop a variety of new businesses. In retrospect, Albion's college town fortunes were driven by graduates and others who appreciated the college's expanding mission and were more committed to it than simply to retail profits.

STRATEGY 4: EXPAND CAMPUS SUPPORT BY INCLUDING UNLIKELY PLAYERS

Urban renewal and small-town economic development are not typically foremost among the priorities one associates with liberal arts colleges. Nevertheless, in our case, members of the campus community played a key set of roles in the revitalization of Albion. Perhaps a survival instinct kicked in when it became apparent that the college could not thrive as blight spread to several edges of the campus property. Perhaps they responded to the recent Strategic Plan that called for local partnerships, or maybe they adopted the slogan "Albion is America" and understood that local issues were a microcosm of national issues. Whatever their motivation, individuals with little or no experience in economic development clearly found ways to make a lasting difference. Charles Moreau, a physics professor, played a lead role in building and opening the microbrewery mentioned previously. Cliff Harris, in the Chemistry Department, organized blues concerts and jam sessions that attracted musicians from across Michigan and surrounding states.[8] Jess Roberts, an English teacher, created teams of middle-school students who promoted literacy throughout the community. Multiple faculty, staff, and students immersed themselves in local politics.

Grant writers at the college assisted town and county entities in preparing applications that resulted in funding for new state and national hiking trails in the community. Alumni established internships for students interested in building the local economy, as several recent graduates remained in Albion to work for the Economic Development Corporation, the Food Hub, and several AmeriCorp VISTA projects. Two of the college's signature programs are relocating from campus to renovated facilities on Albion's main street. The Gerald Ford Institute for Public Service and the Gerstacker Institute for Business have missions aligned with redevelopment work, and the transformation of five storefronts into an educational space changed the dynamic of an entire block, providing much-needed momentum and signaling, again, the college's confidence in the town-gown identity.

When a team of students publicly acknowledged the importance of resident faculty and volunteered to assist with the renovation of abandoned houses, they offered another sign for Albion's civic leadership that the college's students cared and valued a faculty presence in the community. Several donors also remarked that support for community development was one more way to enrich the Albion student experience. As members of the campus community became vested in the town's success and stepped into redevelopment roles they would never have anticipated, they became effective advocates for the community, eagerly anticipating the opening of new businesses and then supporting them. In the span of four years, downtown Albion transformed from a place that students and staff had avoided to a more vibrant, and relevant, community that reflected a new model for college towns of modest means to consider.

STRATEGY 5: MOVE BEYOND HISTORICAL BARRIERS

Working-class towns and elite colleges have not always mixed well, and Albion College and its local community have not always been an exception. Town residents tell stories of scaling the brick wall built to keep them off the athletic fields. Many, if not most, on campus today have never known that wall's purpose, but lifelong residents of the town remember. In 1970 the college moved the president's home from town to a bucolic location five miles from campus. On one level it made sense, with a meadow and brook providing a better view than an aging steel mill. However, that decision created a perception that the college's leader put more value in what he or she saw out the front window than in being a part of the community. Residents of the town reflected the diversity of the workforce in the factories and foundries. In the mid-twentieth century, they had trouble, literally and figuratively, seeing themselves on the campus of an elite college. Current residents remember their grandparents talking of being forced to sit in the balcony of the local theater while college students took the favored seats. They also remember that not all that many years ago their parents bought ice cream at the side window of the local shop while college students went through the front door.

College officials should not have been surprised when many longtime residents expressed skepticism in response to the call for town leaders to work with the college on multiple projects. Reestablishing the president's residence in town was an important first step in building new trust. Locating it adjacent to a closed public school and close to a collapsing steel plant sent several important messages, and they were received. Current and prospective college employees are now more confident about moving into town. Local residents take more seriously the college's intent to help rebuild the local community, and this latter message has been reinforced by making the reopened president's house available for local functions.

New scholarship programs for local students have also made a critical difference. With ten full-cost scholarships given to each entering class, many in town currently know or are related to someone attending the college and living on campus. In return for this support, local students agree to contribute four years of community service. As the college's diversity has come to match the town's, local residents have reach out to provide support to underrepresented students. These actions have created a sense of increased ownership that in turn has produced a new group of community advocates.

When construction projects were announced, there was a great deal of lingering skepticism. Decades of promises had not materialized, and there was an understandable suspicion that this round would be no exception. Even after ground was broken and major renovations were initiated, many residents still predicted that the various projects would never materialize. As those predictions steadily turned out to be false, they were replaced by a concern that the facilities coming online were designed and located more for the benefit of the college than of the town. This notion has been difficult to overcome as it is partly accurate. Many of the earlier projects were conceived and designed by those whose concern and alignment was exclusively with the college, so they tended to focus on areas within walking distance of campus. However, with early successes has come momentum that is bringing developers with a broader range of interests, and we are now observing a new round of projects with loose or no ties to the college. As part of this process, it has been important to create a narrative that emphasizes the important role of the Community Foundation and the local Economic Development Corporation. And, as the development cycle has matured, projects with broad-based appeal, such as a joint college-community after-hours health care clinic, have been added to the original focus on new businesses.

Suspicions established over many decades have not been entirely dispelled in the past few years, and there was predictable frustration when projects were greeted with skepticism rather than enthusiasm, but passion and confidence are proving to be the more powerful characteristics of current campus-community relationships. We have learned firsthand that being located in a small town can be a great advantage for a residential liberal arts college no matter what some of the literature may project. Yet the college and its community will need to collaborate in making sure that the local community can thrive in the face of challenging economic conditions. We view this commitment not only as a moral responsibility for the college but also as a matter of mutual survival. If the Albion experience is any guide, our residential liberal arts colleges are strongest when surrounded by a vibrant community that continues to provide the setting for those serendipitous interactions that create a valuable and meaningful educational experience for both current students and recent graduates.

CHAPTER 7

A Plan for Brooklyn

Engaging Community in the First Year of a College Presidency

MIGUEL MARTINEZ-SAENZ

> *I believe what the world needs now more than ever are living examples of people who strive to live lives of loving service to themselves and to others. I believe sincerely and optimistically that St. Francis College can be a living example of what it means to aspire to live in a beloved community.*
>
> Miguel Martinez-Saenz, inauguration speech, January 2018

St. Francis College, founded by the visionary Franciscan Brothers from Ireland in 1859 to serve Irish immigrants, continues that tradition today in serving many first-generation and immigrant students from New York City and around the world. The institution I joined as president in 2017 already enjoyed strong relationships with community leaders and local elected officials. With an enrollment of 2,300 students, St. Francis is surrounded by much larger institutions, including New York University–Tandon, City University of New York's College of Technology, Long Island University, and Pratt Institute, to name just a few Brooklyn neighbors. St. Francis's motto, "The Small College of Big Dreams," speaks to the numerous achievements of graduates in recent years. For generations, St. Francis College has graduated accountants, teachers, first responders, and more recently, nurses. Society requires these crucial jobs, no matter how innovative and technologically advanced things become. We are a necessary and vital institution. It is imperative that with the changing landscape in Brooklyn and the advent of the Tech Triangle in its downtown, the attributes and strengths of St. Francis College are not left out of political and economic conversations.

Following are six action steps presidents can take in their first year in the office.

START BY MAKING LOCAL CONNECTIONS

In my first two weeks in the position, the college's longtime lobbyist hosted a "Welcome to Brooklyn" event for my family, and the list of attendees from higher education, cultural institutions, and city and state politics was striking. Afterward, we felt as if we were in a small town rather than a city of more than 8 million people. I made it a point to follow up one-on-one with each of the ninety or so people who handed me a business card that evening. From that one reception, I can now trace back many new partnerships that are already benefiting St. Francis students. After meeting an executive from Bronx Community College, we realized that its qualified accounting students could transfer to St. Francis College to take advantage of our master's degree programs in accounting. I also trace a renewed relationship with the Brooklyn Hospital Center to that night. Our nursing students will now intern and be given clinical spaces at that institution. Brooklyn Borough president Eric Adams became a vocal advocate for St. Francis graduates based on conversations starting that night. The borough president keenly understands that many of the college's students come from the borough's underserved sections. To enhance our campus's accessibility to the public, he has committed to helping us secure several grants to support technology upgrades in classrooms and laboratories.

In addition, borough president Adams suggested that St. Francis offer special courses to make it easier for first responders, including police officers and firefighters, to begin or complete their degrees. He offered to help forge connections between the college and the police officers' and firefighters' unions to help the college tailor academic programs to suit their schedules and needs, and he also suggested use of the park outside Borough Hall as an extension of the St. Francis campus. As part of my inauguration festivities, we set up flags from every country in the world to illustrate the diversity and unity of our student body and Brooklyn as a whole. The flag display became an impromptu public art exhibit as

A New President's First-Year Agenda

- Start by making local connections
- Take nothing for granted about relationships or money
- Continue the traditions of your predecessors
- Leverage business-community partnerships immediately
- Honor your religious mission
- Practice radical hospitality

teachers brought their classes to view the display and many New Yorkers and tourists took pictures with their home or favorite flags. The college plans to host more student activities in this area with the aim of partnering with the entire downtown Brooklyn community and highlighting its college town identity.

TAKE NOTHING FOR GRANTED ABOUT RELATIONSHIPS OR MONEY

New York State recently introduced the Excelsior College Program, which promises free tuition to city and state colleges and universities. Ninety percent of St. Francis College students qualify for this program, and the college must now do a more thorough job of informing our students about the value and benefits of a private-college degree. Although we have done extensive outreach with many people in the community, there are still some elected officials with whom I have not had the chance to meet one-on-one. An example of how this has held St. Francis back was apparent in a recent trip I made to that state capital in Albany in April 2018. One Brooklyn elected official asked what kind of outreach we were doing in her district, and we were disappointed and somewhat embarrassed to learn that we had not received a single application from the high schools in her district. While outreach to that district has been moved to the top of our recruitment list, this discovery demonstrates clearly how many agenda items we have had to address in the first few months of this presidency. The main lesson learned has been not to take relationships with local elected officials for granted and to follow up on every phone call and concern as a new president. The new chief executive must forge and maintain an open dialogue that keeps these town-gown partners apprised of your vision and engaged in activities on campus. For example, we now invite the local City Council member to the Poetry and Prose Reading that results from the Senior Citizens Creative Writing Class which that member helps fund.

Elected officials are a gateway to new cohorts of prospective students, and the entire presidential leadership team needs to meet them, remember them, and reach out to them and the communities they represent. Also, independent colleges need to remind their governors and state lawmakers of their role in the higher education ecosystem. For St. Francis College, this includes sharing the results of studies like the one conducted by the Equality of Opportunity Project which found that students coming from low-income families have an increased chance of later making a sizable income if they attend St. Francis.[1] As reported in the *New York Times*, out of almost six hundred selective private colleges, students from St. Francis were offered the nineteenth best "chance a poor student has to become a rich adult."[2] The Equality of Opportunity Project (now Opportunity Insights) found that a student coming from the bottom fifth of incomes had a 49 percent chance to reach the top fifth of incomes as an adult.

CONTINUE THE TRADITIONS OF YOUR PREDECESSORS

One of St. Francis College's most revered presidents, Frank Macchiarola, had served as schools chancellor for the New York City Department of Education,[3] making it logical for me to reach out to then-schools chancellor Carmen Fariña. Chancellor Fariña's husband is an alumnus of the college, and she recognizes the college's prominent role in the community. She was extremely helpful in giving candid feedback on how the college could strengthen and expand its degree programs in education so that we can graduate the teachers New York City public schools will need over the next two decades. Chancellor Fariña was generous with her time and advice, and provided me with a lengthy list of people I should follow up with, including the resident of Queens College, Felix Matos Rodriguez, and various regional school superintendents.

I went to the meeting with the chancellor with the hope of gaining pipelines of New York City high school students for St. Francis College, but I left with much more, including a sharper, more realistic vision of how we can best help our students who want to become teachers. The Department of Education needs more special-education teachers to help students with dyslexia and ADHD (attention deficit hyperactivity disorder). New York City schools need more physical education and bilingual teachers. As a result of this meeting, the St. Francis is now deepening its commitment to producing teachers better equipped for New York City schools by focusing on certification in two critical areas: special education and English as a second language.

Another wise piece of advice for new presidents is to let their actions speak more loudly than words. As an example of this point, in 2017 St. Francis shared its campus facilities with 140 distinct nonprofit organizations and government entities that utilized our spaces for more than 750 events, including such organizations as the Caribbean Cultural Theater, the Child Abuse Prevention Program, and the New York City Department of Education. St. Francis also hosts a For Seniors program offering Tai Chi, swimming, film screenings, and classes in writing, computers, and art. The practice of bringing the community into our buildings with greater

Colleges and Universities in Brooklyn, New York

- ASA College
- Boricua College
- Brooklyn College
- Empire State College
- Kingsborough Community College
- Medgar Evers College
- New York Community College of Technology
- New York University, Tandon School of Engineering
- St. Francis College
- St. Joseph's College, New York
- The College of New Rochelle, Brooklyn Campus
- Touro College

frequency resonates with our local elected officials and has resulted in increased funding to upgrade those host spaces in order to better serve future students and community groups.

The goal that has guided us in these activities has been to build on the relationships established by our predecessors. Here too, we are learning to take nothing for granted. Building foot traffic by hosting community groups has raised the college's profile in numerous, positive town-gown ways. We have introduced ourselves to constituencies that did not realize we are located in Brooklyn Heights. Elected officials are often guests of these groups, giving us several opportunities to strengthen those relationships. Likewise, the long-term goodwill is priceless, as a mother or father whose child swims in our pool during grade school, for example, may return several years later when it is time to look for colleges.

LEVERAGE BUSINESS-COMMUNITY PARTNERSHIPS IMMEDIATELY

As the college president, I was invited to sit on two local boards, the Brooklyn Chamber of Commerce and the Downtown Brooklyn Partnership. Like most chambers of commerce, the Brooklyn organization promotes economic development across the borough and advocates on behalf of its member businesses. In addition, the Brooklyn Chamber is currently the largest and fastest-growing chamber of commerce in New York. St. Francis College is capitalizing on this opportunity by remaining engaged on the Government Affairs Committee and attending advocacy events in New York City, Albany, and Washington, D.C.[4] During my first year, I also participated in NAICU (National Association of Independent Colleges and Universities) and CICU (Commission on Independent Colleges and Universities) events, the national and state organizations that advocate on behalf of independent colleges. Our vice president for government relations is active within these organizations and has also formed a local informal group comprising government relations representatives from New York City colleges and universities that meets every other month. Since St. Francis College is one of the smaller participating institutions, these alliances provide valuable support. Also, the larger institutions have sometimes been attacked for their tuition levels, and St. Francis has taken the lead in countering that message by explaining the rationale.

The Downtown Brooklyn Partnership is a nonprofit local-development corporation that serves as the primary champion for downtown Brooklyn as a national yet sometimes underappreciated business, cultural, educational, residential, and retail destination. The partnership understands the value of a new kind of college town branding and actively builds bridges between Brooklyn's higher education institutions and local innovation firms in order to connect our students to job and internship opportunities. Downtown Brooklyn is home to more than 42,000 undergraduate students, and St. Francis College students benefit from access to its Partnerships Job Board events and to office visits in which student groups visit Brooklyn's most entrepreneurial firms to gain exposure to real-world applications of the skills they are developing in the classroom. Having ties to these organizations helps our students significantly by providing a way for the college to develop and expand its student internship program, as membership in multiple business and education organizations creates a larger pool of potential connections. Being active in these groups also demonstrates to local business and civic leaders that the concept of a college town, even within one of the world's largest cities, is a powerful tool with which to achieve both student enrichment and corporate growth.

Another New York Story: Manhattan School of Music

Manhattan School of Music (MSM) celebrated its one hundredth anniversary in 2017. An internationally renowned conservatory, offering degrees in classical and jazz music as well as musical theatre, it enrolls almost one thousand students, and its faculty perform or otherwise work in the New York Philharmonic, the Metropolitan Opera, Jazz at Lincoln Center, and Broadway productions. During his first years at MSM, **JAMES GANDRE**, its current president, completed $25 million in renovations to the school's campus, successfully reached the end of its largest capital campaign, saw the election of half of the current trustees, and expanded the enrollment

(continued)

by nearly 15 percent. In 2018 Gandre responded to a few questions we put to him.

How does Manhattan School of Music take advantage of Manhattan as its college town?
We have utilized the breadth of New York City, our "college town," actually, from our earliest days as a college. Our artist faculty largely are drawn from the city's great performing institutions. In addition, our students regularly perform throughout the city and region, including with the New York Philharmonic, New Jersey Symphony, Harlem Stage, Orchestra of St. Luke's, American Ballet Theatre, New Jersey Performing Arts Center, and Alliance Française. We also bring myriad guest lecturers and master-class artists to the college each year who are both New York artists and international artists performing in New York at Lincoln Center or Carnegie Hall, for example.

As president, what has been a successful strategy for you in developing partnerships and relationships with civic and corporate leaders in New York City?
What I have found most successful in presenting ideas to our civic partners is some kind of win-win situation. In one case we had a performance space that was needed, and the organization could provide instruction to our students with no money changing hands between our organizations. In some cases we may be able to provide students to sing for a large choral work that would otherwise not be done because the organization needs to watch its budget.

What is the single most important piece of advice you would offer to other presidents and provosts in developing successful town-gown projects with the leaders of the city or town in which they are located?
I recommend that before reaching out to a civic organization with an idea or a plan, no matter how timely, the president first study the recent history and present goals of the local organization and make sure they align clearly with those of your college or university.

HONOR YOUR RELIGIOUS MISSION

As important as meeting and building relationships with members of the local Brooklyn civic and business communities was my establishing a strong and visible partnership with the Brooklyn Catholic community, particularly the college's founding order, the Franciscan Brothers of Brooklyn, and the Diocese of Brooklyn and Queens, led by the bishop of Brooklyn, Nicholas DiMarzio. As an independent Catholic institution, St. Francis has always maintained a strong relationship with the diocese. Welcoming students of all backgrounds and faith traditions, I am committed to sustaining these connections as well as strengthening and expanding our ties with the Catholic and interfaith communities in New York City. In 1884 the trustees of St. Francis received permission from the state legislature to "establish a literary college" and confer diplomas, honors, and degrees. In June 1885 St. Francis College conferred its first bachelor of arts degree, and seven years later the first bachelor of science degree was granted.[5] When I began my tenure as president, I was warmly welcomed by the Brothers as well as by Bishop DiMarzio. The college's previous presidents had formed strong relationships with the bishop, and it was my goal to continue that tradition as president both professionally and personally.

During my first months as president, I was met with gracious hospitality by many in the Catholic and Franciscan community. The Franciscan Brothers who live in the friary near our campus shared their time with my family and me, and this helped me to learn more about the Brothers as individuals, the ministries they are involved in, and what led to their vocations. I gained a better understanding of this particular Franciscan order and an appreciation for their commitment to help the underserved populations in Brooklyn. Bishop DiMarzio and I met over breakfast at his residence and discussed ways in which the college and the diocese could collaborate with and support each another. The bishop has a keen interest in the issues related to immigrant communities and has done a great deal of work in the area of immigrant and migrant rights. It is an important topic to the college, as well, as our student population has historically drawn heavily from immigrant communities with a number of first-generation college students. The bishop and I considered how to best work together to offer ministry and spiritual support to our student body. This led to the creation of the Office of Mission, Ministry, and Interfaith Dialogue here on campus with the vision to reinforce our commitment to our Franciscan values. Staff members will help advance the programs and events organized for all members of the college community as well as our neighbors in Brooklyn.

Staying connected to and engaged with the Catholic Franciscan community also involves active, high-profile participation in the organizations that support the Catholic mission and Franciscan Charism.[6] As the new president, I was invited to contribute to an ongoing series of webinars sponsored by the Association of Catholic Colleges and Universities (ACCU). This activity has helped to establish partnerships with other new presidents and taught us more about what ACCU does to support the network of Catholic colleges and universities throughout the country. It has been an invaluable resource to me and my staff in pinpointing ways that we can learn and share best practices pursued on other Catholic campuses and in continuing to reinforce creative town-gown initiatives in our Brooklyn community. Toward these ends, I attended the annual meeting of the ACCU in Washington, D.C., in 2018 and joined the Association of Franciscan Colleges and Universities (AFCU).[7] This group, made up of twenty-four Franciscan institutions, opened an important window on how other campuses engage, discuss, and promote the Franciscan Charism on their respective campuses and in partnership with their towns and cities. Early in 2018, I met with Fr. Kevin Mullen, OFM, the Provincial of the Franciscan Holy Name Friars, along with the presidents and board chairs of the two other New York Franciscan institutions, St. Bonaventure University and Siena College. Friar Kevin wanted to explore how our three New York Franciscan schools can partner in sharing resources, ideas, and collaborative projects. Our initial partnership planning meeting occurred in the fall of 2018.

We stay connected with our Franciscan roots and in contact with the Franciscan Brothers of Brooklyn also through periodic meetings with the superior general of the order, Bro. Christopher Thurneau, OSF, and with the principals of Saint Francis Preparatory Academy and St. Anthony's High School—two institutions established and run by the Brooklyn Brothers. We meet at least once a semester to discuss events where the Brooklyn Brothers are the linking thread. Yet Brooklyn holds one of the nation's most diverse populations, and a few years ago St. Francis sponsored the creation of an interfaith prayer room for all denominations. This facility has proved especially useful for the college's Muslim students, who constitute one of its fastest-growing populations. A lesson learned in this president's first year has been that although our name, our mission, and our values may be based on the Franciscan Charism, we still need to emphasize, both in recruiting new students and in forming our town-gown collaborations, that all students are welcome.

PRACTICE RADICAL HOSPITALITY

When I became president, it was important to me as its new leader to focus first on enhancing the culture and climate at St. Francis College. In preparing for my inauguration, I wanted to engage all college constituencies in an authentic embodiment of the college's mission. To accomplish this, the leadership team formed an inauguration committee chaired by a member of the Board of Trustees and consisting of administrators, faculty, Franciscan Brothers, and students. We chose the theme "Radical Hospitality" and hosted a series of events that began by welcoming students to the start of the spring semester with a Cuban feast served by the leadership team. We held two orientations sessions, lunch and dinner, so that our evening students could also participate.[8] We designed a webpage announcing all of the inauguration events, and in addition to the flag display mentioned earlier, we also hosted two performances of *Lyrics from Lockdown* by Bryonn Bain, a Brooklyn-born activist and spoken-word poet.[9] Bain's fight for justice for those incarcerated mirrors my own work teaching in prisons, and the college recently celebrated the graduation of its first three students from a post-prison program.[10] The performance was followed by a conversation with the supervisor of education from the nearby federal detention center, who is collaborating with the college to provide an expanded role in educating inmates at that location.

The inauguration committee also incorporated a day of community service into the event with a focus on hosting underserved children at the college. We partnered with Big Brothers and Big Sisters and other community groups to expose young children to a college town experience of sorts, because we wanted them to know that a college education is a legitimate possibility and something to work toward. They were invited to tour our science laboratories and television studio, and they concluded the day by watching our Division I men's basketball team play a home game. As we're a Franciscan Catholic college, we also held an inaugural Mass, striking a celebratory note by processing in our academic robes from the main building down the middle of the streets of Brooklyn Heights to a church several blocks away.

The formal inauguration was the final event during which the college and the community came together to form a new kind of college town within the city. My comments focused specifically on St. Francis's plans to join with our many external communities to enrich the lives of our students. As a final touch, in order to engage the public, our advertising agency suggested that we announce my presidency in ads on the New York City subway system for two months of town-gown awareness. Each of the inaugural events gave us, by design, an opportunity to highlight the history and future potential of St. Francis College. Each person involved served as an ambassador sharing her or his vision for St. Francis with the larger community as we begin to design new models for the college and its partners to share greater resources and achieve greater goals.

CHAPTER 8

Right Place, Right Time

Presidential Vision and Political Realities

SUSAN HENDERSON AND AARON ASKA

INTRODUCTION: SHAPING COLLEGE TOWNS IN URBAN AREAS

Jersey City's odyssey from an overlooked, polluted factory town to the back edge of Wall Street continues as marginalized pockets of the city such as the Greenville Section are revitalized. Anchored by New Jersey City University (NJCU), the new housing and retail outlets that are transforming Greenville also serve as a revenue source for state-of-the-art facilities for NJCU's recognized music, dance, and theater programs. The journey would not have been possible had it not been for the campus's recognition of the potential in a new college town strategy combined with its long-standing commitment to serve a community on the move. Over a period of years, the NJCU leadership coordinated a group of dedicated, underleveraged business, civic, and community leaders into a team of partners that worked creatively and tirelessly with the president and NJCU's governing boards to shape a new model for campus-community relations—and action.

All university presidencies are the same, yet all presidencies are also different. Hence, a new president must celebrate her or his institution's strengths and opportunities, fall in love with the new place, listen to whomever he or she can, gain a deep understanding of the institution's history and culture, and then make key decisions. Early on, after carefully listening and questioning, the president must identify the right partners and build a team that has the skills needed to move the institution forward. New Jersey City University's identity is deeply woven into the history of its host city. Founded during the Revolutionary War as a fort and site of a number of skirmishes, Jersey City quickly grew into the conduit for Manhattan just across the Hudson River of food, tools, materials, manufacturing, and labor. The city was known for its rail yards and ferries that connected the rest of the country to the center of the financial world. Factories such as chromium hubcap producers and pencil makers dotted the landscape alongside longshoremen's homes. However, as tunnels and bridges were developed and manufacturing became international, Jersey City became a place of rotting piers and abandoned factories.

Insightful developers in the 1970s saw the value in developing the city as a bedroom community for Manhattan and an extension of Wall Street. Increasingly, financial transactions were done in Jersey City for the firms on Wall Street as a generation of renters and homeowners grasped the value of living close to the city without incurring the extreme costs associated with downtown Manhattan. Thus, since 2000, many financial institutions and other Manhattan-centric companies have moved their offices to Jersey City to take advantage of less expensive real estate and a ready workforce.

Historically, Jersey City State, now New Jersey City University, had served principally as the local, affordable public institution of higher education, preparing teachers, business managers, police officers and firefighters, and nurses. As a commuter school with limited residential space, NJCU served the populace in its near vicinity, yet its workforce and community were clearly evolving. Within just a few years, the city and the community surrounding NJCU became strikingly more diverse with an in-migration including immigrants who came to fill the jobs needed by the burgeoning business district. These included workers in the data analytics, logistics, international business, and health care fields. With a growing ESL program and partnerships with numerous K–12 schools, NJCU provided critical support for new residents while continuing its commitment to serving the traditional needs of the local community.

Colleges and Universities in Jersey City, New Jersey

- Eastern International College
- Hudson County Community College
- Hudson County Schools of Technology
- New Jersey City University
- Rutgers University, Satellite Campus
- St. Peters University
- University of Phoenix

LESSON LEARNED: KNOW THE TIMES AND PLACES FOR PRESIDENTIAL LEADERSHIP

With the explosions in new housing, relocated businesses, and numbers of new immigrants, and the associated need to make higher education more relevant and affordable in its area, NJCU needed new facilities, academic programs, and support services to meet the demands coming from its changing demographics. Without dramatic changes, the university could not continue to be an essential and valued resource for a city on the move. Out of these developments emerged new thinking about Jersey City as a new kind of college town, along with new opportunities for the NJCU presidency to shape both campus and community identities. Especially significant was the fact that higher education in New Jersey had become decentralized, allowing local initiatives to take root and flourish. Hand in hand with this decentralization, New Jersey's public-private partnership (P3) legislation provided NJCU and colleague institutions with a highly effective tool for innovation in addressing the facilities and resource demands arising from the rapidly expanding community and city needs.

To get big things done, a team with the requisite skill sets must be assembled. At NJCU the first priority was to hire a vice president with knowledge in real estate and construction as well as experience with P3 projects. In addition, the university needed someone with experience with construction projects that require support and cooperation from legislators, developers, and investors. We brought in someone from outside the institution who had these qualifications. As the president's role itself was

P3 Legislation

"P3 Legislation" refers to laws passed by state legislatures, authorizing infrastructure projects that utilize public-private partnerships and ultimately benefit both private and public interests. According to The National Council for Public-Private Partnerships, "33 states, the District of Columbia, and Puerto Rico have passed laws authorizing some types of P3s," but the council is hoping to expand the purview of these laws to include the development of more varied types of infrastructure projects.

Source: "Model Law Gives Template for State P3 Legislation," *National Council for Public-Private Partnerships*, January 24, 2016, https://ncppp.org/model-law-gives-template-for-state-p3-legislation/.

Urban College Towns: Three Lessons from New Jersey

- Know the times and places for presidential leadership
- Move the university to its students
- Treat developers and investors as colleagues and partners

also evolving, other college town players were identified, including Jersey City's mayor, county legislative leaders, the university provost and resident deans, and, off campus, real estate lawyers and developers, business leaders, and community representatives. The NJCU Board of Trustees and Foundation Board also assumed greater roles and responsibilities, including essential approval for each developmental step. With this enhanced, yet focused, team in place, the president outlined the ultimate purposes of these initiatives: To take advantage of P3 funding, to secure other funding sources, and to build new facilities in order to provide the appropriate educational spaces for new academic programs that addressed many joint campus-community needs. New Jersey is the third-largest logistics hub in the country and has a vast population in the Northeast Corridor. Jersey City, long the back edge of Wall Street, has expanded to include major national and international financial firms. Many of the arts have blossomed in Jersey City in the past few years, yet the city lacks appropriate spaces for performances. Health care needs have grown with the aging population and the demand for exceptional services from patients and their families. In response to these growing opportunities, NJCU has created new programs in data analytics, cybersecurity, global business, logistics, nursing and health sciences, security studies, environmental and life sciences, and educational technology. Businesses in these areas need a diverse and educated workforce, and NJCU is positioned to provide that by working with local businesses to craft "boutique" programs for their future employees that include a robust internship experience.

The region's workforce demands require students from beyond the immediate community, including international students who find the robust diversity enriching at NJCU. With this in mind, the vice president of administration and finance and the Student Affairs leadership identified a growing need for more and better housing for NJCU students. Our local students and those from other regions are increasingly cost-conscious, with more than half being Pell eligible. As at other institutions, budgetary priorities are focused on providing scholarships, supporting students, and ensuring a quality education. As President Susan Henderson has noted, "the NJCU community is personally dedicated to and accountable for ensuring that each and every student receives a high-quality education and first-rate experience that leads to timely graduation with minimal debt. . . . NJCU students also earn about 22% more than the national average income 10 years after graduation."[1] New programs that need new facilities are often left adrift or compromised by the onerous costs of construction and lack of state support for facilities construction and maintenance. P3 projects can mitigate risk and lower the cost to the student through ground lease revenue from projects that also enrich a community, socially and programmatically.

The town-gown partnerships that the university's leadership created in ongoing collaboration with Jersey City planners, developers, and elected officials have resulted in a campus where visitors feel safe and welcome and where students can choose from an array of academic programs that meet their needs while living in attractive, affordable housing. Along with an expanding set of cultural opportunities, these offerings are gradually revitalizing the Jersey City community as well as the university's main campus. They have given NJCU the facilities and revenue streams it needs to offer the new academic programs and student services in demand, and they have enabled the institution to meet the increased demand for student housing. As well, the university has relocated its School of Business to the waterfront right across the Hudson River from Wall Street. In short, effective, sustained campus-community planning and partnerships have given NJCU the means to meet these challenges even though the university originally lacked sufficient capital funds.

LESSON LEARNED: MOVE THE UNIVERSITY TO ITS STUDENTS—THE WATERFRONT PLAN

In response to the growing need for relevant business degrees on the Jersey City waterfront, home to an increasing number of financial institutions, NJCU decided to rent space in part of a building housing financial and other businesses. The twenty-year lease, with a renewal for an additional twenty years, provided the institution with the means to build out a state-of-the-art facility for the current business education program with the flexibility to update for future needs. With the hiring of a person with extensive financial experience as a governor of the New York Stock Exchange to be dean of business, academic programming mirrored the innovative facility development. According to Business Dean Bernard

McSherry: "This is a defining moment for the School of Business. Our presence in the midst of New Jersey's financial capital and our proximity to Wall Street positions NJCU to attract top faculty and to give our students a competitive edge for global experiential learning."[2]

Local legislators and government leaders were thrilled with these decisions and with the university's willingness to look to novel funding sources for facility development. As state senator Ray Lesniak said at the time, "Government resources can no longer do the job by themselves, but by bringing the business community in with higher education, they can work together to provide the financing that we no longer can."[3] Our own state senator, Sandra Cunningham, chair of the Higher Education Committee noted at the groundbreaking, "Look out and see Wall Street just across the water. I think it is a stimulating way to help students grow as they're talking about business and finances."[4] Also at the ceremony, President Henderson noted:

> With the growing influx of new businesses in Jersey City and the school's location in the heart of the financial district, NJCU has an important role to play in the economic vitality and expansion of the region. Under Dean Bernard McSherry, the NJCU School of Business will be able to take the lead in these efforts. The NJCU School of Business will be part of the business community in an exciting world-class environment where students will study with top scholars and practitioners and learn to become future business leaders. The benefits of this new development are beyond measure for students, faculty, and corporate partners."[5]

As another outcome of this innovative waterfront-based town-gown planning venture, the location and focus of the School of Business caught the attention of NJTV, the state's public television station and a partner with the PBS station in the New York Metro area. The station approached NJCU about doing a nightly business news report and locating the studio in the Business School, with a view of the World Trade Center. The program has been highly successful, and provides valuable insights for New Jersey businesses. According to Dean McSherry, "Having NJTV's business news broadcast to the metro area from a studio overlooking Wall Street at the NJCU School of Business sends a powerful message. This is an opportunity to let the business community and students everywhere know that NJCU is the place to go for business news and business studies in New Jersey."[6]

LESSON LEARNED: TREAT DEVELOPERS AND INVESTORS AS COLLEAGUES AND PARTNERS

NJCU's main campus is located in Jersey City's Greenville section, which consists of single- and multifamily residences. During the city's exponential growth phase, this relatively large section was decidedly overlooked. To help with the revitalizing of Greenville, NJCU worked with city officials and entrepreneurial developers to accomplish major change over a ten-year period. NJCU purchased several parcels of land now known as University Place. City leaders immediately recognized the property as a potential game-changer for community revitalization, eagerly joined the initiative, and played a major role in the development of the infrastructure, including roads, utilities, landscaped areas, and a new public plaza. The first phase of the project was the residence hall. Mayor Steve Fuiop recognized the importance of this project for the community at the ribbon cutting: "When you have more students living here, more students active in the area, it energizes the streetscape. It energizes not only the residential component, but the retail component, and we couldn't be more excited about what this project means today and what it means for the long-term side of Jersey City."[7] Aaron Aska, who was intimately involved in all of the facilities projects and continues to lead the development of University Place, noted, "This is only the first of many projects. The residence will be situated on a 22-acre West Campus redevelopment site, which will also include retail, a supermarket, a fitness center, tennis courts, and an academic building. In many ways, this privatized student housing project represents a bridge that connects [NJCU's] past to [its] future."[8]

The University Place project would not have been possible without private investors who saw the value of market-rate housing in a neighborhood on the rise. At the dual residence hall ribbon cutting and market-rate housing groundbreaking ceremony, Jeff Sica, Circle Squared founder and president, said, "The opportunity this development offers our investors is a chance to be part of something that will completely transform a neighborhood. At Circle Squared, we do more than connect investors to real estate deals managed by the best in the business. We connect them with communities that these development projects enhance."[9]

An event of this magnitude could not have happened without numerous university partners. As in other regions of the country, diminishing support from state governments for operational needs exacerbated the funding needs for updated and new facilities. Some state grant money was available each year that could be matched with institutional monies (obtained from reserves or loans) until 2012, when the state implemented the Higher Education Capital Program, the first in twenty years. Some of the funds required matches, others were outright, and all needed to fit in the state priorities for economic impact.

This disparate and uneven capital funding mechanism for higher education refocused the attention of both the New Jersey higher education community and legislators on a rational and innovative funding model for capital development. This gave rise to public-private partnerships made possible through the New Jersey Economic Stimulus Act of 2009 and the New Jersey Economic Opportunity Act of 2013. Reflecting an alternative, flexible capital funding model, this legislation has enabled state and county colleges and universities to enter into various P3 arrangements. The statutes were intended to provide the regulatory framework to respond to the varied capital needs of public four-year institutions and provide the opportunity for public institutions to partner with private developers for the purpose of constructing, financing, and operating institutional facilities without the public entity assuming the cost of financing or the related debt.

NJCU used the P3 legislation to develop University Place, and in 2016 the residence hall was completed. Since then, ground has been broken on the apartment units. One of the benefits of the P3 legislation is that it allows the state's public institutions to directly contract with developers to shift the operating and financing risks to these partners. The private partners are responsible for assembling their own finance, design, and development teams for the benefit of the public entity. The New Jersey P3 laws prohibit public institutions from financing privatized projects, and the private partners must comply with various labor-friendly provisions such as negotiating project labor agreements and paying prevailing wages. These projects required the unwavering support of the university's Board of Trustees as well as the support of its Foundation Board. To achieve additional savings, the privatized student housing project was structured through an affiliated university foundation that became the borrower for and owner of the project. Not only was it important to gain trustees' approval, but numerous approvals were required from the university's foundation board of directors, the New Jersey Educational Facilities Authority, and the New Jersey Economic Development Authority. These entities were critical to the success of NJCU's P3 projects.

While the student housing project laid the foundation for the other P3 projects in terms of their structure and compliance with the New Jersey statute, P3 projects undertaken since then have been even more complex and required the expertise of new teams of seasoned developers. As one example, an RFP (request for proposal) was developed for three distinct commercial blocks that now constitute University Place. NJCU retained a special real estate legal advisor responsible for the creation of the project development and ground lease agreements. Three developers were selected, and two of the three developers are poised to develop more than six hundred apartment units on four discreet blocks. Although the student housing project laid the building blocks for these commercial developments, each project has been unique and has required clarity about what a new kind of college town can become as NJCU and its leadership team has grown and evolved.

CONCLUSION: WHAT WE LEARNED AND WHAT WE WOULD DO DIFFERENTLY NEXT TIME

Over the past decade, even NJCU's strongest plans still needed modifications, sometimes many modifications, to achieve lasting success. Presidents and senior administrators need to remain agile and creative. For example, prior to the financial closing of NJCU's major student housing project, its foundation discovered that the institution did not have title to the two existing student housing buildings that were critical to the overall enterprise. If these legacy residential facilities were not included, the financial projections would not sufficiently incentivize the developer to engage in the transaction. In response, the city modified its strategy and decided not to pursue developer subsidies in the form of redevelopment area bonds (RABs), opting instead to provide the subsidies directly to the university in the form of an infrastructure bond. The amount of the subsidies remained the same, but the RABs would have been politically unpalatable in the city at a time when several municipal seats were up for election. This convergence of political will and economic realities motivated all team members to work together and be flexible and creative to ensure the P3 projects remained viable.

In addition, since the P3 application deadline, the economic landscape had markedly changed, several key assumptions had to be revised, and previously approved applications needed amendment. In one case, one of the developers modeled its financial pro formas on paying a 7 percent PILOT, later revised to 10 percent.[10] This revision could have derailed one of the projects, and the university made various concessions on ground-lease rent and extended the term from fifty to seventy-five years. In another instance, a developer decided to eliminate one of its proposed tenants and replaced its originally designed parking garage with surface parking. This revision to the parking component required all parties to

West Campus Master Plan, New Jersey City University. Office of the Vice President and Chief Operating Officer, NCJU.

return to the negotiating table and devise a mutually beneficial result. In the end, the principal reason for choosing the New Jersey Economic Development Authority as the oversight agency with approval authority for all changes in the project was its flexibility, which ultimately enabled this series of agreements instrumental to NJCU's growth and success.

In retrospect, hiring a master developer, Strategic Development Group (SDG), was critical to the success of University Place. One of the most important lessons the university learned was that we needed an agent to coordinate the execution of the multiplicity of legal and financial agreements not only with developers but also with state agencies. SDG was paramount in assisting the university in successfully executing those agreements, but in hindsight it may have been more prudent to structure the agreement with SDG whereby they were paid over a longer period, as there remained ongoing tasks to be completed after the agreements were signed. A series of milestone payments would have been preferable in order to encourage continuity in the group's involvement at a reasonable cost. However, as things turned out, SDG grasped the importance of the evolving college town concept for both the campus and the local community and often worked over and beyond the contractual requirements.

From the president's perspective, the final master plan ended up differing in many ways from the original concepts devised more than a decade ago. Yet, while the previous NJCU administration needed land to expand academic programs and also hoped to revitalize the surrounding community, the new University Place has finally become just that—a space for expanded university programming and residences as well as a long-sought revitalization of the community through market-rate housing and retail. An advantage of the new plan is the increased revenue flow that resulted from the P3 work that funded significant academic spaces without increasing the financial load on our students. For the campus, the local community, and most important, NJCU students, a new form of urban college town has been created, and it would not have happened without the right timing, the right partners, and a cohesive yet flexible vision.

CHAPTER 9

Community College Towns

Five Ways Presidents Can Leverage Their Resources

KEVIN E. DRUMM

INTRODUCTION: COMMUNITY COLLEGES AND THE NEW MODEL FOR A COLLEGE TOWN

Can a community college legitimately anchor a college town? Can a community college contribute significantly to a college town with a research university sitting nearby? What about a football team and a residential population? Is either necessary for a new American college town? As political leaders increasingly press public colleges and universities across the nation into service as forces for economic development, strategically helping to build a healthy college town is a key option for presidents, provosts, and other leaders to consider.

A community college may view strategic economic development in at least three dimensions: (1) strategic planning may focus on academic programs that help grow the local economy, a fairly standard approach for many community colleges; (2) strategic planning may focus on increasing the economic mobility of students; and (3) strategic planning may focus on building the core elements of a college town primarily for economic development itself. This chapter will focus on the last-named dimension: strategically acting to build a college town.

Community colleges depend greatly on the economies of the regions they serve. Those community colleges that receive either municipal or county funding (this author's among them) depend even more on their local economies than those that do not receive local funding, but both governance models rely heavily on the local population for funding if only through tuition and fees. Growing economic regions tend to have growing populations, and contracting regional economies tend to have stagnant or shrinking populations that will in turn erode a community college's market base.

Kevin Carey, in a recent *Chronicle of Higher Education* article, noted: "Colleges and universities are positioned to capitalize on the collapse of the blue-collar economy." As the nation further develops the service sector in the wake of a shrinking blue-collar economy, community colleges situated in communities with an existing foundation for a college town may choose to work with local leaders to both develop a plan and to help build a college town environment in their community. Carey further observed, "I believe that the idea of the university is stronger than ever. We love our colleges not for what they are but for what they represent—beauty, truth, justice, each generation's profound obligation to the next. Colleges are what great societies build."[1]

In the late twentieth century, most downtowns across America experienced some decline, and often major decline, especially in small metropolitan regions.[2] Providence, Rhode Island, and Pittsburgh, Pennsylvania, are two smaller cities that achieved national attention for their rapid decline, but both have remade themselves in the service economy in part as attractive college towns with major universities at the forefront of their growth: Brown University and Johnson and Whales University, among several others, in Providence; and the University of Pittsburg and Carnegie-Mellon, among others, in Pittsburgh. Each city has re-created itself despite massive manufacturing sector losses.

The Binghamton, New York, region is home to roughly 200,000 people today and to Binghamton University (no football team), Davis College (no football team), and SUNY Broome Community College (no football team). It was once also home to manufacturing giants such as Endicott-Johnson shoes and IBM. "E-J" employed more than 30,000 at its peak but is now entirely gone. IBM, with nearly 20,000 employees in the Binghamton region at its peak of computer manufacturing, is now down to fewer than a thousand employees in software and consulting. Consequently, the greater Binghamton area was hit particularly hard by the manufacturing sector's rapid decline from the 1960s to the '90s.

KEVIN DRUMM

What is the single most important piece of advice you would give to a new college president on her or his first day about working with a mayor or city planner on a town-gown project?

Know the economic and workforce trends of your region.

By the time I arrived as president of SUNY Broome Community College in 2010, the population of Binghamton proper had declined from roughly 75,000 people at its peak to 45,000. SUNY Broome receives county funding, and by 2010 the tax base to support the college had eroded significantly. But that year a new student residence opened in downtown Binghamton next door to Binghamton University's downtown center, and as the community college president I began speaking out about strategically building a college town in Binghamton rather than simply chancing that it might continue to happen organically. In presentations to community groups, in op-eds, and in speeches, I pressed the idea of building a college town as deliberate economic development.

It turns out I am not alone as a community college leader thinking about intentionally building a college town. Jon Connolly, president of Sussex County Community College in New Jersey, was asked about his attitude toward building a community college town. "Three years ago," he responded, "the Town of Newton, [New Jersey,] undertook a campaign to promote itself as a 'college town.' This campaign was the result of a concerted partnership between the college and the town and began with an idea from one empowered college employee."[3]

FIVE WAYS PRESIDENTS CAN MAKE A DIFFERENCE

Start at the Beginning and Build Shared Support

So, if you want to strategically build a college town, where do you start?

First, you have to sell the idea, on campus and with your trustees, that not all of your investment should be on campus and that the future of your community is the future of your community college. Shortly after I was hired in 2010, I began the process by talking about the idea of a college town in early interviews with local media and in my first op-ed as president. Selling the vision is critical for a community college, though not so much for many state universities, which rely on their state or larger geographic region for their students, as Binghamton University does in Binghamton, New York, our community college's nearest SUNY neighbor, just a few miles away. The university's success is not tied to the region's success. In fact, the university has been steadily growing for many years in spite of the region's economic decline, while SUNY Broome struggles mightily just to maintain enrollment (80 percent of revenue) in the wake of a long-declining local population and a somewhat improving regional economy. Therefore, helping to build the community, however it might happen, is critical to the future of SUNY Broome Community College. And helping to build a college town, as one major focus for economic development among four or five strategic areas, has become a priority for the college and also for local political and industry leaders.

Determine a Downtown Project on Which to Focus Investment

So, just what makes a college town?

In 2004 the *Journal of the American Planning Association* published a study of the best downtowns in North America.[4] The authors asked urban planners from across the United States and Canada what were the best downtowns in North America. Their responses indicated that "only a small number of North American metro regions possess a successful downtown" and that, of those successful few, a large proportion were college towns.[5]

The authors did not set out to study college towns. They asked urban planners across North America which were the best downtowns. It turned out, in studying the characteristics of the nineteen top downtowns in North America, the urban planners found that a key characteristic common to the majority was having a college downtown or within a few miles. Other characteristics also emerged that led the American Institute of Architects (AIA) to conduct an observational study of what, besides having a college or colleges nearby, made the top downtowns so attractive. What the authors discovered provides a roadmap for how to intentionally build a college town and community colleges can participate if they choose. We can't participate at the level of a large, public or private university, but we can participate and it is happening around the country.

The top downtowns cited by urban planners were, in alphabetical order: Asheville, North Carolina; Athens, Georgia; Boise, Idaho; Burlington, Vermont; Charlottesville, Virginia; Chattanooga, Tennessee; Fort Collins, Colorada; Halifax, Nova Scotia; Iowa City, Iowa; Kingston, Ontario; Madison, Wisconsin; Rochester, Minnesota; San Luis Obispo, California; Savannah, Georgia; Santa Fe, New Mexico; State College, Pennsylvania; Victoria, British Columbia; and Wilmington, North Carolina. "In the majority of instances where downtowns are successful," according to Anirban Adhya in the *AIA Journal*, "a picture of integration [emerges] where the downtown and campus have coalesced into a strong and vibrant interface."[6]

Find Willing Partners

At SUNY Broome, working with local economic development groups led to projects aimed at strategically helping to build Binghamton, New York, into a cool college town. Some projects already had sprung up organically after the local university built a downtown center in an effort to help turn around a decaying inner city in the wake of losing tens of thousands of

Five Ways Presidents Can Make a Difference in College Town Planning

- Start at the beginning and build shared support
- Determine a downtown project on which to focus your investments
- Find willing partners
- Look for opportunities on campus to further the vision
- Benchmark other college towns

traditional manufacturing jobs. A privately funded student housing complex was built next door, and eventually other private housing projects sprang up. Restaurants began opening and new pubs popped up like dandelions in spring. As SUNY Broome became involved strategically enhancing the college town, it built on an organic effort already begun. But as a major entity in the community, it was the community college that pushed local leaders into investing in the college town concept, and so the college had to put its resources where its vision was and ultimately invested in two major downtown projects.

SUNY Broome has also partnered with Binghamton University on a downtown project where the university recently opened a traditional business incubator on the first two floors and SUNY Broome operates a student business incubator on the third floor of the new building. We are also renovating a historic building just a block from the incubator where a new Culinary and Events Center will be located in the heart of downtown Binghamton. SUNY Broome, founded as Broome Tech in 1946, hadn't operated in downtown Binghamton since the campus was moved to an immediate suburb just a few years after it opened. Studies show that college towns, as well as the most successful downtowns, take strategic advantage of their historic buildings.

KEVIN DRUMM

What is one of the most important lessons that you learned either from researching and writing this chapter, or from your broader, ongoing work with elected officials on college town projects through your career?
Learn about the assets already in place and find partners to fill in what's missing for a college town.

Historic preservation is one hallmark of identified successful college towns. SUNY Broome is renovating this 1904 Carnegie Library building in downtown Binghamton, New York into the Culinary & Events Center. SUNY Broome

Architectural rendering of SUNY Broome's new Culinary & Events Center. SUNY Broome

Other community college leaders have adopted similar partnership strategies. President Paul Young of the Northern Wyoming Community College District, with campuses in two small cities, Sheridan and Gillette, told me:

> For us it is about creating win-win engagements with our community and other nonprofit local partners and city leadership. We're getting better at this as we gain experience creating complex partnerships. So,

> as we are faced with questions as to how to add updated and enhanced experiences for our students, we also ask how can we help enliven and strengthen our community in the process. We've had three very successful ventures so far with our performing arts at our downtown theater, culinary arts in an existing catering and restaurant facility in town, and agriculture programs jointly offered at a local UW [University of Wyoming] facility. In each case we were looking to create real-world experiences for applied programs and we saw opportunities to integrate these programs into existing operations in the community by leveraging both government and existing private assets with the campuses' growth plans.[7]

This Wyoming example is instructive because, except in Laramie, community colleges are the only colleges around which to build a college town in the state. Laramie is home to the University of Wyoming, the only university or public baccalaureate college in this large state. (Wyoming has one other, tiny, private, specialized baccalaureate college.) The state's eight community colleges are each at least a hundred miles from another college, and those colleges are typically in another state. The eight towns in which Wyoming community colleges are located have unique opportunities to build college towns around their institutions. The same is largely true for Sussex Community College in New Jersey, mentioned earlier, and many other rural community colleges around the nation.

Look for Opportunities on Campus to Further the Vision

SUNY Broome is located on the outskirts of the city of Binghamton, separating it from the zone where the northern suburbs of Binghamton end and the farmland begins. At SUNY Broome, we recently built a residence hall on our campus. Although the previous master plan slated the building of a residence hall at the back of the campus, we built our "Student Village" right out front and directly across the street from a convenience store, an Applebee's, a Cracker Barrel, a movie theater, a pizza shop, a Starbucks, a stir-fry restaurant, a credit union, and a church. Overnight we created a suburban college village on the edge of Binghamton by strategically placing a residence hall on the edge of campus near the many amenities typically used by college students.

Benchmark Other College Towns

Other characteristics of college towns determined by the studies cited above include accessibility by automobile (good parking); head-on retail competition with suburbs (individual stores versus malls); accessibility of surrounding amenities; public transportation; bike paths; twenty-four-hour activity; pedestrian-friendly access; cultural activities (art, music, and food); civic events; green space; high-density residential living; a public-sector presence (state capital or county seat); historical character; nearness to prominent geographic features, social services, and a high density of the creative classes.

All of the above characteristics provide opportunities for community colleges to become directly involved in building a college town as part of a local economic development strategy. Only five of the top downtowns cited in the planning and architectural studies were state capitals, so being a capital is not a prerequisite. Most of the top towns were not particularly socially diverse, which is good news for more rural towns with only a community college nearby. Notably, none of the top towns had experienced significant structural renewal; older buildings had been restored rather than razed and replaced. Retail facades tended to be continuous, and all the towns had exceptional retail and hospitality establishments including boutiques, restaurants, bars, and cultural and entertainment venues.

Nearly all the top college towns have a distinctive natural feature nearby that has been capitalized on strategically, most often a water feature. Green space can be key here. States like Wyoming would have great advantage with their vast natural beauty, as would other rural states. Binghamton, New York, quickly becomes rural at the edge of its urban core. Its downtown sits at the confluence of two major rivers, the Chenango and the Susquehanna, that have become a focus for development. Several projects have sprung up recently along or near the rivers. Gratifyingly, Binghamton has recently appeared on national lists of the nation's top college towns, so it appears the strategy is taking hold.

Additional characteristics found by the studies included a high number of hotel and motel rooms. In the Binghamton area three major hotels (one of them historic) have been recently renovated downtown, and others have sprung up in the suburbs around the university's main campus. There are several near SUNY Broome as well.

KEVIN DRUMM

What is one way you believe American college towns are changing, or have changed during your career of working in and with them?

Over the years, college towns have become both more prevalent and important to the U.S. economy.

Public-sector financial support for revitalization projects (prevalent in New York and Wyoming) was also highlighted in the studies. Public-private partnerships, public art, convention centers, a variety of restaurants, attention to natural amenities, and concentrated efforts to market the downtown were all emphasized as well. Virtually all of these aspects of a college town suggest opportunities for community colleges to focus on college town economic development thrust in collaboration with other leading entities in their communities.

CONCLUSION

It may seem counterintuitive to some, but community colleges are uniquely situated to drive a college town vision for their communities. Those that provide the only higher education game in town form a unique community asset on which to capitalize further. This is a hallmark of modern-day economic development: capitalize on your existing assets first while working to attract or open new businesses. The community college is clearly one of those top local assets in any region where they are located; thus community colleges must be integral to any economic development effort, and building a college town can constitute the legs of the economic development stool.

As the nation's economy becomes increasingly specialized, as *where* one studies in college becomes less important than *what* one studies, and as the cost of earning a bachelor's degree continues to rise, the importance of community colleges to their communities should only grow. Further, community colleges are by, for, and of the community, so who better to drive economic initiatives.

Finally, anyone invested in economic development is aware of the importance of attracting the creative classes to one's community. While community colleges may not be in the business of attracting large numbers of creative people, other than primarily for some faculty and staff positions, these institutions are focused on helping their communities to educate and retain members of the creative classes. This is another impetus for strategically working on building a college town. College towns are by their very nature magnets for those members.

Looking ahead, higher education seems poised to become more integrated in the fabric of our society and less a separate ivory tower sequestered on a brick-and-mortar campus. The fantastic growth of distance learning and the demise of one small private college after another shows no signs of abating, and these patterns suggest that "the community's college" may be the only college left in many communities in the not-so-distant future. Large percentages of our students aren't ready for online course offerings at the beginning of their college careers; eighteen-year-olds make up only a small portion of the online market. Affordable community colleges may therefore become increasingly desirable for traditional, classroom attendance, while distance learning eventually monopolizes the degree completion market, if it doesn't already. So who will be left to anchor a community college town if not a community college? It's hard to build a college town around the internet.

It remains to be seen what prominence community colleges may have in the future and whether they will become the most likely anchor for a college town, but there's no time like the present for preparing for such a future. It won't happen if community colleges don't begin taking part in building college towns where possible.

All of the best downtowns named in the studies had a high density of the creative class, as described by professor and author Richard Florida.[8] And of course it helps to have a college or university handy to attract the emerging creative class in the first place.

PART III

BEYOND THE PRESIDENT'S OFFICE

Expanding Missions and Leveraging Resources

CHAPTER 10

How Planners Work

Best Practices from Keene State College and Keene, New Hampshire, in Balancing Community Relations

JAY KAHN

INTRODUCTION: ACHIEVING PERFECT (IMPERFECT) HARMONY

At the conclusion of the 2007–8 academic year, the city of Keene and Keene State College (KSC) were starting to celebrate the college's one-hundredth anniversary. The city of Keene had grown to be the 23,000-person hub of a 76,000-person county in southwestern New Hampshire. The college had matured into one of New England's leading public liberal arts colleges, with more than 5,000 students, nearly half of whom were drawn from outside New Hampshire.

The history of a supportive town-gown relationship began prior to the college's 1909 founding. The city had worked for two years to secure the location of a new normal school in Keene (in competition with three other locations) in part by granting the state funds sufficient to acquire two of the most precious and prestigious pieces of property on the west side of the city's Main Street, only two blocks from Central Square. One, the Hale property, had been owned by a New Hampshire governor, and the other, the Catherine Fiske House, had been the home of the second women's finishing school in the United States, established in 1814. The college added both properties to the national historic registry in the 1960s. Today, Hale houses the president's and other administrative offices, and the former Fiske House is the president's residence and is used for formal entertaining.

The 2007–8 academic year concluded a yearlong discussion between a working committee established by the mayor and the college president to draft a new municipal services agreement for both parties. Any acrimony that had arisen in discussions about the college's contribution to the city for municipal services was now set aside. The traditional mutual support provided by one party to the other was captured in the college's Centennial celebration kick-off event titled "In Perfect Harmony," a reenactment, starring campus and community leaders, of the city's 1907 debate over allocating funds for the state's acquisition of land.

INITIAL DISCORD: WHO DEFINES LAND USE

Beneath the surface, though, a firestorm had erupted over the question, Who should control the use of land across from the two original gifted properties? By 2007, the college had grown from the original seven acres to 190 acres, expanding away from downtown in southerly and westerly directions. However, use of college-owned land on the east side of Main Street, where the college owned three formerly residential properties, had not been publicly discussed until the college was approached by two property owners who wanted to sell their land directly across from Hale and the president's residence. These two parcels, contiguous to the other three, would essentially create a block stretch across from the school's original historic properties.

Construction of a new roundabout to replace a lighted intersection that borders the college and the city's downtown had left these two properties without street parking. Each had some parking to the rear used by students who live above professional offices on the first floor. The first-floor tenants of both buildings were closing their businesses, prompting discussion about how the land could best be used to complement this important intersection.

The town-gown disconnect was one more of timing than of neglect. The college's master plan, approved by the University System of New Hampshire (USNH) in 2004, had involved all campus constituencies as well as the City Council and local alumni. The college's previous master plan had launched an unprecedented period of facility and grounds improvements and opened up the campus for community use, bringing regional and national design and construction awards; visitors were by then calling it the most attractive public college in New England. In 2004 the primary facility need voiced by city representatives was additional college housing, which the plan recommended. USNH trustees acted quickly to respond to this need by issuing a bond to construct another 350 beds on campus, including property acquisition that squared up the campus's boundaries where two new residence halls would be built. The college's master plan maintained a commitment not to expand north, toward downtown, but the plan did identify repurposing property the college had

Perspectives on Effective Town-Gown Relationships from the Society for Campus and University Planning

MICHAEL MOSS, CAE, is the president of the Ann Arbor–based Society for College and University Planning (SCUP). In collaboration with its board of directors, he is responsible for providing leadership and vision for the organization and guiding the development and implementation of its strategic plan, programs, policies, and practices.

- SCUP advocates an *integrated* approach as the most successful form of institutional planning. It engages all stakeholders in the planning process, the campus and its local community are influential stakeholders, and both thrive in a new model of the American college town.
- Finding a shared, *common purpose* between the academic mission of the college or university and the civic good of the community goes a long way in creating harmony and may make other matters of concern, such as economic development or student behavior, an easier conversation down the road.
- College town leaders, both civic and campus-based, need to recognize that engaging the college's or university's desire to contribute to the common good starts in the local community. Community and institutional leaders can leverage the academic and social purposes of the town and gown and advance a thriving community.
- Examples that link academic experiences to the community include student-led field research, internships, and service learning in the course of students' educational experience. Faculty scholarship may also be a point of connection.
- Finding common purpose in shared strategic initiatives also helps the campus and the local community achieve key long-range objectives, support operational effectiveness on both sides, and ensure that both can grow independently and in collaboration.

purchased in 2002 on the east side of Main Street for a new administrative building, an alumni center.

When the college had an opportunity to acquire the abutting properties on the east side of Main Street in 2007, it saw that the new administrative building could be built in a way that also met additional goals: enhance its gateway, provide the fourth and final anchor building to the city's new roundabout, announce the importance of alumni at the college's front door, and provide functional space along Main Street that could be used by the college and community. The new Alumni Center was to house the alumni, advancement, and college relations offices, relocating each from buildings that lacked accessibility for people with disabilities. Beyond that, the college and its trustees envisioned the new Alumni Center as a way to raise student awareness of the alumni network they would join upon graduation, raise alumni engagement with students (through career advising and mentoring), and contribute to the college's strategic initiatives through fund raising.

After the master plan was adopted, the City Council in 2005 created the Heritage Commission, one of whose charges was to "review and comment on any application for a demolition permit for any building or structure in the city in which the proposed demolition is greater than 500 square feet of gross floor area, and the building was constructed more than 50 years before the date of application for a demolition permit, or is eligible for listing in the National Register of Historic Places, or located in an established historic district."[1] KSC's tenth president, Helen Giles-Gee, arrived on campus in fall 2005. Her first year focused on establishing college goals and building relationships with campus and community constituents. Her energy, vision, and commitment were embraced on and off campus. By 2006, alumni leaders were responding by developing their own set of goals, including a new alumni center for which they would raise funds and through which they would continually contribute to connecting current students to their predecessors for job networking and mentoring. An Alumni Center planning committee was established by the presidents of the college and the Alumni Association.

In spring 2007 the construction market raced ahead. A potential $6 million project failed to attract the large architectural designer pool that previous campus projects had gathered. Fortunately, it did attract local architects who had worked on historic preservation projects. The firm selected was Weller and Michel Architects of Keene, New Hampshire. Their work with the design team produced plans that were presented to the campus community and University System of New Hampshire trustees in May 2007. The college would raze the three contiguous buildings closest to the roundabout on the east side of Main Street and construct a new alumni center. The design used an efficient footprint, leaving green space and adding parking to the rear that would link to an existing ninety-car lot. Its three-story facade resembled a late-1800s "Empire" style, with a mansard roof similar to other buildings on Main Street primarily to the north of the college toward downtown.[2] The president and the vice president for finance and planning presented the project for the trustees approval, which was received in June 2007.

Alumni Center, three original houses. Tom Weller, Weller & Michel Architects, Keene, New Hampshire, and Eckman Construction, Bedford, New Hampshire.

BEST PRACTICE: PRESERVE NEIGHBORHOOD IDENTITIES

That same month, the Heritage Commission appeared at a City Council meeting, claiming the college was violating in spirit, if not fact, a commitment to sustain the historic look of Keene's Main Street. The City Council asked the college president and VP for finance and planning to attend the next council meeting, where it was agreed that city and college officials and the architects would attend the next Heritage Commission meeting. The Heritage Commission viewed each of the buildings as historic—more than fifty years old and contributing to the historic feel of Main Street. The view was not unanimously shared; some city councilors had described the two newly purchased buildings as something out of a Sears Roebuck catalogue, narrow and deep. In fact, they had been built by the owner of the third building, at 232 Main Street, in the early 1900s as rental properties and were clearly not as stately as nineteenth-century homes on Main Street that had front porches stretching across their frontage with attractive front yards. Prior to the meeting, both parties independently sought the opinion of the State Department of Historical Resources. The department's state architect indicated to the college that he also questioned the historical contribution of at least two properties, but the department declined to mediate a local disagreement.

The first two meetings failed to achieve common ground. The mayor suggested that the college build behind the existing buildings and link to them. However, the middle building's first floor had been a dentist's office for the preceding thirty-five years, and a hazardous materials review identified that mercury, used in tooth fillings, was present on all surfaces and in the structural beams. The extent of demolition and renovation required to all the buildings and the changes necessary in elevations made this option impossible.

The Department of Historical Resources did identify historic preservation consultants, and all parties agreed to one with extensive experience who had previously worked for the department. The city manager and college VP agreed that it was important that the city and college share the cost of the consultant's services, so that each would play a part in defining the project's scope and would receive the consultant's report. That report was received six weeks later in November 2007. The consultant found that each of the buildings contributed to the historic nature of Main Street, but that the oldest of the three was of greatest significance. The college had two choices: relocate the proposed building to a parking lot on campus, which would push more cars into surrounding neighborhoods, or propose a Main Street design that would not undermine fund-raising efforts and would win the acceptance of the Heritage Commission and city officials. The agreement to pursue the Main Street option while retaining the most historic of the three buildings was made in December 2007. Of the proposed solution, the consultant said, "What's important is that the image of the neighborhood be preserved."[3]

The consultant's report provided some additional design clues, including the suggestion that building height, setbacks, and residential scale be maintained. The original design also had picked up on replicating the window elevations, porches, and columns of neighboring buildings. The first redesign reduced the building's height from three floors and a mansard roof to two floors with a gabled roof. While both styles can be found on Main Street, the new concept matched more closely the residential scale evident as one moves away from downtown. More difficult was figuring out how to maintain setbacks and provide parking, because the reduction in height and integration of the most historic of the properties required the footprint to spread in order to integrate floor height changes and achieve disabled accessibility. This expanded footprint was required because of the need to match the new ground-level entry with existing first-floor elevations, which were eighteen inches higher. At the second

Seven Best Practices for College Town Strategic Planning

- Preserve neighborhood identities
- Use sustainable design principles
- Gain community support
- Engage trustees
- Prepare for surprises
- Build trust and celebrate success
- Stay focused on collaboration and communication

level, the interior height of the new building required a ramp that dropped twelve inches to meet the lower level of the older building. These ramped interior transitions increased the ratio of unassignable square footage, but it also presented an opportunity for more attractive gathering space leading to the function hall on the first floor. The total building grew from 18,500 square feet to 21,200 square feet.

BEST PRACTICE: USE SUSTAINABLE DESIGN PRINCIPLES

The building design also had to mitigate runoff into the city's storm water drainage system, and the larger footprint reduced the ability to store water on site. A creative civil engineering solution was to use a porous asphalt paving material for the parking lot that allowed for below-ground water detention. An eight-foot-deep detention area was filled with sand up to a two-foot stone layer below the final porous asphalt (with a larger aggregate stone). This mitigated the storm water runoff and allowed for more on-site parking for Alumni Center guests and college staff.

Another lower-cost solution was use of faux-slate roof shingles. The material for the faux-slate was recycled plastic including punch-outs from baby diapers. While there was some price premium over an architectural shingle, the faux-slate matched other older properties at the college. Exterior materials were already in the college's tradition, such as the red brick and residential clapboard cladding, both of which melded with existing Main Street residences.

BEST PRACTICE: GAIN COMMUNITY SUPPORT

After eight designs, the college and its architects chose a schematic design that met the program, fit the site, and achieved the criteria set forth in the historic preservation consultant's report: height, setback, and residential scale. Before presenting the design to the city, the president met with an alumni focus group that included design team members to test the likely final design. The alumni liked the integration of the original 232 Main Street house into the new portions of the center, the function hall, and office corridor housing administrative functions on the first and second floors. They also liked the sweeping entry that provided the length needed to ramp the at-grade elevation of the new building with its function hall to the height of the old building with the administrative offices. Many alums had fond memories of the 232 Main Street house, formerly the Newman Center; hence, its repurposing as the Alumni Center, archive, and reading room had sentimental value for them. The focus group meeting ended with a discussion of which alums would be the best spokespersons for future presentations.

The president and VP for finance and planning returned to the Heritage Commission in January 2008. Commission members expressed sincere appreciation for the college's having worked to achieve the recom-

Colleges and Universities in New Hampshire

Community Colleges

- Great Bay Community College
- Lakes Region Community College
- Manchester Community College
- Nashua Community College
- NHTI, Concord's Community College
- River Valley Community College
- White Mountains Community College

Public Institutions

- Granite State College
- Keene State College
- Plymouth State University
- University of New Hampshire
- University of New Hampshire at Manchester
- University of New Hampshire School of Law

Private Institutions

- Antioch University New England
- Colby-Sawyer College
- Dartmouth College
- Franklin Pierce University
- Hellenic American University
- New England College
- New Hampshire Institute of Art
- Northeast Catholic College
- Rivier University
- Saint Anselm College
- Southern New Hampshire University
- Thomas More College of Liberal Arts

mendations in the consultant's report. The commission chair's report to the City Council stated: "The process is an example of what collaboration and cooperation can accomplish. The City and the College have both recognized their important roles as stewards in protecting the historic Main Street area. This reflects well on both the College and the City. The Keene community, as well as the College students and faculty, can see the College administration and City officials acting together in a responsible and respectful manner."[4]

The report went on to request that KSC modify its master plan to state that it "will not purchase additional properties on the east side of Main Street" and "will not purchase additional properties on the west side of Main Street which have frontages on Main Street."[5] The college president indicated she would consult with the USNH Board of Trustees on adjustments to the college's master plan.

The City Council received the report at its February 2008 meeting. The daily *Keene Sentinel* newspaper reported that "College administrators drew praise from councilors for their willingness to compromise when they presented revised plans for a scaled-down version of the project to the council committee."[6] One year into the design of the Alumni Center project, the college had received key alumni and community seals of approval for achieving strategic town-gown objectives.

BEST PRACTICE: ENGAGE TRUSTEES

Administrators often want to avoid going back to boards of trustees after having received a project approval, as it can cast doubt on the trust that trustees place in their administrators. In the period around 2008, this was occurring more often, primarily due to rapidly escalating commodity prices and market uncertainties. Not only had the Alumni Center's square footage increased, but estimators calculated that the original $6.1 million project would likely cost $8.2 million. Little did they know how a global recession would affect construction prices in the following year.

The tipping point was the alignment of goals: the college's strategic planning goal to diversify funding streams; the Alumni Association's goal to create an Alumni Center and achieve closer engagement with students; and the USNH trustees' goal for the system's campuses to bolster fundraising infrastructures. The Keene community's support provided the necessary endorsement of the project's importance to both the city and the college. It signaled that fund raising would not be impaired by an ongoing dispute over historic contributions. The USNH trustees needed to consider the college's requests to increase the project budget and for internal borrowing to augment funds raised from KSC alumni by $2.1 million. For Keene State, community fund raising had grown, while alumni fund raising had lagged behind that of its peer institutions. The trustees were expanding the toolkit for campus presidents to ramp up their fund-raising abilities. The Alumni Center was an important investment in building the college's alumni engagement and the annual-fund revenue stream. A revised $8.2 million budget was approved in June 2008.

The Alumni Center construction documents were finished in early 2009, but by then the construction climate had shifted dramatically. To take advantage of the depressed construction market, the college opted for a competitive bid for a general contractor rather than selecting a construction manager as had been done in previous projects. The results rewarded the choice of method: the construction contract was below $5 million, which with alternates and change orders rose to $5.4 million. Total project costs, including equipment, testing, design, and commissioning, closed at $7 million.

Trustees also approved the president's recommendation to amend the master plan to specify no further acquisitions on the east side of Main Street. The Alumni Center was the only improvement in the master plan intended for that location. However, the president noted, the master plan did include acquisition of a couple of corner properties on the west side of Main Street that, when acquired, would give the college ownership of all properties along Bruder Street. The president communicated with the Heritage Commission that the college would follow through with this acquisition if the corner properties became available.

BEST PRACTICE: PREPARE FOR SURPRISES

Every project has a moment of new discovery, and this is true particularly with renovation projects. The Alumni Center's moment came when the contractor began deconstructing the 232 Main Street building. Once the attic floor was removed for a new mechanical system and lead paint and asbestos were abated, contractor staff observed something remarkable about the old colonial-style structure. Every vertical two-by-four had been severed and raised five feet, nine inches. The 1860s-vintage building had originally been a Cape Cod design. This fact showed up on no Keene Historical Society records nor in the report of the historic preservation consultant. The structure would never support the additional weight of the new design. The contractor estimated it would cost $40,000 to knock down the old building and pour a new foundation to replace the old stone foundation. If we retained the old facade, it would be able to support only cladding and windows. A new foundation would be needed, pinned to the old foundation, and all new supports would be placed on it. The additional costs were doable. The college administration never flinched; having made a commitment to preserve the original 232 Main Street building, the college would rely on its floor plan and facade to inform the final construction even if it cost more.

The supporting structure was not the only item the college had to pay more for in order to retain a historic look. Tin ceilings, preserved columns, and fireplace surrounds needed to be historically replicated. The porch needed to be rebuilt because the Alumni Center porch was only eighteen inches above the ground, so College Product Design faculty cut the column base down to twenty-four inches to match the original base and created a column cap to make up the distance to the porch ceiling.

BEST PRACTICE: BUILD TRUST AND CELEBRATE SUCCESS

The Alumni Center groundbreaking occurred on Reunion Weekend in June 2009, during the college's centennial year. At the following October's Homecoming, past and current students and staff were invited to sign a beam that was installed at the entry of the Alumni Center, and dedication occurred in June 2010. At the ceremony the mayor of Keene exclaimed, "This building is great," and emphasized how the Alumni Center complemented the city's investment in the roundabout. Indeed, both parties had risked their community image at this intersection, and only through accommodating each other's interests were they successful. The city had considered college student safety concerns in building the roundabout and adding speed tables on the college side of the intersection, and the college had considered the city's historic preservation concerns in maintaining a residential-scale building at its intersection with the roundabout.

Keene State College's Alumni Center project offered several teachable moments. When faced with on-campus renovations, the college had an admirable record of restoring properties and blending historic elements into updated classroom and residential facilities. The emerging role of the city's Heritage Commission brought on the first time the college needed to account for historic preservation, and the elements of historic preservation were addressed in the next college master plan. The most significant outcomes were preservation of pride and trust that the college would do the right thing and do it tastefully while the city maintained its independence. Both parties recognized that mutual respect creates value.

Keene State College Alumni Center, after renovation. Tom Weller, Weller and Michel Architects, Keene, New Hampshire, and Eckman Construction, Bedford, New Hampshire.

BEST PRACTICE: STAY FOCUSED ON COLLABORATION AND COMMUNICATION

Cities use zoning the way colleges use master plans; both guide future development and investment. Housing zoning is generally about single- or multifamily occupancy. Zoning can also be used to direct the type of housing desired in an area.

The college's enrollment grew faster than its on-campus housing capacity. The growth was due to in-coming student yield rate increases and higher retention rates thanks to better academic advising, and also to faculty engagement and use of institutional research data. On-campus housing priority was given to in-coming students, while upper-division enrollment growth spread into the abutting neighborhoods to the east of campus. New on-campus housing investments required acquiring more land, incurring debt, leveraging the college's future resources, and driving up campus housing prices and the overall price of attendance.

The private sector was filling some of the need. Single-family homes in the abutting neighborhoods could be turned into cash cows when owners rented to four college students paying double the price of the mortgage. Some homes owners took the quick-cash route and sold to landlords, both in town and out of town. Rising property values provided an increased tax base for the city. However, low-priced housing was evaporating, and tensions between family-owned properties and student rental properties were increasing. The city wanted the college to consolidate the student housing footprint, which posed a free-market dilemma.

Two options existed. On one hand, the college could build on existing residential-life properties. On-campus low-density family housing, built after World War II when families lived on-campus while adult members attended college, were the logical sites. Family housing could morph into nonfamily upper-division student apartments—an inefficient use of land and a poor housing arrangement. Replacement with higher-density housing would provide a poor financial return on investment because only the net gain in new beds built revenue growth and because increased operating and debt-service costs would require raising housing rates. Raising on-campus housing rates would work well for the private sector, which would also raise off-campus housing prices. But the overall dynamic would raise the price of attendance, making the college less competitive.

The other option was private development. Could the college and city attract private developers to build higher-density housing to consolidate the off-campus student housing footprint? Sometimes this option requires a public-private partnership whereby the college, in order to reduce developer risk, guarantees an occupancy rate, leases land to the developer, or helps promote rental to its students. From the city's side, tools like infrastructure development of utilities, pedestrian sidewalks, lighting, and roadway and intersection improvements can be pledged from increased tax revenues. Zoning requirements such as setbacks, on-site parking, and design restrictions can be waived. These steps reduce the developer's construction costs or increase the number of occupants and revenue.

An area north of the college was zoned as a mixed business district. Some of the properties were quite run-down; others were unoccupied and for sale. Ralston Street provided a link to the college on one end and, on the other end, to a former railroad switchyard redeveloped for commercial and retail space, just one block from downtown.

In 2010 the city manager and the Keene Planning Department proposed a Sustainable Energy Efficient District (SEED) overlay for this area north of the college.[7] The SEED zoning district included incentives that enabled developers to construct up to five levels, build out the property to within ten feet of property lines, and require less landscaped space, resulting in more on-site parking. The idea was shared with the town-gown committee, and the college's vice president for finance and planning testified in favor of the district.

The college, for its part, prepared a request for information (RFI), posted it on its website, and sent it to national, regional, and local developers. It held a preproposal workshop where it promised, "If you build it, we won't."

Three years later, four apartment-style projects had been completed, totaling 475 new beds and adding nearly $20 million to the city's tax base. Ralston Street was rebuilt to accommodate storm water drainage, and new pedestrian walkways and lighting improved safety for those traveling to and from the campus. The transition from on-campus to off-campus housing also linked to commercial and retail businesses and downtown Main Street. As enrollment decreased due to demographic changes, it was rental housing in east-side residences that posted vacancy signs.

The collaborative town-gown efforts had again led to a win-win. Low- to moderate-income housing can now be restored to owner-occupied residence as the highest and best use. The off-campus housing stock is now located in more modern, safer, and sustainable properties closer to the college and more closely integrated with commercial and retail businesses. Student-nonstudent neighbor conflicts are down significantly, thanks both to location of off-campus housing and to improved college communications with off-campus students.

PROGRESS INTERRUPTED

So let's review the underpinnings of these two victories for town-gown relations. The tenth college president, who served for seven years and who previously had chaired the Society of College and University Planning, supported an integrated, college-wide planning process for determining academic, financial, capital, and information technology priorities. The vice president for finance and planning and a respected faculty member cochaired the college-wide planning process. The VP for finance and planning and the city manager had a twenty-year working relationship. A town-gown committee cochaired by the city Manager and the VP brought leaders from both institutions together to share issues as they evolved. Mayors, city councilors, and college leadership changed, but institutional relations were sustained.

The New England climate is rough on track and field sports. The basketball court–sized gymnasiums provide early-season practice space. To get regulation-sized spaces, campus grounds keepers and athletes push snow aside, but the climate remains cold and raw. This is true for both college and community school athletics.

Keene State College is a member of the Little East Conference, which includes public colleges from five of the six New England states. Since joining the conference in 1999, KSC has won the Commissioners Cup every year for best overall performance in seventeen sports. While KSC sustained great success among New England public undergraduate institutions, its teams struggle to move beyond the first round of NCAA post-season competitions. More successful northeastern public institutions have in-door facilities for field sports, which enable teams to start their spring seasons earlier. The college president had administrative experience in the New York and New Jersey public sector, primarily with undergraduate institutions that had the indoor field venues necessary to help them achieve premier status for Division III athletics.

The creation of an indoor field venue provided another opportunity for a town-gown partnership. A college-led study that included city and community leaders produced a proposal for a 120,000-square-foot multiuse facility that included a skating surface and a two-hundred-meter track with a field and court inside that could be used for graduation ceremonies, convocations, and conventions. Of the five potential locations the study identified, participants preferred a site between the college and downtown, filling in another former railroad yard currently used for surface parking. The land was donated to the college in 2012 on the condition that it be used primarily for indoor sports activities. The skating function, filling a community need, was ultimately separated from the project and built by a nonprofit on the second-best site, near the east-side residential neighborhood. Hence, the proposed college facility would be approximately 100,000 square feet and would cost an estimated $25 to $30 million.

The multiuse indoor track and field space, mostly on one level, would make a large footprint that also had a high roofline, about forty-five feet—a facility easily built on an empty field (another option explored in the study), but more controversial if built on a site near downtown and the college. The near-downtown site had the advantage of drawing increased traffic for commercial and retail businesses and restaurants, and the disadvantage of being out of character in the downtown historic district and creating pressure for additional parking.

Four years after the 2009 start of the study, two proposals were in play: that the college use its bonding capacity to build the multiuse indoor track and field structure and the city build the parking; or that the city and college work with the Monadnock Economic Development Corporation on a New Market Tax Credit to build both the in-door facility and the parking deck under a newly formed independent organization.

With the proposals still in draft stage, the partners began to change. The president resigned to take another presidency. A new mayor and city council were elected. The USNH board chair, chancellor, and vice chancellor for finance all changed. The VP for finance and planning became the interim president for a year until a new president was appointed in summer of 2013. By 2016 the VP and the city manager had retired from their positions. In other words, the relationships that facilitated fraught discussion and decisions, and a widely accepted college plan and planning process that facilitated shared decision making, were breaking down.

The new president's facility priority became on-campus first-year student housing in a living-learning–centered residence hall. It's a spectacular building and no doubt attractive to prospective students. However, this priority change put all other facility needs on hold and risked the college's remaining at debt capacity. It also placed newly added off-campus housing at risk. And when enrollment began to decline after the new residence hall opened, the college needed to close a couple of older residence halls, which resulted in net operating deficits and more intense competition for residential occupancy locally. The multiuse indoor track and field community space on donated land moved off the radar.

FINAL THOUGHTS

Relationships take years to build and moments to break. That seems obvious in all facets of life, but it also applies to institutional relationships. When the city manager and the college's VP for finance and planning left, so did twenty-five years of institutional memory.

Changing priorities accelerated the loss of institutional memory. Commitments, trade-offs, and past concessions could easily be disregarded. The community shifted its focus to constructing an ice arena and arts facilities at a greater distance from the college.

Financial contingency planning in competitive markets is essential. All organizations need to undertake stress tests and share the results with stakeholders. Understanding context for decision making is arguably the best way to understand the decisions.

Take time to reflect and celebrate what has been accomplished. Memories and facts fade, and without ongoing reflection, we fail to celebrate and communicate the good.

CHAPTER 11

How Architects Envision College Towns Today and Tomorrow

Ten Best Practices for Integrated Design

STUART ROTHENBERGER, KRISAN OSTERBY, AND PATRICK HYLAND JR.

INTRODUCTION: SETTING THE STAGE

Every campus must be a place where people thrive and develop meaningful connections. As architects and planners who serve higher education, we have learned through our careers with DLR Group that our most important campus contribution lies in elevating the human experience. This includes the perceptions and activities shaped by the local community. Students desire seamless access to learning and discovery. Neighbors, businesses, and city officials seek opportunities for shared amenities, services, and revenue potential—along with answers to safety, security, and infrastructure capacity concerns. In the face of expanding online learning options and decreasing funding for physical improvements, strategies for creating welcoming facilities and vibrant open space for place-based learning become critical to successful recruitment, retention, revenue generation, and durable campus-community partnerships.

The physical campus is a learning landscape and network of physical systems. At the integrated design firm DLR Group, we believe that buildings, open space, and infrastructure embody institutional values, history, and traditions. Every campus tells a story, and the best campuses provide a holistic setting for an integrated academic and student-life experience. Planning and design for the new American college town must acknowledge, explore, enhance, and celebrate the specific qualities of each campus and its host community. Investments in existing buildings and grounds, as well as new development, must reflect and sustain the institution's mission, programs, and sense of place.

Creating a lasting beacon of shared campus and community values provides an important tool for student and economic success. Facilities, open space, and infrastructure embody an institution's well-being and cultural DNA and project its collective physical brand message. They offer a window on the range of services, programs, and activities available campus-wide. Likewise, they depend on their setting for both an inviting perimeter and a vibrant economic and social life. The best campuses have community edges that invite visitors *in* while simultaneously encouraging students, faculty, and staff members to venture *out* to engage with their neighbors.

Members of our firm are frequently asked how best to create a campus that supports its local town or city. Over the course of our fifty-plus-year history—and across our global offices—we have learned key components to consider and advocate.[1] We have seen common concerns emerge across multiple campus projects. A thread that runs through them all is the quest for frugality, efficiency, and partnerships that achieve the betterment of the greater community. Institutions are refreshing and repurposing their existing building stock for the future in order to compete, work within tightening budgets, and reinforce their brand reputation.

In this chapter we share a range of examples that address both public and private institutions across a wide range of regions. We highlight the campus and community leaders who manage and affect the project vision, design, and construction. Depending on the type of facility, we identify the stakeholders on campus and in town who are key to know. We describe valuable best practices to embrace and pitfalls to avoid. Many projects encounter bumps in the road; we share ways to redirect a project to negotiate those bumps. And for these fiscally challenging times—when all institutions are wary of hidden costs in any college town project—we address financial concerns along with innovative solutions to consider.

CREATING PHYSICAL AND PROGRAMMATIC QUALITY WHILE ADDRESSING DEFERRED MAINTENANCE: UNIVERSITY OF MOUNT UNION

Mount Union is a traditional liberal arts college, founded in 1846, with approximately 2,000 undergraduate and 250 graduate students. It is one of the two largest employers in Alliance, Ohio, and high school football games are held in the college stadium. Although Mount Union is not nationally prominent, its role as a resilient community resource and point of pride is a model for other residential colleges in small rust-belt

Best Practices for Town-Gown Planning and Design

- Creating physical and programmatic quality while addressing deferred maintenance
- Enhancing wayfinding and the gateway experience curb appeal
- Fund raising and partnerships to implement specialty facilities
- Inviting partners to new learning and research spaces
- Transforming libraries and learning commons
- Promoting community engagement through new approaches to campus arts facilities
- Teaching old residence hall models new tricks
- Focusing on convenience, access, and diversity for student-life spaces

communities. The forces it faces are typical: the higher education landscape in Ohio and the Upper Midwest is increasingly competitive as the traditional pool of middle-class students reaches a demographic plateau. Private and public colleges in the region are now vying for the same students.

Mount Union realized that a strong heritage and community support did not guarantee survival. It undertook a strategic plan in 2010 to transition from a college to a university and added programs for engineering (undergraduate), nursing (undergraduate), physician assistants (graduate), physical therapy (doctorate), and education (graduate). The university's critical question for DLR Group was how to evolve its facilities and address deferred maintenance to support these new activities.

Mount Union had a hearty supply of built stock from nearly every era of campus development. Although the buildings were structurally sound, they needed new mechanical, electrical, and plumbing systems, energy-efficient glazing, and roofs. They also needed to be adapted to new learning configurations, technology, and amenities for active learning, team-based learning, collaboration, and interdisciplinary programs. Critically important to the Mount Union experience, 1950s-vintage facilities, including the library, science, and arts buildings, defined the academic core. To set the stage for transformation, Mount Union undertook a master plan to physically support its strategic plan, explore the need for new facilities, and identify places for future buildings to enhance programmatic density and vitality. In this process, the DLR Group team took advantage of underutilized existing buildings and open space to make additions and renovations.

A key strategy was to exploit and enhance unique Mount Union campus features. The university purchased all internal streets from the city of Alliance. For many of the acquired rights-of-way, the streets were abandoned and transformed into green space and pedestrian ways. Rather than purchase ad hoc perimeter parcels, Mount Union chose to control the campus appearance and provide a welcoming experience by redesigning and maintaining the street grid that connected the community with the campus core. The campus perimeter was reinforced by acquiring strategic parcels, defining "campus thresholds" through integrated facility and open space design, and designating a network of diverse green spaces.

The combination of new and repurposed space for health sciences on the edge of campus addressed deferred maintenance and provided a powerful attraction to the second major employer in the town, Alliance Community Hospital. Gallaher Hall for Health Sciences was added onto the existing science building, Bracy Hall. The new facility was strategically positioned to support undergraduate nursing, physician assistant, and physical therapy programs. Adjacencies between departments, programs, and the hospital were critical to support the overlapping requirements for core classes between disciplines and applied learning. The building addition and programs were placed to create a science and health quad. Located on the campus perimeter, facing the hospital, the quad provided an easy flow for students and staff between classes and internships.

ENHANCING WAYFINDING AND THE GATEWAY EXPERIENCE CURB APPEAL: PINNACLE BANK ARENA, UNIVERSITY OF NEBRASKA, LINCOLN

Pinnacle Bank Arena is located across the street from the University of Nebraska, adjacent to Lincoln's famed historic Haymarket District, and is the centerpiece of a new $340 million development.[2] The facility provides the campus and the city with a dynamic multipurpose venue that delivers an amazing experience. DLR Group's design for the facility took full advantage of its site by featuring a multistory glass-fronted lobby. It gives outside passers-by a peek at the activity taking place on all levels of the building and encourages inside patrons to look out at the university, the new Haymarket development, downtown Lincoln, and Nebraska's state capitol beyond.[3] Designed around the ability to host University of Nebraska men's and women's basketball games, the venue also easily accommodates concerts, ice events, high school state tournaments, and nearly every other type of event imaginable.

Pinnacle Bank Arena enlivens its historic district in Lincoln near the University of Nebraska with special events, lighting, and transparency at the neighborhood scale. DLR Group

The 16,000-seat arena encompasses approximately 470,000 square feet. The Event Level features dedicated locker suites for the university's teams, numerous other locker facilities, event staging areas, storage, and a dedicated student entry for Husker basketball games. In addition to general patron seating and amenities, the lower seating bowl features 900 club seats with a dedicated Club Lounge located immediately behind them on the Main Concourse. The Premium Level features thirty-six 12-person suites and 24-person loges, along with generous lounge space and other amenities such as a custom pizza oven.

The site chosen for the arena, originally a tangled web of railroad tracks, was sandwiched between two still-used lines. To meet the scheduled opening day, a large portion of the facility had to be constructed while those lines remained active. Several columns supporting the seating bowl and long-span roof structure were located only inches away from a strict right-of-way. Had any portion of the work violated that right-of-way, severe penalties would have been incurred and would have placed the schedule in jeopardy. Once the adjacent rails were finally moved, there was little time to construct the perimeter of the facility, so a unique steel and composite structure was used to expedite the distinctive phasing approach.

The severely constrained site also forced creative thinking in order to accommodate the desired seating capacity. A "stacked" seating bowl, with overhangs and steep rakes, was employed to fit all seating areas inside the boundary defined by the rail lines. What was initially a challenge became an opportunity to create an intimidating "wall of fans" surrounding the playing court, helping to give the home team a distinct advantage. Before opening the arena for the 2013 season, the Nebraska Cornhuskers had never gone into a men's basketball season with all tickets sold out. Pinnacle Bank Arena positioned them to achieve that feat.

In addition, placing a "modern" arena immediately adjacent to a nationally recognized historic district in the hope of integrating the two posed a series of challenges. Through careful site planning and choice of massing and materials, a facility was created that enhanced and enlivened the existing district without overwhelming the character of the beloved nearby brick warehouses. Transparent facades and metal cladding on the side of the arena fronting the historic district lessened the facility's impact and helped to create a strong link between old and new.

The interiors concept emerged from a comment made by Mayor Chris Beutler, who said he wanted the facility to be "the state's arena."[4] Tasked with that goal, DLR Group researched Nebraska's geographical significance. The well-known Platte River emerged as an important factor in the state's history, so the patterns and motifs employed in the facility heartily reference its braided river features. This theme was carried throughout the public areas and create a strong bond between users and the place they are proud to call home.

FUND RAISING AND PARTNERSHIPS TO IMPLEMENT SPECIALTY FACILITIES: SCHOOL OF ARTS AND ENTERTAINMENT, VALENCIA COLLEGE, EAST CAMPUS

As the inaugural winner of the Aspen Institute's Prize for Community College Excellence in 2011, Valencia College in Orlando, Florida, is nationally recognized for its innovation.[5] Its film and entertainment programs are also a national benchmark. A new School of Arts and Entertainment Building on the college's East Campus further enhances the school's educational opportunities and strengthens its community and industry partnerships. DLR Group's facility programming and design leverage various forms of fund raising for new building construction, equipment, and staffing. They also reflect important strategies for additional revenue generation.

The 30,705-square-foot state-of-the-art facility accommodates increased enrollment in Valencia's popular film technology, music and sound technology, and digital media programs. It also fills an educational gap in the region by providing unique training and applied-learning opportunities. Finally, it prepares students for immediate employment and production careers, provides a place to experience real-world training, and pairs students with local industry experts—a winning combination for all parties. Located near premier film production enterprises, the East Campus provides both seamless connections to industry partners for hands-on learning opportunities and the skills needed in the ever-evolving production field. Employers in the Orlando region's arts and entertainment industry are looking for people who are creative, entrepreneurial, and up-to-date on the hottest trends in technology. Partners of the program include Walt Disney World, Universal Studios, the University of Central Florida, and JPMorgan Chase & Company.

The building spaces and equipment required funding mechanisms that went beyond traditional public revenue sources. Unique and highly specialized facility features include blended learning spaces, a 2,500-square-foot sound stage, a film screening theater with 120 seats, two recording studios, editing suites for film and music editing, and a digital media production studio. Facility and equipment funding was secured through a variety of sources. The building program and design was a key communication tool in making the case to the public and multiple partners. Perkins federal grant dollars supported those equipment dollars that met the federal and state requirements for these funds. The college was awarded two other rounds of grant funding in addition to Perkins dollars to purchase specialized equipment. Equally important, the Valencia College Foundation funded the purchase of additional specialized equipment.

Looking beyond initial construction costs, Valencia realized it was essential to secure funding for ongoing maintenance, operations, and upgrades as the programs change over time. The building is designed to encourage additional revenue streams associated with the arts and entertainment program. For instance, students can work with a guest director on a full feature film. Multiple specialty spaces such as a sound stage and post-production rooms create opportunities for expanded public-private partnerships. Two recording studios are available for rent to generate additional revenue for the program. Framed by a plaza and a lake, an exterior performance stage supports campus use as well as encouraging an ongoing set of local community partnership–driven events.

INVITING PARTNERS TO NEW LEARNING AND RESEARCH SPACES: GOODWIN HALL OF BUSINESS, BENEDICTINE UNIVERSITY

Over the past twenty years, Benedictine University in Lisle, Illinois, has grown from 1,500 to more than 10,000 students. The university has sustained and re-created itself to keep up with changing student needs, its community context, and its partners. The vision for the Daniel L. Goodwin College of Business was born out of this transformation and evolving global reach. Since the initial class of 39 business students graduated a little more than forty years ago, more than 10,000 students have earned business degrees, and some 2,000 enroll annually in the College of Business's various programs. A dedicated and flexible place was needed to expand and showcase business education, partnerships, and student development for both the college and the university.[6]

Working with the college's dean and department faculty, DLR Group programmed and designed the new facility to reflect the college mission to "build a better world through business," support the university's focus on business partnerships, coordinate with services abroad, and establish the college in emerging markets at its international sites in China and Vietnam. Altogether, the building bolsters academic programs, related research, and hands-on, forward-thinking business training with corporate partners. It also integrates amenities that professionals employ at the workplace every day to ease the transition from college to career. The building is the most progressive and largest academic facility on campus. It encompasses 125,000 square feet and includes twenty-one learning environments, three computer classrooms, and two distance-learning classrooms to connect students across the globe. Classrooms are designed with no limitations, and collaboration flows through an integrated media system, allowing all students to connect and share their work digitally and wirelessly. Through this interaction, the university extends its reach farther than ever before. Students sitting in Lisle, Illinois, have no barriers to becoming instantly immersed inside an active business in any country across the globe—or connecting synchronously between the university's main campus, twenty other Illinois learning sites, two national branch campuses, two international sites, and online programs.

The Goodwin College of Business is designed to host an array of events, foster student organizations, offer hoteling for local and global businesses, and host public or private events. The Center for Corporate Partnership, which includes an Executive Partner's Suite, is a space where university officials can bring local, national, or international businesses to campus for collaborative teaching-and-learning sessions. The Competency Assessment room, part of the Executive Partner's Suite, is a multipurpose room for corporate employers, student-run business events, video coaching, and project team rehearsals. To ensure the Center for Corporate Partnership can support a wide variety of events into the future, the building has convertible space for twelve additional classrooms, a mixed-use gallery space, and a fourth-floor banquet room.

The College of Business's new facility was also designed to reflect the tradition of the existing built environment. It unites adjacent buildings with upper-floor walkways and serves as a backdrop for the new Quad—a campus "outdoor living room" framed by a circular walk. Its expanse of grass and trees, comfortable benches, and attractive night lighting encourages outdoor gatherings, enhances institutional identity, and welcomes community members to campus by design and by programs.

TRANSFORMING LIBRARIES AND LEARNING COMMONS: MARICOPA COMMUNITY COLLEGE SCOTTSDALE CAMPUS LIBRARY BUILDING RENOVATION

The Maricopa Community College Scottsdale Campus was the only community college in the United States developed on tribal land in the 1970s. The property was leased from the Gila Nation on its Salt River Reservation. The original campus facilities, including the library, were designed by one architect and used the same materials—cast concrete structures, tilt-up concrete panel walls, brick accents, and clerestory windows, all in a mid-century modern style. Since that time, the college has taken a hands-off attitude toward directing architectural design. Each facility has been different, depending on the architect and building purpose, and the landscape has been used to tie the campus and buildings together with colors, graphics, and accents that meet the standards of the Gila Nation.

Although iconic in appearance, the original library interiors had not changed since construction. They were ill-suited to the college's expansion from 1,000 to 10,000 enrolled students and 3,000 special-interest learners. The average age of students was twenty-six years, but the library was serving all ages, from high school students in dual-enrollment courses to senior citizens gaining new knowledge. Students represented all races and ethnic backgrounds and came with an unlimited variety of interests and purposes. The library they entered was old, uninviting, and filled with stacks—typical of a forty-year-old building. The collections and programs had outgrown the space, the stacks were outdated, over capacity, and inefficient. Staff had purchased new stacks with varying design themes and the interior layout was a hodgepodge. The structure offered no space for online research, only one classroom, and no active-collaboration space. Accessibility standards went unmet and universal design features were missing.

In addition, the land use around the college had changed dramatically. Since the school's original construction in what was then relative isolation, a freeway had been built nearby and the surrounding corridor had transitioned from open reservation land and Sonoran Desert to a mixed-use zone of offices and retail. The college now hosted an entirely commuter student body within an environment completely automobile-centric. Although the library theoretically served the campus and community, it appeared to turn its back on incoming students and tribal members. These perceptions fueled public support for funding the library renovation. Bonding was authorized by taxpayers from the entire district and then earmarked for specific projects—including the library—identified by the college for each campus. In response, DLR Group's planning and design were reviewed by the Gila Tribal Community to assure that it met current tribal design standards to achieve permitting.

To convert the library into a flexible space that was responsive to the local community and conducive to twenty-first-century learning, the building was completely redesigned. What began as a project to "refresh" the facility dramatically expanded as soon as construction began. Asbestos abatement, a deteriorated steel structure, and a contractor who failed to perform laid the foundation for an innovative approach to the project's budget, schedule, and design. While the college worked its way through legal proceedings and additional funding requests, it devoted time to expand user group feedback, tour peer institutions, incorporate the evolution of online access, position changing technology, and strengthen interior art and place-making through the input of a local designer.

Learning spaces developed for students and staff were also opened to the public. Then, to invite public users to stay and encourage students to be productive and faculty to embrace flexible teaching methods, the furniture was chosen to be entirely moveable and rooms were made very simple to reconfigure. Large tables encourage students and outside visitors to spread out to work with materials and devices, and library staff at a redesigned, expanded front desk welcome both students and local community users more effectively.[7]

PROMOTING COMMUNITY ENGAGEMENT THROUGH NEW APPROACHES TO CAMPUS ARTS FACILITIES: SUE & FRANK MAYBORN PERFORMING ARTS CENTER, UNIVERSITY OF MARY HARDIN-BAYLOR

The University of Mary Hardin-Baylor (UMHB), a small Christian college in rural Belton, Texas, lacked an adequate facility to serve its College of Visual and Performing Arts majors or to hold extracurricular activities for approximately 3,900 full-time students. While DLR Group was programming and designing a new Performing Arts Center, the university was adamant that the facility was for institutional use only. During the construction process, however, multiple community groups approached the university requesting to use the center's signature performance and reception spaces, and the University Foundation and its fund-raising team began to appreciate the potential for hosting events, generating revenue, and strengthening relationships for donor opportunities.[8] DLR Group assisted the university throughout this process, and through this programmatic and design evolution, UMHB gradually seized the opportunity to strengthen its community connections and develop multiple, unprecedented financial and program partnerships.

Since no other academic building is located at the edge of campus, the building site at the corner of Main Street and Martin Luther King Junior Avenue positions cultural events and arts programs at the university's front door. In addition to the historic college gate and iconic front lawn, the new facility provides a community gateway along Main Street and adds vibrant events and activities to the primary campus entrance. By establishing multiple linkages with the neighborhood around it, the university more efficiently engages with patrons and stakeholders. Accordingly every major space in the Performing Arts Center has been designed to function in multiple ways, including the lobby, which is equipped to double as a concert space. The many multifunctional rooms allow the center to be used as both a teaching facility and a venue for community and national touring musical and theatrical performances through the academic year. Finishes in dressing and rehearsal spaces were upgraded to account for outside group and touring group use.

The center's prime location near downtown Belton—along with the college's expanded performing arts programming—promotes restaurant and business activity by attracting additional customers. The center improves the quality of life in this small community by offering new options for residents to enjoy local performances in lieu of traveling to Austin or other larger cities for shows and entertainment.

TEACHING OLD RESIDENCE HALL MODELS NEW TRICKS: PANORAMIC STUDENT HOUSING DEVELOPMENT, CALIFORNIA COLLEGE OF THE ARTS

Student housing has traditionally been developed within an academics-dominated community where students frequent on-campus dining and adjacent campus amenities. Developing student housing in a town center or a highly urban context encourages students to engage with and patronize the greater community. The new, eleven-story Panoramic residential tower in San Francisco's South of Market District offers a new format for

Panoramic Student Housing delivers community on the ground floor with a mixed-use approach to amenities and the public realm. DLR Group

student housing. Located outside the confines of the California College of the Arts campus, it supports student desires for a sense of community, answers a need for affordable student housing, and encourages interaction between student residents and the greater San Francisco community. The Panoramic consists of 120 "micro-units" and 40 suites that, combined, provide four hundred beds.[9]

Micro-units are small suites and studio apartments that feature a full galley kitchen, one or two beds, a dining nook, built-in storage solutions paired with a closet, and a full private bathroom. The facility provides urban housing that is less expensive than traditional condominiums and apartments, and such cost savings for students can be a significant bonus for institutions and their partners that are developing within an urban core. In addition, city planning departments often view micro-units more favorably than other infill housing projects, because they can significantly boost potential housing density on a smaller site.

Although the Panoramic was not initially a student housing project, it was a perfect match for California College of the Art's needs. Stemming from an opportunity to capitalize on in-migration for San Francisco's rapidly expanding tech sector, where workplace design and lifestyle trends were highly conducive to micro-units, the developer's original goal was to bring new housing opportunities to those who might otherwise be priced out of the city. But the unit efficiencies, communal spaces, and maintenance methodologies aligned perfectly with the student housing market. As a result, Panoramic Interests partnered with the college to provide the tower as housing for its satellite campuses across the city. The tower's proximity to Bay Area Rapid Transit stations and bus stops, along with the prevailing trend for multimodal and shared transportation, eliminated the need for large-scale dedicated parking for tenant cars. Bicycle storage was provided.

FOCUSING ON CONVENIENCE, ACCESS, AND DIVERSITY FOR STUDENT-LIFE SPACES: O'HARE ACADEMIC CENTER RENOVATION AND EXPANSION, SALVE REGINA UNIVERSITY

Salve Regina University is landlocked along the historic Cliff Walk in Newport, Rhode Island, surrounded by prestigious private landowners and valuable residential property. The university recognized it was not feasible to expand its campus and construct major new facilities to improve students' experience, support student well-being, and meet student-life and academic needs for its enrollment of approximately 2,200. University leadership preferred to improve existing facilities both aesthetically and functionally to fit the campus context and programs and to respect the venerable surrounding college town. The renewed O'Hare Academic Center at Salve Regina University emerged from this mindset.[10] The building renovation and expansion provided an opportunity to meet strategic university goals and objectives while acting as a good neighbor within the historic setting. Considered the university's flagship academic facility, the building expanded by 23,000 square feet to provide critical updates to educational spaces and create an unprecedented improvement in student life.[11]

The addition to the O'Hare Center reflected the impossibility of adding to the nearby campus Student Center—housed in a historic mansion that could not provide large event space, expanded retail venues, or flexible collaboration space. Thus, the addition and its new entry linked campus social spaces with academic spaces and infused student life into the academic core. It created an anchor for Salve Regina student life as well as a location to build community among students, faculty members, and Newport neighbors. It achieved this by providing a diverse scale and variety of hard and soft interaction spaces, along with independent retail and dining that are separate from the university dining plan. Sightlines between newly-situated departments and programs were critical considerations, presenting a view into Salve Regina's culture and campus life both to students and visitors alike. Glassed-in rooms provided acoustic privacy for meetings while allowing natural light into the building's core. These features combined to create a new campus crossroads and "beehive location," an interior "Main Street" that welcomes students, faculty, and community members alike.

The O'Hare Academic Center was reclad to respond to its high-profile location next to the Breakers—one of Newport's and the nation's most iconic visited mansions. Although the project is complete and successful, the university and the planning team had to negotiate with a highly political and emotional community during the planning and design process. After an extensive communications effort, the project ultimately passed the Ochre Point Historic District's neighborhood review and approval hurdles. The team utilized videos, site visits and tours, evening meetings, and "360-degree" engagement to win support from the surrounding community. The programming and design were refined to include neighborhood-requested space for night classes, public lectures, and public meetings. In addition, a conference center embedded in Salve Regina's business program provided a boardroom-like atmosphere that cultivated local relationships, supported applied learning, facilitated internships, and offered authentic connections to Newport businesses.

The facility is now a major community resource and a university recruiting and retention tool, giving neighbors and students a home base that feels comfortable and safe. Communal areas, including an expanded café with indoor and outdoor dining options, offer landscaped terraces overlooking the university's oceanfront grounds and courtyard along the Cliff Walk that invite local community members onto campus.

CONCLUSION: BUILDING THE NEW COLLEGE TOWN

From an architect's perspective, there is no end in sight to the expanding opportunities to strengthen place-based learning and partnership strategies while helping institutions return to their community roots. Large or small, public or private, highly urban or semirural, land grant and community colleges are all realizing that the norm is now 360-degree engagement, democratized higher education, and sharing of scarce resources. At the turn of the twenty-first century, campuses and buildings that opened their programs and their doors to embrace the public were the exception; now they are the rule. Working with planners and architects, institutions are increasingly eager to discover the distinct story they can reveal in their physical sense of purpose and sense of place as they enhance their connections to the community that grounds them in their mission. If the common saying that learning happens everywhere is true, it is critical to realize the academic, economic, environmental, and emotional value of facilities that offer a return on programmatic, financial, and relationship investments.

The key to achieving this new college town perspective is taking advantage of the time it takes to do things differently: listening deeply to community ideas, keeping an eye open for blending access and services, viewing the student and community experience as a continuum from K–12 to retirement, and recognizing that any facility investment has the potential to deliver learning, resources (physical, human, and monetary), and partners.[12]

CHAPTER 12

What Mayors Think

Local Politicians' Views of College Town Opportunities and Expectations

KATE ROUSMANIERE

INTRODUCTION: MAYORS AND THEIR COLLEGE TOWNS

As the mayor of a small college town in which the university enrollment is more than double the number of permanent residents, I am often reminded of Canadian prime minister Pierre Trudeau's famous description in 1969 of his country's relationship with the United States as "sleeping with an elephant. No matter how friendly or even-tempered is the beast, one is affected by every twitch and grunt."[1] I think of this metaphor when the issue of town-gown relations in my town arises. The elephant is the university, and "every twitch and grunt" is, for instance, a change in its academic calendar or its student requirements for residency. Furthermore, it sometimes appears that the sleeping elephant does not even notice that it has just jolted its partner.

Conceptually, this is what town-gown relationships can look like from a mayor's perspective: we are sleeping with a big beast, however friendly or even-tempered, that does not pay much attention to us, and the two of us often approach an issue, project, or problem from completely different positions. And yet we value the beast and like it. College town mayors surveyed for this chapter unanimously expressed happiness with their jobs and with the vibrancy and stimulation offered by a local college, community college, or university. As one colleague observed: "The creative energy and synergy of a university brings the world of ideas, culture, and possibilities to us." Another commented on the flexibility and change offered by a university neighbor: "Because students, faculty, and visitors are always arriving and departing, there is a strong sense of openness to new ideas and practices." Some mayors who also work, or have worked, at a higher education institution find their city job particularly rewarding as

Mayors Who Contributed to This Chapter

Todd D. Barton, Crawfordsville, Indiana (Wabash University)
Tim Kearney, Borough of Swarthmore, Pennsylvania (Swarthmore College)
Steve Patterson, Athens, Ohio (Ohio University)
Kate Rousmaniere, Oxford, Ohio (Miami University)
Jerry Smith, DeKalb, Illinois (University of Northern Illinois)
Jim Throgmorton, Iowa City, Iowa (University of Iowa)
Lucy Vinis, Eugene, Oregon (University of Oregon)

they begin to see a 360-degree perspective of the community and are able to make connections across town and gown.

The mayors contributing to this conversation appreciate the many good things about our college and university partners: student engagement in the community, the culture and sporting events that the university offers citizens, economic development, social diversity. At the same time, we all hear regularly about the immeasurable but very persistent "us-them" problems: staff who resent professors; stereotypes about "townies" and "rich students"; and conflicts over which is more valuable for our town—a Walmart or a bookstore? We feel every twitch and grunt that the school makes, and we sometimes wonder why the college or university does not recognize the great unspoken questions: Why aren't they paying attention to us? Don't they know what this will mean for us? Why didn't they think about us when they planned a huge sporting event on the same night as the high school prom, or rebuilt their streets in ways that cut off access to a residential community?

BEING A COLLEGE TOWN MAYOR: LESSONS IN LEADERSHIP

The job of mayor depends a lot on the size of the municipality and the type or form of government. In most large cities, the mayor is an independently elected full-time chief executive officer in charge of a deep staff. Most small, rural towns, including many college towns, often follow the council-manager or weak-mayor system, in which the mayor is selected from an elected council while a professional administrative staff person, such as a city manager, is the true head of the executive branch. "Weak" does not necessarily mean ineffective; a good small-town mayor is a community leader thoroughly engaged in community issues and concerns.

Serving in a part-time position, with no or only a minimal stipend, this type of mayor has less executive authority and more symbolic or cultural authority. As a "weak" mayor in a council-manager organization, I play a primarily ceremonial role—I conduct a lot of weddings, read proclamations, cut ribbons, and visit any community organization that wants me. To me, this role of community outreach is a major part of the job as my public presence helps to build trust between the community and local government. As I am also a full-time faculty member at the local university, I am in an advantageous position to build this trust by enhancing communication and understanding between the two organizations. To do this effectively, I need ongoing help and support from both town and gown in collaboration.

Michael Fox, coauthor of chapter 2 in this volume, has written extensively about municipal relations in town-gown settings, and he refers to the necessary mind shift of college town leaders from *government* to *governance*, emphasizing the strategic importance of relationship building, joint problem solving, and collective strategic planning.[2] Town and university leaders need to recognize their interdependence in all of their work and develop new tools for development—tools that may shift away from "business as usual" practices toward coordinated community planning, public-private partnerships, and entrepreneurial economic development. Such enterprises may require amended guidelines and relationships from a wider set of stakeholders, including community members, students, alumni, and private industry. The concept of government versus governance offers the kind of relationship-based problem solving that observers contend is reflected in the most effective college towns according to the theory that the people closest to the problem are also the people closest to the solution. As the political philosopher Benjamin Barber put it in his 2014 book, *If Mayors Ruled the World*, mayors are the level of government closest to the majority of citizens and most responsive to their daily needs, such as streets, water, and safety. Accordingly, mayors can work pragmatically, relying on civic trust, community engagement, and direct communication more than national leaders, and in that way they represent the best of democratic practice.[3] In *Our Towns: A 100,000 Mile Journey into the Heart of America*, James and Deborah Fallows studied more than two dozen small towns and offer portraits of how community-oriented, problem-solving local leaders offered resilient, flexible, and dynamic solutions to local problems.[4] Such communities draw on local strengths in higher education, the arts, and health, and draw on concepts like small-town urbanism, public-private partnerships, and community engagement to revitalize their towns' strengths and to develop new opportunities.

Making It in Massachusetts: How the Historic City of Salem Has Successfully Partnered with Salem State University

KIMBERLEY DRISCOLL has been the mayor of Salem, Massachusetts since 2006, and under her leadership the city, with a population of 43,000, has achieved two milestones: a vibrant, revitalized downtown and an activated waterfront. **TOM DANIEL** has been Salem's director of planning and community development since 2016, and served for five years as the city's economic development manager. In these positions he has addressed a number of town-gown issues, specifically campus growth and transportation.

Currently, what are the most significant town-gown issues confronting you as the mayor of the city of Salem?
The top town-gown issues are traffic, parking, and campus growth. Since communication is so important in addressing any issue, we established the Salem State University Neighborhood Advisory Committee to better foster communication between the city, the university, and its neighbors. The committee is charged with keeping communication open between the stakeholders and determining the best way to keep the public informed.*

What shared economic development activities does the city of Salem engage in with Salem State University?
The city and Salem State University (SSU) collaborate in multiple ways on economic development activities. These are some recent highlights:

The Salem State University Assistance Corporation (SSUAC) was created by a special act of the Massachusetts legislature in 1994 in order to

- Promote the university's orderly growth and development;
- Assist the university in securing physical and financial resources necessary for the acquisition and development of properties important to allowing SSUAC to fulfill its purposes; and
- Manage and operate the Enterprise Center.† The Enterprise Center leases space to entrepreneurs and offers programming to help business of all sizes succeed. The special act designates the Mayor and the City Planner as members of the SSUAC Board of Directors.

The city and SSU are both active members of the Salem Partnership. The partnership works on specific long-range economic development initiatives for Salem and the region, focusing on courts, ports, and transportation. The Salem Partnership also actively participates in "Quality of Life" initiatives, with an emphasis on making Salem a better place to live and

(continued)

work,‡ the Salem Chamber of Commerce, and the North Shore Alliance for Economic Development.

As mayor, how do you get the university's attention?
The mayor has regularly scheduled discussions with the Salem State University president. In addition to the boards and organizations noted above, the two interact in other areas. There is a mutual understanding of the importance of communication and collaboration.

Describe one of the most successful collaborations between the city and the university to address an issue.
The city and SSU have a long-standing collaboration on education. For more than one hundred years, a public school has been on the SSU campus. Although the school is moving off campus in 2018, SSU's commitment of professor and student support will continue. The Salem public school system has faced several challenges over the past decade, and SSU has been a key partner in making significant and lasting improvements to the district.

*"Mission Statement," Salem State University Neighborhood Advisory Committee, *Salem.com*, https://www.salem.com/salem-state-university-neighborhood-advisory-committee.

†"About," Salem State University Assistance Corporation, Enterprise Center at Salem State University, accessed October 20, 2018. https://enterprisectr.org/about/salem-state-university-assistance-corporation-governing-body/.

‡"Home," The Salem Partnership, accessed October 20, 2018, https://www.salempartnership.org/.

Such work is not easy, as it can challenge community cultural norms and government practices. Innovative partnerships between colleges and their home towns and cities require deep trust between the organizations. College town mayors, for instance, can use multiple forms of help from the local university to argue for what some full-time residents might see as a wasteful or trendy initiative that could disappear with the next mayoral election. And well it might, unless the university is there to help. It is wise to remember that one mayors' appreciation of higher education's diversity and flexibility does not always translate to a long-standing set of relationships in a community that is suspicious of change and has nostalgic visions of their town.

University leaders also need their college town mayors. Alumni may well remember the challenges of their first stint of independent living in off-campus housing more than their first year in a residence hall. For current students about to embark on that experience of off-campus living, city public and social services, including first responders, become their off-campus educators, and often their lifeline. For prospective students and their parents, donors and visiting dignitaries, the college town provides an important context for a broader understanding of the university's mission. Together, city and university leaders can make a college town stronger and more resourceful for both long-term and temporary residents.

MAYORS' ROUNDTABLE: BEST PRACTICES AND SOME PITFALLS TO AVOID

Of the town chief executives surveyed for this chapter, five were mayors of medium- to small-size towns with public state universities, and two were mayors in towns with a private liberal arts college. All mayors were asked to respond in writing to ten questions about their experience as civic leaders of a college town, addressing issues such as city structure, principal challenges and opportunities in town-gown relations, their formal and informal relationships with the college or university, and their top three recommended practices for presidents, provosts, and deans to consider on the higher education side. Mayors were also asked what they liked most about being mayor in a college town. I also gathered ideas informally from a number of college town mayors at the 2018 International Town & Gown Association Conference in Columbus, Ohio. Key themes that emerged from talking to these leaders included the challenges of land use, economic development issues, student culture, and the importance of regular, meaningful communication with top campus decision makers.

The topics of land use, economic development, and student culture present college town mayors with consistent and unique tensions between the university and the local community. The culture of off-campus student housing is a consistent worry, both in terms of short-term issues—garbage, public safety, traffic and parking, alcohol and drug violations—and in terms of the long-term impact of deteriorating housing stock, the decline of formerly family-friendly communities, and the development of an uneven housing market with a shortage of stock for families, faculty, the elderly, and moderate-income workers.

Mayors also described community concerns regarding university expansion of facilities that can destabilize local neighborhoods and offend local culture. A classic university "twitch and grunt" that drives local people crazy occurs when the university rightfully makes plans on its property that upsets the local community. Certainly the university has the authority to demolish its own campus park or building, or to redesign a campus road to improve student safety, or to expand its food service options so that students have less need to leave campus for meals. But if it neglects to tell the community of such changes in advance, the resulting social and financial impact on the community can be devastating. In such cases, writes one mayor, the city "is left with few options in a situation not of our creation. It's another chapter in a power dynamic that is hard to shift."

Economic development issues are also unique for college town mayors. Because in many college towns the downtown and the campus bleed into one another almost imperceptibly, commercial activities in the downtown are often dedicated to undergraduate students, most notably in restaurants, bars, and youth-oriented clothing shops. While such a market keeps one sector of the local economy happy, other sectors are marginalized or chased away. College town mayors struggle with trying to respect the economic needs of a college or university community while dreaming of a more balanced market for year-round residents and visitors. In some communities, an active Visitor Bureau can help achieve this balance by promoting the college town's strengths to those who are not students.

All of the mayors interviewed applauded a number of town-gown shared activities, including university sponsorship of service learning projects that enlist volunteers, interns, and consultants in a wide array of nonprofit and public-sector roles. This work serves an additional purpose of engaging students with the external community, and in some college towns students have significantly impacted the quality of life with their volunteer work and entrepreneurial efforts. Many colleges promote such service learning activities as the star program of their community engagement, and most mayors agree that this work is important in that it provides the necessary labor for social services, yet they realize that the ultimate purpose of such university initiatives is the enhancement of student experiences as much as the resolution of community needs.

Accordingly, mayors were particularly proud of coordinated efforts between city and university structural and administrative services, including police, fire, public transportation, high-speed internet, and joint support of entrepreneurial business incubators working in coordination with regional economic development organizations, as well as university financial investment in community public parks, recreation trails, and cultural events. Of particular note were joint community-university efforts for outreach to incoming students to address off-campus binge drinking and house parties. In-depth communication is critical to the success of such efforts. Even as mayors described ongoing joint meetings between senior campus and city officials, a welcome, open-door policy with the college or university president, and regular staff meetings to discuss planning, economic development, and neighborhood issues, they also wondered who was really making the decisions on campus. Some described occasions when a joint vision was shelved due to dense fiscal and regulatory limitations, and they puzzled over conflicting messages about university purview, responsibility, and restrictions. Perhaps, some mayors remarked, we need to find a way to talk with people *around* the president who are really in control, such as provosts, CFOs, or auxiliary-services vice presidents.

Thus, although most city leaders believed that they had ready access to university leaders, including the president, many noted that the impact of this accessibility was limited by the university's complex legal and fiscal structure, or by the fact that a particular mayor may serve only one term, or by the possibility that a college president may depart suddenly. As one mayor wrote, in spite of all the positive coordination, "there is a long history in the city of feeling that the university proceeds with plans without adequate notice or engagement with the town or its neighbors who are impacted by their choices."

MOVING FORWARD: SUMMARY RECOMMENDATIONS FROM MAYORS FOR HIGHER EDUCATION LEADERS

The mayors' main recommendation for college and university presidents was to develop ongoing, proactive, and substantive lines of communication about both long- and short-term plans. "Relationships are important," one wrote, "but information is the key to successful partnerships." Other recommendations include putting incentives in place that prioritize faculty, staff, and student investment of significant time and service in the local community. In addition, a joint town-gown committee should be authorized with a memorandum of understanding to formalize existing collaborations and partnerships and to stimulate future endeavors. Recommended, too, was a presidential appointment of one active college or university staff person to be the main spokesperson and business liaison for community relations, someone who would be a constant presence at city council, neighborhood, and other meetings.

Presidents also need to provide the community and its mayor with clearer explanations about how processes work. Higher education finance and law are confounding to most people, and in the case of joint projects, rumors can often be clarified by simply explaining existing policies. Can the college subsidize a salary for a joint city-college position? If not, why not? Does the university code of conduct explicitly apply to students off campus? If so, can the city partner with the institution in adjudicating off-campus violations? Who actually owns that city street that runs through the campus, and can community members have a say in redesign plans? Should they? To what extent does a tax-exempt college provide payments or services to the city in lieu of taxes? Presidents are also urged to continue and expand their role in supporting economic and workforce development in the extended community, to engage proactively with the city's strategic planning, and, for public institutions, to marshal the city's support in campaigns to increase state funding, since many municipalities, too, have experienced reduced state support.

Presidents are advised to hold reasonable expectations, as the town-gown relationship existed long before they, or their mayors, arrived. And optics matter: the visual presence of the president traveling to the town for meetings may seem only symbolic, but this symbolism is significant to successful town-gown relations. The president and the president's staff should be present and visible in their town or city on a regular basis. Membership and participation in town-gown organizations at the state and national level, particularly the International Town & Gown Association, is also highly recommended, as the ITGA is the annual venue where college town issues are raised and debated most productively; it is also the association most effective in offering best practices for leaders on both sides.

Several mayors interviewed for this chapter noted that for many years their towns had essentially coexisted with the college or university, but that over the past five to ten years circumstances had changed and now there was an active drive to enhance the relationship in ways that benefit the college, the students, and the community. Today, both colleges and towns are seeking to serve as an anchor institution, rather than a passive neighbor, via more creative and collaborative governance models.

As one mayor described it, the town-gown relationship "takes our community to the next level and provides us with opportunities we wouldn't have otherwise." However, it also requires careful work and understanding from both the town and the college or university. Finally, all mayors agreed in their recommendations that higher education leaders work slowly, methodically, and seriously on the development of town-gown relationships. Trust must be built and maintained, and regular, meaningful communication is a central part of that trust.

CHAPTER 13

Money Matters

Creative Financing for Campuses and Their Communities

RICK SELTZER

No matter how creative an idea is, it usually comes with a price, and especially so when it involves college presidents and the construction of a new building. Colleges and universities across the nation are constantly developing strategies to finance new buildings both on and off their campuses. In some instances, it means convincing donors in unexpected places to support a much-needed expansion or a program with local school-aged children. In others, it means negotiating an acceptable arrangement with a private business that provides students with an important service. Whatever the scenario, I have most likely written about it during my time as a reporter for *Inside Higher Ed*. As one initial takeaway, it has become abundantly clear that presidents, provosts, and CFOs need to beware of unintended consequences and unexpected blowback tied to the way they pay for their favorite projects—even in cases where leaders have the best of intentions, and even in cases where they are attempting to do something in the best interest of the larger community.

Developers drive hard bargains, and donors seeking anonymity can quickly become sources of controversy. In the process, institutions can find themselves sucked into an unfamiliar tangle of local political grudges and regulatory scrutiny. The following stories are not necessarily cases in which higher education administrators made bad choices or committed cardinal sins by pursuing cockamamy financing schemes. The goal of this chapter is not to second-guess any particular financing mechanisms, whether they be public-private partnerships, vendor contracts, donor agreements, or other arrangements. Rather, the goal is to show that the price of carrying out a good idea is not measured simply in dollars and cents but also in the opportunity it provides to learn from colleagues' experiences.

University administrators who are used to navigating balance sheets, student recruitment, and shared governance on campus might struggle to see the wide and nuanced range of drawbacks tied to financing a good idea, but any drawback at any stage should be taken seriously so that leaders can make the best decision during future initiatives. Leaders should not turn their backs on out-of-the-box ideas and creative financing mechanisms, but they should be exceedingly cautious before signing any deals, because even carefully developed funding plans can carry unexpected tripwires.

EVEN DONATIONS FOR A GOOD CAUSE COME WITH STRINGS

A program called Ignite and Run at Grinnell College in Iowa had local school-aged children enrolling in courses taught by college students. In its first three years, the program hosted 580 students taking 105 different classes.[1] Its aims included boosting children's readiness for higher education by exposing them to a college campus in hopes of making them feel more comfortable in the environment. The program would seem to fit well with Grinnell, an institution that has heavily emphasized social responsibility throughout its history, including when it was a center for abolitionist activity. Unfortunately, the program did not prove to be so simple, because it drew some of its money from husband and wife donors Pete Brownell and Helen Redmond, and Pete Brownell spent a year as the president of the National Rifle Association. His local company, Brownells, called itself the "World's Largest Supplier of Firearms Accessories and Gunsmithing Tools."

Soon after Brownell was elected NRA president in 2017, Grinnell alumni took notice of his position. Debate followed about whether the college was conferring legitimacy on the NRA by accepting money from its president. A similar discussion might not have cropped up at every campus in the country, but it was intense at Grinnell, an institution with progressive roots. An online profile the NRA posted about Brownell helped to fuel outrage because of the way it referred to the college. It described Grinnell as a place that had not always been a "bastion of pro-gun sentiment" until Brownell taught faculty members about guns:

> Pete and his family live in Grinnell, a town of around 10,000 east of Des Moines in central Iowa. The spick-and-span community likes to refer to itself as the "Jewel of the Prairie" and is home to Grinnell College, an excellent Midwestern liberal arts school. Brownell likes to point out that the college hasn't always been a bastion of pro-gun sentiment, and this

RICK SELTZER

What is the single most important piece of advice you would share with a college or university president about to undertake a significant college town project with a mayor or city planning team?

No matter how well intentioned, politicians and planners are only two narrow parts of a community. While working with them may be important, it doesn't mean you'll have the support of all constituencies—or that you should ignore those with legitimate interests, concerns, or input regarding a project.

omission of pro-gun common sense presented Pete with an obvious hometown problem to rectify.

"We started by opening up a dialogue," Brownell said. "It wasn't that the folks on the faculty really hated guns, it's just that they didn't know anything about them."

So Pete volunteered to lecture on Second Amendment issues and, in time, managed to start a shooting club on campus. Then, when several of the professors expressed a desire to help with wildlife habitat enhancement on Brownell land bordering the company shooting range, the CEO sensed an opportunity to open even more philosophical doors. When the educators finished with the hands-on work involving plants, seed and soil, Pete introduced them to the shooting range.

For most it was a first. And, as is generally the case, the majority of the faculty left Brownell's property giddy with excitement over having actually fired a real handgun. Today these same educators are regulars at the range. The newly committed gun owners have been known to take their guns with them when they return to New York for civic events. The professors hate to miss out on even a few minutes of range time, and the previous anti-gun sentiment at the college has been offset by an open-mindedness that never would have exited [*sic*] without a little push from Pete.[2]

This passage eventually disappeared from the NRA website. Grinnell representatives declined to say whether they were involved in the takedown—or to share more information about Brownell's donation. What representatives would say is that the college is not endorsing its donors when it links their names to programs they support, but is only expressing gratitude. Nevertheless, Grinnell made several changes to its donor acceptance policy as the debate unfolded. The policy was changed to include guiding principles: that Grinnell not encourage gifts deemed inappropriate because of a donor's "personal or financial situation" and that the college accept gifts that could reasonably be expected to benefit its mission. Alumni representation was added to a Gift Acceptance Committee. A measure called for a program's constituents to help vet a gift if it was to benefit that program. That result left many unhappy on both sides. Anti-NRA forces wanted a rejection clause in the new policy, while others worried the college was moving down a perilous path toward accepting only gifts deemed by popular opinion to be morally clean.

Since Grinnell's leadership did not provide much comment on the Brownell gift, it is not possible to know exactly what administrators were thinking when accepting the money Brownell and Redmond gave, but it is possible to see why the money might have been attractive. Brownell was a local businessman offering funding for an exciting program benefiting students in the college town community. As he had attended the University of Iowa, this gift represented a broadening of Grinnell's donor pool beyond its own graduates. Nonetheless, he turned into a lightning rod. The larger point was not whether Brownell's involvement in the NRA was acceptable or not, or whether anti-gun alumni were standing on the right or wrong side of history. It was that Grinnell found itself caught between the two sides, and its existing policies made it difficult to handle the situation.

Ultimately, the lesson here is that many constituencies on and off a campus believe they have a stake in upholding their college or university's reputation. They need to feel that they have properly vetted gifts and donors, and they also need to believe that they have a recourse if a donor is found to be out of step with an institution's principles. Ideally, an institution will not have to return a gift or change its policies in order to quell a public outcry, but sometimes that outcome cannot reasonably be avoided. Thus, for presidents and trustees, often caught up in the primary goal of securing funding, it is critical also to remember that many donations come with an undeniable cost. In the words of Eliza Willis, a professor of political science at Grinnell who helped coordinate Grinnell's discussion about its gift acceptance policy, "It's a hard debate, but we can't just take money from everyone."[3]

SCIENTISTS SUSPECT DONORS' MOTIVES

The donor's identity and intent can bring criticism from scientists and those who have no direct relationship to a university. In September 2017, the University of California, Irvine, found itself receiving intense criticism from different corners of the scientific community for taking money from donors in order to name its College of Health Sciences, which focuses on "interdisciplinary integrative health."[4] Two of the university's longtime donors, Susan and Henry Samueli, pledged $200 million to name the college. Medical researchers quickly balked at the focus of the new enterprise, which was also said to be tasked with incorporating "integrative health research, teaching and patient care" in its schools and programs. Many viewed "integrative health" to be a rebranding of alternative medicine, which has earned a reputation of not being supported by science.

The Samuelis, owners of the Anaheim Ducks of the National Hockey League, brought to the table a long history of backing integrative medicine. In 2001 they wrote a $5.7 million check to found the Susan Samueli Center for Integrative Medicine at UC Irvine. The same year, they opened a Virginia-based institute studying alternative medicine. Susan Samueli has traced her connections to alternative medicine back three decades, when she caught a cold while in France. A friend told her to try aconite, a homeopathic remedy, and Samueli found herself cured. The couple also gave homeopathic methods credit for keeping their children healthy without giving them antibiotics.[5] Henry Samueli has also proclaimed his own belief in integrative health. At an announcement of the couple's $200 million gift, he even referred to the Samueli Center for Integrative Medicine at UC Irvine as "Susan's center" and said he asks his wife for help with homeopathic remedies whenever he feels a cold approaching.

About $30 million of the couple's gift was earmarked for facilities, equipment, and technology. The rest was bound for an endowment funding faculty chairs, scholarships, fellowships, research projects, curricular development, and clinical services. The Samuelis were not to have a say in the choice of faculty members who would hold endowed chairs, but they or their representatives were invited to serve on an advisory board for the college and an advisory board for the Susan Samueli Center for Integrative Medicine, which was being renamed the Susan Samueli Integrative Health Institute. UC Irvine officials insisted the institute would be evidence-based, with Vice Chancellor for Health Affairs Howard Federoff telling the *Los Angeles Times* he would never allow anything to take place if he believed clinical evidence was lacking.[6] He also argued that physicians and scientists need to keep an open mind, saying some treatments dismissed in the past have been found effective in certain situations.

Some academics at the university seemed unconcerned about the issues raised. Jay Gargus, professor of physiology and biophysics, professor of pediatrics, and director of UC Irvine's School of Medicine Center for

Autism Research and Translation, chaired the Academic Senate for the College of Health Sciences at the time. He took part in meetings early on in the process of winning the $200 million gift. Gargus said the medicine in question would be rigorously reviewed by the Academic Senate. The Samuelis' comments about homeopathic remedies at the "infomercial launch" of the gift might be troubling if someone was not familiar with the university, he said. However, the university was not spared from criticism when the gift was announced. "What is clearly happening here is an attempt to put a giant thumb [on] the scale of science and medicine through money," wrote Steven Novella, an academic clinical neurologist at the Yale University School of Medicine, on the blog *Science-Based Medicine*, where he was executive editor.[7] Novella titled his post "Quackademic Medicine at UC Irvine."

This situation is an extreme example of the wide-ranging tension between donors who may want to influence universities and universities themselves that want to operate independently while still recognizing that they need different, and constant, sources of funding. "How much are you willing to, potentially, bend mission in order to progress on other things?" asked Noah Drezner, an associate professor of higher education at Columbia University Teachers College, when interviewed about this issue for *Inside Higher Ed*.[8]

IT TAKES MONEY TO MAKE MONEY

Publicly traded companies are typically large employers that want to build goodwill in communities in order to attract customers and keep stockholders happy, and what better way to do that than to close deals providing much-needed services to college and university students? For example, many banks pursue agreements that place a branch on campus and a financial product in the hands of thousands of undergraduates. In one common arrangement, banks create partnerships with higher education institutions that allow students to connect their campus-issued identification cards to checking accounts. The student enjoys the convenience of having to carry only a single card, plus all the benefits of a bank account. The bank receives a new customer early in life. The college often receives a local bank branch and some lucrative payments. However, as the following example demonstrates, not everyone was happy with the partnership signed by several campuses and the San Francisco banking giant Wells Fargo.

In early 2018 the bank came under scrutiny for the student card deals it had struck. When the *Wall Street Journal* analyzed fees that banks charged

RICK SELTZER

What is one key way you believe college towns have changed over the past generation?

Many college towns seem to be facing a growing number of questions about their core identity as American life changes: What are they, what do they want to be, what institutions will lead them, and what will they value?

to students at colleges, it determined that Wells Fargo charged twenty-two of the highest average fees levied during the 2017 fiscal year.[9] A follow-up investigation I conducted for *Inside Higher Ed* examined Wells Fargo accounts linked to twenty-nine different colleges for the same year.[10] Across those twenty-nine colleges, students at the University of Florida paid the lowest average cost in fees, $31.51 a year for 37,353 active accounts. Students at Florida A&M University paid the highest annual average, $67.99 across 6,219 accounts. The median costs were much lower than mean costs, so a small subset of students were likely paying much higher fees than the overall student body. The fees Wells Fargo pays are determined by negotiations between a college and the bank. The fees students pay are determined by how they use their accounts. They can rack up fees for activities like using out-of-network ATMs. How much did Wells Fargo pay campuses in return? Again, it depended. The smallest cash consideration the bank paid was $10,421, to Fayetteville State University in North Carolina. The most it paid for the year was $340,000 to Texas A&M University, which had the most accounts of the group analyzed—more than 38,000. At Sacramento State University, Wells Fargo paid $119,764 in 2017, and it collected more than $650,000 in fees from Sacramento State–connected accounts.

Whether these are good deals depends on a number of factors, of course. The agreement's backers at Sacramento State and Wells Fargo have argued it gives students an on-campus banking option where one might not otherwise have been available. They add that, because the bank leases space on campus, Wells Fargo is paying the university more than government-mandated disclosures show, and that it has agreed to some important restrictions on how it markets additional services to students on campus. Yet it is also important to consider the student perspective. The average fee for an account holder at Sacramento State was $47.35. In contrast, PNC Bank had a deal with Penn State leading to average fees of $14.32 for 13,216 students. PNC had a deal with the University of Illinois that had 10,903 active accounts paying average annual fees of $15.03.

Wells Fargo's deals came under scrutiny because of the bank's other well-documented issues in the late 2010s. It attracted the attention of U.S. senator Richard Durbin, who sent a letter to Wells Fargo's CEO asking the bank to stop any plans it had to expand on college campuses. "I will be watching your bank's process in improving its company policies and practices with great interest, especially with respect to your treatment of America's student consumers," Durbin wrote in 2018.[11] In sum, deals with for-profit companies can provide important resources for colleges and universities and useful access to services for their students, but it is still wise to test the market to discover whether an even better deal is out there waiting.

SCHOOLS IN THE SPOTLIGHT

Few things are as important to a community than its K–12 school system. Parents and employees weigh schools heavily when considering where to live, as schools serve as a center of civic life as they put on plays, host athletic events, and serve as polling places. When a school is struggling, the local college or university often tries to help. College and university missions tend to align with those of schools, and in many cases an area's college produces a large number of the teachers who go on to work in its K–12 schools. However, beyond simply graduating large cohorts of teenagers, schools are also a complex intersection of local governance, state policy, federal policy, and employment law.

Ball State University in Muncie, Indiana, found itself in the middle of those difficult issues in early 2018. The local public school system, Muncie Community Schools, had long been losing students since its enrollment peaked at nearly 20,000 students in 1967. By 2018 the schools enrolled just over 5,200 students. A 2017 study found the system's facilities were less than 75 percent occupied the year before, and the occupancy rate was predicted to fall to 68 percent by 2030.[12] Of greater concern to state legislators, $10 million from general-obligation bonds in 2014 had been earmarked for school maintenance. But the money went instead to funding operating costs for a system facing intense budget pressures. The financial crisis rankled Indiana's Republican-controlled legislature. Lawmakers drew up a plan to give control of the schools to Ball State University, the state's fourth-largest public university. It would have replaced the school system's elected board, made up of five members, with a board made up of seven members appointed by the university. Ball State leaders supported the idea. Historically a teacher's college, the university already had numerous programs at Muncie schools. The university's president, Geoffrey S. Mearns, said the university's future was tied to the future of

Muncie and that Ball State had an obligation to support its home city and community. Many faculty members hoped to expand programs they believed would help children. The state was offering some additional funding for the school system if Ball State took over.

The proposed deal gave Ball State several important protections. Although the university would control the school system through the remade board, the two would be legally and financially separate entities. Ball State would not be required to recognize collective bargaining rights for the local teachers' union. This was seen by some as a shot at teachers' rights to unionize, and it came in a state where the traditional public school model was already under pressure from state law. Indiana law allows neighboring public schools and charter schools to compete with each other for student enrollment. Ball State itself authorized public charter schools, and it ran the K–12 Burris Laboratory School and a residential high school for gifted juniors and seniors called the Indiana Academy for Science, Mathematics, and Humanities. As a result, Ball State found itself in a politically dicey situation, potentially serving as the vehicle for shattering a decades-old paradigm for public education in Muncie. And it was doing so with very little ability to guarantee local residents that they would have a say in the way it would run the district. Ball State president Mearns cast the idea simply as the university doing what it could to help the local schools. "We're not trying to establish either a statewide model or a nationwide model," he said. "What we're attempting to do is address a significant, profound challenge in Muncie and bring together the experience and expertise of our campus."[13]

The measure became law during a special state legislative session that spring, setting in motion a process in which Ball State moved to appoint five new school board members from applications submitted by the community, one from nominations by Muncie's mayor and one from nominations by Muncie's city council. The university also moved to create a Community Engagement Council of volunteers and to send a senior administrator to be a liaison to the school system. President Mearns recommended that the board report to the public, not to him. "They are a public school board; they'll have public meetings the way any school board would," he told Indiana Public Media. "Again, the only difference is how they get to that seat, not how they operate once they're in that position."[14]

As soon as the plan went into motion, Ball State attempted to assure teachers. It announced that it expected to hold salaries and benefits steady for employees during the first year of Ball State control. But the final law did give the university the option of not recognizing the existing teacher's union.[15] Ball State's eventual success or failure in running the local school district would likely affect how the move is viewed in the long run. Putting aside the open question of how the experiment would work out, the situation exposes the risks universities take when agreeing to radical new community partnerships—risks to both their own reputations and the communities around them.

Although a university-run school district is exceedingly rare, Ball State would not be the first to try the practice. Boston University (BU) ran public schools in nearby Chelsea, Massachusetts, for about twenty years ending in 2008. That design was similar to the one proposed for Ball State in that the university's finances were kept separate from the school district's. However, it was markedly different in that the Chelsea School Committee, a locally elected board, kept power to override BU's decisions on major policy issues. Nonetheless, BU's experience is informative. Administrators said BU encountered a wide range of entrenched problems in the local school system. They believe they improved schools' financial and operating practices. A university thinking about taking over public schools must look closely at what it is getting into and know how much authority it has, said Doug Sears, vice president and chief of staff to the president at BU. Sears was also superintendent of Chelsea Public Schools for five years while BU controlled the district, and he is a former dean at the university's School of Education. "My biggest cautionary tale is that a lot of ideas in higher education right now just aren't very good," Sears said. "I'm very proud of what we did. I think we did not get the credit for it."[16]

DEVELOPERS PLAY HARDBALL

Developers can offer colleges and universities some interesting—and attractive—ways to finance major projects. Various permutations of public-private partnerships, lease-and-sublease-back agreements, and other arrangements can allow institutions to access new sources of private capital, pay less than full price up front for new facilities, and avoid the headache of managing those facilities once they are built. The benefits can be attractive, especially for an institution seeking to build projects that are more ambitious than the usual slate of dormitories, academic space, and athletic fields. Many universities have been exceedingly happy with projects for building mixes of academic, residential, and retail space. Yet drawbacks can lurk. Take, for example, Bethune-Cookman University, which built a new, 1,200-bed dormitory in a deal with a developer. Construction costs totaled $85 million, which drew some questions because they were originally projected at only $72.1 million. Drawing even more questions was the way the university would pay for the construction:

a lease-and-sublease-back agreement estimated to cost more than $306 million over forty years.

A former trustee called the deal the type "that boards and presidents cannot allow to happen," saying due diligence and vetting are required to "make sure you never put yourself in this type of financial situation."[17] Scrutiny of the deal mixed with other concerns about Bethune-Cookman's governance, and the university's president, Edison O. Jackson, announced his retirement in 2017. The upheaval did not end there. By early 2018, Bethune-Cookman was suing the dormitory's developer and several of its former administrators, including Jackson, over the expensive deal. The suit alleged the developer had made improper payments to Bethune-Cookman officials while the dormitory price tag jumped.[18] Weeks later, the developer countersued, denying claims in the university's lawsuit, defending the lease-and-sublease-back agreement's total cost as akin to a thirty-year mortgage, and saying the dormitory project was "largely independent" of the university's difficulties with governance and finances. The developer also sought damages including rent, late charges, and interest, along with possession of the dormitory, the appointment of a receiver to run the dormitory business, and an injunction requiring Bethune-Cookman to fill the dormitory before leasing space to students elsewhere.[19]

The lawsuits made an already undesirable situation even messier. The reality is that big-money construction contracts come with high stakes for both university and developer. They can benefit all involved, but universities need to scrutinize them closely and be prepared for the possibility of unexpected, and unwanted, results. That is why savvy town-gown planners learn to read the fine print and pay full attention to the companies they do business with in order to determine if the up-front construction costs and the price to pay them back over time are worth it.

LESSONS LEARNED FOR COLLEGE TOWN PLANNERS

The most important lesson learned in the examples described above is one simple idea: Think through contingencies. Thinking through contingencies is deceptively hard work because the upside is always exciting and the downside always looks messy. The thought process becomes even more challenging for a college president or provost trying to work with the institution's surrounding community, whether that consists of local businesses, donors, schools, or developers. Each constituency brings its own unique desires and needs to a situation, lengthening the list of contingencies that will need to be considered. It is also wise to remember that the way a program is paid for shapes both that program's operations and the way it is perceived by the campus and the external community. In cases of philanthropy, those trying to raise money likely hope donors have the best intentions or are attaching only a few reasonable strings to the money they are giving. In reality, that may not always be the case—and the larger community will not hesitate to question a donor's intentions. College and university leaders would be wise to consider both whether donor relationships are appropriate and how they will be viewed by a diverse range of interested parties, including local residents, students, faculty, trustees, and alumni. Perception is reality to the broader public, and it should not be brushed off. Deciding not to take the money should always be an option on the table.

Planners should also question the sources of money. Even if a for-profit company pledges to uphold strong values and provide a needed service, it remains an operation established to prioritize its own owners or shareholders. Asking whether a contract is really the best deal available could have benefits for a college, its students, and the broader community alike. Whether it is Wells Fargo offering banking services or a private company pushing a public-private partnership deal, administrators have to take a step back and ask if the agreement is in the best interests of all involved. This calculation becomes even more complex if the interests of different parties do not align—if, say, a university can get the most money from one company for banking services, yet it will then potentially mean higher fees charged to students. It can be harder to walk away in such situations. Renegotiating a contract with a company could jeopardize or disrupt services on campus, and scrapping an expensive real estate transaction might mean delaying completion of a much-needed residence hall or chemistry laboratory. History shows that the alternatives can be worse, however. Bethune-Cookman faced long-term expenses and significant administrative upheaval, at least in part because of its controversial residence deal. Grinnell faced questions about its core identity because it accepted money for a school program from a well-known firearms titan.

In sum, community-minded financing is not simply about what a college's administration and its board may want and are willing to pay. It is also about what the surrounding community needs and perceives the best price to be. The process of making these decisions is painful even when they are confined to the campus quadrangle; they become exponentially more challenging when they spread out into surrounding towns, cities, and school districts. As a rule, while there can be remarkable upsides to creative financing, tread carefully.

CHAPTER 14

Hidden Opportunities and Challenges in the College Town Job Market

ANDREW W. HIBEL AND KELLY A. CHERWIN

INTRODUCTION

If Old Main is not the heart of Penn State, it is certainly the soul of the university. Old Main captures the spirit of the university community and the essence of higher education. For generations, virtually every top academic and administrative leader at Pennsylvania State University, including the university's president, has had an office in Old Main. From within its walls, these leaders have made the decisions that have catalyzed Penn State.

Old Main on the campus of Pennsylvania State University, University Park. Wikimedia Commons

A summary of the history of Old Main on the Penn State World Campus website paints a perfect picture of the building:

> Old Main has been a prominent landmark for the Penn State University Park campus for many years. On cold winter nights, you can find students catching snowflakes on its lawn, and in the spring a good game of Frisbee. It also is one of the most photographed places in University Park, second only to the Lion Shrine. The path Old Main took through its 150 year history was riddled with obstacles, fires, and rebuilds, but the building still holds the same symbol of Penn State pride.[1]

In the spring of 1996, the founders of HigherEdJobs.com were housed in the "garden level" of Old Main, in Penn State's development offices. The genesis of the company was forged when the founders, having recently secured their first professional positions in academia, bonded over their shared experiences and began formulating ideas for how they could serve others trying to navigate employment opportunities in higher education. In 2000 HigherEdJobs.com opened its first offices at Penn State's Research Park. Since then, HigherEdJobs.com has both served college towns and competed to hire candidates in a college town. The experience of its founders and staff has taught them that, for most people, working in a college town is more than simply pulling into the parking lot of a nondescript building; rather, it is being a part of something that brings meaning to their lives. This chapter describes how the qualities of college towns create both exclusive opportunities and unique challenges for employment in higher education.

PRIOR DEFINITIONS OF AND DISCUSSIONS ABOUT COLLEGE TOWNS

To understand the effects of a college town on the recruitment of university employees, a discussion of the characteristics of these towns is needed. In college towns, schools are usually the dominant employer in the community and, as such, have many distinctive qualities. The original rise of the college town may have been premature. Indeed, many college towns grew prior to the growth of primary and secondary schools. John Thelin, in his book *A History of American Higher Education*, shows that the growth of the college town in the early nineteenth century often happened without the infrastructure to support a population of students: "A peculiar feature of the college-building impulse is that it took place

ANDREW W. HIBEL and KELLY A. CHERWIN

How do you think college towns have changed over the course of your career?
There is a greater divide between rural and urban communities. The rural college town is becoming more similar to an urban college community than the community that surrounds it. It is not just town versus gown anymore; it is also town versus town.

prior to, and with more enthusiasm than, the initiative to establish primary- and secondary-school systems. . . . Civic 'boosterism' for establishing a town with a college probably led to an excessive proliferation of colleges."[2]

In analyzing the defining characteristics of the college town, we should acknowledge that the original development of these communities may have been without planning for needed fundamentals and with "premature zeal"; this partly explains why these communities' origins don't necessarily fit the pattern of other towns. Blake Gumprecht, in *The American College Town*, offers a traditional definition: "I consider a college town any city where a college or university and the cultures it creates exert a dominant influence over the character of the town."[3] Gumprecht's definition accounts for the strong influence that these leading employers hold over their communities. This characteristic is something that shapes virtually every college town, from those hosting major state universities to those with small private liberal arts colleges.

The fact that schools in major metro areas are often among their communities' largest employers helps better distinguish another characteristic of college towns for employee recruitment: varied workforce skills. College towns are unique communities. Noncollege towns, whether major metropolitan areas or small towns, also have dominant employers, but their communities do not always have the other characteristics of college towns. In our view, college towns reflect the college or university's ability to attract and retain the faculty and staff that make up its workforce. Historically, schools have been a primary employer in their community, and their status afforded them multiple benefits. As Thelin explains:

> The prototypical American campus of the twenty-first century, whether a college or university, was a formidable organization in its local and state community. Often a college was the largest employer in what was,

> of course, a "college town." This presence even extended to major cities: Johns Hopkins in Baltimore, Brown University in Providence, Harvard in Cambridge-Boston, the University of Kentucky in Lexington, Indiana University in Bloomington, Northwestern University in Evanston, and so on. Part of this heritage was that the American campus continued to enjoy a variety of tax benefits, including exemption from local property taxes and federal and state income taxes. But the size and success of the American campus also meant that between 1970 and 2000, these traditional privileges were subject to continual review and renegotiation.[4]

Today, many colleges and universities are still significant employers in their communities. Institutions are the largest single private employer in eleven of the fifty states, third after Walmart and health care.[5] However, these examples may run contrary to the realities of recruiting and maintaining the labor force needed to preserve and enhance institutional competitiveness.

HIGHEREDJOBS.COM DATA AND THE NEW MODEL FOR COLLEGE TOWNS

HigherEdJobs.com is one of the most widely used sources for colleges and universities to recruit faculty and administrators, and its job postings data provide a new model for assessing the realities of recruiting in a college town. To provide insights into how schools are actually going about recruitment, HigherEdJobs.com staff chose thirteen anonymous schools to be evaluated. A cross section of various types and sizes of institutions were included in this sample according to the standard Carnegie classification of institutions.[6] No schools specifically named in this chapter were part of this cohort. All towns had populations between 15,000 and 200,000. These "college towns" posted 8,217 jobs in 2016, which constituted the analyzed data.

As table 14.1 shows, 75 percent of jobs posted at these thirteen schools were in the administrative category, 23 percent in the faculty category, and 1.5 percent in the executive category. The jobs were posted in the forty-six major administrative classifications and twelve major faculty classifications. The top ten administrative classifications by number of postings accounted for more than 62 percent of the postings. These categories, along with the top five faculty classifications, are presented in tables 14.2 and 14.3.

Table 14.1. Breakdown of Job Postings by General Category

	Percentage
Administrative	75.5
Faculty	23.0
Executive	1.5

Table 14.2. Top Ten Administrative Classifications, 2016

	Number of job postings
Laboratory and research	773
Computing	605
Secretary	469
Facilities	466
Business	418
Health	241
PR and marketing	234
Student affairs	221
Development	218
Human resources	198

Table 14.3. Top Five Faculty Classifications, 2016

	Number of job postings
Liberal arts	389
Science	262
Fine and applied arts	227
Business	189
Agriculture	188

The thirteen colleges we analyzed were located in a variety of college towns, which were categorized as shown in table 14.4. Four of the college towns had a population of less than 50,000 people (class A), six had populations between 50,001 and 99,999 people (class B), and three had populations greater than 100,000 people (class C). Employees of the college or university made up between 0.58 and 36.34 percent of the total town population (see table 14.5).

Findings from the HigherEdJobs.com posting data are discussed further in the "Essential Considerations" section at the end of this chapter.

Table 14.4. Categorization of College Towns by Population

Class	Population (2016 census)	Number of towns
A	<50,000	4
B	50,001–99,999	6
C	>100,000	3

Table 14.5. College or University Employees as a Percentage of College Town Population

College town	Size categorization	Percentage of population (2016 Census)
A	Class C	6.22
B	Class B	13.37
C	Class B	0.58
D	Class A	4.78
E	Class A	1.53
F	Class A	36.34
G	Class C	4.51
H	Class B	17.99
I	Class B	7.83
J	Class C	13.27
K	Class B	0.92
L	Class A	1.88
M	Class B	4.78

CHALLENGES AND OPPORTUNITIES FOR COLLEGE TOWN EMPLOYMENT

As the title of this chapter suggests, the job market in a college town presents both opportunities and challenges. Variables such as the community's size, location, and economic health are several of the factors that can play a part in the job market. Consequently, these factors can be an advantage or disadvantage when it comes to recruiting talent for an institution. Representatives from HigherEdJobs.com spoke with several institutions to discuss their recruiting experiences vis-à-vis the surrounding or nearby college towns. When asked about what opportunities in Boulder, Colorado, make it easier to recruit, Tracy Hooker, the human resources director in Employee Services at the University of Colorado (CU), replied that her university leverages location as an advantage: "Denver and its surrounding areas are one of the fastest growing areas in the country."[7] Mark Rickenbach, professor and chair of the Department of Forest and Wildlife Ecology at the University of Wisconsin–Madison, echoed this sentiment: "In addition to UW-Madison being a world class university, an advantage that Madison has in recruiting is that it has been voted one of the most 'livable' cities in the United States."[8]

When it comes to the population of the college town and how it affects recruiting, one could say that the right size is in the eye of the beholder. Deborah Haynes, who heads the Department of Health and Human Development at the University of Montana, told us: "Generally the small-town size of Bozeman is more of an advantage, [but in cases where the smaller population may cause hesitation] we talk to candidates about the easy drive to metropolitan areas and the direct flights to such places." She noted further: "The fact that Bozeman is a well-educated community and has a high number of quality entertainment venues because of our tourist industry is a major opportunity for the University to help in their recruitment efforts."[9] To address concerns about the high cost of housing in Bozeman, the University of Montana assists newly hired employees in order to improve their recruiting efforts. The university is proactive in searching for and evaluating rental housing to make sure that out-of-state hires are not unhappy when they arrive.

Distinct attributes of college towns can be important draws for candidates, as well. Albert A. Liddicoat, vice provost for academic affairs and personnel for California Polytechnic University (Cal Poly), San Luis Obispo, credits the advantages offered by San Luis Obispo as a home city in attracting talent to the university, especially the "vibrant downtown and the distinct college feel." In addition, he said, "the larger community is entrepreneurial and outdoor focused." Even with all of the positive community attributes of San Luis Obispo, Cal Poly faces challenges in recruiting. Liddicoat mentioned that "the smaller communities can also be a challenge due to the lack of amenities and the diversity often found in larger cities." He continued, "For both faculty and staff who relocate to the area and who have partners looking for work, it can be particularly challenging, especially given the high price of housing and limited professional jobs in the area. In addition, Cal Poly is the only university on the coast between Santa Barbara and San Jose, and therefore faculty have fewer opportunities to collaborate with local peers." However, Cal Poly's strong national reputation continues to attract highly qualified faculty. "Many people choose to live in San Luis Obispo," Liddicoat observed, "because it aligns with their lifestyle and they are willing to make some compromises to live in such an idyllic area."[10]

Although many college towns are desirable locations in which to live, tighter markets could pose a threat to recruiting for certain positions, particularly faculty positions. Tracy Hooker notes that challenges in recruiting at CU are "a low unemployment rate of the area and the nature of specialized research positions." To tackle these challenges, Hooker says, "University of Colorado markets and brings awareness to their rich benefit packages." In terms of trying to fill unique positions, the university "partners with other organizations to post jobs in order to gain traction as well as posting on an internal job board where cross-campus opportunities are posted to encourage internal growth."[11]

A factor increasingly important to candidates is diversity on campus and in the surrounding community. This is one area the University of Wisconsin considers a challenge. "Wisconsin is not extremely diverse," Mark Rickenbach admitted, "and this can be an issue when recruiting candi-

ANDREW W. HIBEL and KELLY A. CHERWIN

What is the single most important piece of advice you would give to a new, likely inexperienced college president, just starting out in the position, about working with a mayor or city planning group on a town-gown project?

A new president must collaborate to build a consensus within their institution first and then in the local business community before going to their elected offices and their staff. One must be rock-solid in the internal consensus and the business community consensus before going into the more fluid political community.

dates." To overcome this disadvantage, the university and the community work together to create opportunities for a more diverse community on and off campus. Rickenbach said a key to his success in finding the right candidate is complete honesty with them about the university. As the department chair, he believes it is his role to highlight the positive attributes about the university and the community, but he also discusses the challenges and explains how the university addresses those challenges. "The last thing you want to do is try to show them something that [the university] isn't."[12] Candidates are repeatedly urged to be honest in an interview, and employers should do the same. Landing a job under false pretenses and hiring under false pretenses can be a recipe for disaster.

WHY THE SYMBIOTIC RELATIONSHIP BETWEEN THE COLLEGE AND COMMUNITY IS IMPORTANT

It is no surprise that universities can have a large impact on their communities' local economy. The Ann Arbor Area Convention and Visitors Bureau reports that 53 percent of all visitors to the Ann Arbor, Michigan, area, with its related local spending, are coming for a reason associated with the University of Michigan.[13] As for the University of Michigan's impact: "Aside from the thousands of jobs and additional payroll circulated throughout the community, the University's research activities generate new socially beneficial discoveries and create new 'spin out'" companies at a rate of one new private company every month. Further, 60 percent of new companies launched by U-M in the last ten years have remained in the Ann Arbor area."[14]

Many communities and their colleges realize the benefits of working together. The International Town & Gown Association (ITGA) was created to support institutions and communities that work to enhance this collaboration. The city of Oxford, Miami University, and the greater Oxford community—all ITGA members—offer this perspective: "We seek to create a community in which the City of Oxford, Miami University and the greater Oxford community are not seen as distinct, but rather spaces where boundaries are blurred—both by our own community members and those from the outside."[15]

In an article published in the *Journal of Economic Geography*, authors Jaison R. Abel and Richard Deitz argue that colleges and universities are more likely to contribute stability to a region than other industries since the higher education sector is less susceptible to downturns.[16] In their view (expressed in another article):

> Policymakers are increasingly viewing colleges and universities as important engines of growth for their local areas. In addition to having direct economic impacts, these institutions help to raise the skills of an area's workforce (its local "human capital"). . . . This contribution is significant because regions with higher levels of human capital—measured by the share of the working-age population with at least a bachelor's degree—tend to be more innovative, have greater amounts of economic activity, and enjoy faster economic growth, and workers in these regions tend to be more productive and earn higher wages.[17]

ESSENTIAL CONSIDERATIONS FOR THE FUTURE OF RECRUITING IN A COLLEGE TOWN

Given the data analyzed in the sections above, it is clear that leaders need to consider some key points when recruiting in a college town. What factors need to be considered in order not only to hire the most qualified people but to keep them?

1. *Highlight the authentic "feel" of the campus community.* Although it may be hard to quantify this factor for candidates, the *feel* of the campus community and the experience of working in the college town is highly important when considering whether to live and work there. As Rickenbach stated previously, showing candidates the true feel of the campus is crucial. This point is demonstrated through results from a survey conducted on the HigherEdJobs.com website, where 945 individuals responded to the following question: What is the most attractive feature of working at a university in a college town? The results are presented in table 14.6.

   Although important factors such as cost of living, type and distance of commutes, and job opportunities for spouses resonated with some respondents, the overwhelming majority considered factors related to the college town's atmosphere to be most important when considering working in a particular community. Thirty percent of respondents named the relationship and connections between the community and the college or university as the most attractive feature of working in a college town, while nearly half named the feeling of community on campus and close relationships and collaboration between colleagues. Emphasizing these aspects of the college town environment is key in recruiting and retention efforts.

Table 14.6. College Town Features That Job Searchers Find Most Attractive

	Percentage of 945 respondents
Job opportunities for partner or spouse	4.76
Type and distance of commute	7.30
Affordable cost of living	8.57
Relationships and connections between the community and the university	30.37
Feeling of community on campus and close relationships and collaboration between colleagues	48.99

2. *Schools place two-thirds of postings for one-fourth of job areas.* This finding from the job posting data above is significant. The majority of college and university's posted positions are only for a small percentage of the needed skills. In other words, three-quarters of all skills needed on campus are being recruited only one-third of the time. For most skills, when recruiters are looking to fill positions, there is a smaller number of postings and thus candidates. The rarity of these postings, combined with being located in a college town, can make the recruitment of these positions more difficult.
3. *The variance in employee percentages is not affected by size categorization.* The percentages of all three size classifications (A, B, and C) varied greatly. Our results showed that regardless of the size of the town, the percentage of employees working at the university varied by college town features they valued.
4. *University leadership needs to evaluate their community's affordability.* As the results show, affordability is not a major factor when it comes to candidates considering working in a college town. Only 9.1 percent named this as the most important factor. However, as several institutions mentioned, the cost of living in their college towns is actually quite high and can be viewed as a challenge in recruiting. Emphasizing the aspects of working in a college town that seem most important to candidates, such as the connections between the community and university or the feeling of community on campus, can counterbalance concerns over affordability.

5. *Employers should consider core skills in expanding their pool of quality candidates.* As the HigherEdJobs.com team discovered, some universities may experience challenges in finding candidates for certain specialized positions or candidates who are willing to consider a smaller college town community and sacrifice larger-city amenities. What can leadership do to increase the applicant pool at their universities and hire more efficiently? David Lewis, president and CEO of the human resources outsourcing and consulting company OperationsInc, urges hiring managers at universities to think outside the box and consider core skill sets. Core skills can broadly be defined as competencies an individual needs to master in order to be successful in the job.

   "Employers sometimes get stuck in a mindset of strict requirements regarding number of years of experience the candidate must possess, their grade point average, the school from which they graduated, or key words on their résumé," Lewis observes. "However, this may drastically limit many qualified applicants and this method of adhering to strict requirements doesn't always translate to the best hire." How does a hiring manager or human resource officer refashion a job posting to include core competencies? "The easiest way to do this," Lewis replies, "is to evaluate the traits of a person who has already been successful in that position. Ask, 'What makes them good, what did I like about them, what skills did they use to succeed?'"[18]

   Once you determine the core skills necessary for the position, you can craft a job description around those requirements rather than just keywords. For positions that have not had a predecessor, Lewis recommends determining "the culture and DNA of the organization." This can be done through personality profiling of key members, or "warriors," of the organization. By identifying high performers and collectively summarizing their winning characteristics, a job description can be created that includes core competencies needed to fit within the organization. "This type of predictive index," Lewis says, "can tell you who you should or should not hire or who *will not* fit into an organization. If your company is oil, you know to stay away from water." In Lewis's opinion, "people who are given the opportunity and hired based on core skills are often more hungry and more appreciative and the result is a quality hire."[19]

The faculty and staff recruitment for college towns will continue to evolve with and respond to the technological and workforce changes in

ANDREW W. HIBEL and KELLY A. CHERWIN

What is one lesson you learned about college towns while researching and writing your chapter?

Colleges and their surrounding towns share a special relationship that impacts faculty and staff recruitment. As technology advances and college culture shifts, successful institutions will need to adapt their recruiting strategies to better meet the needs of both the campus and the external community.

coming decades. The diffuse nature of the talent pool that is a college's lifeblood will continue to need to respond to technology's effect of making employment opportunities easily available and widely applied for. The next wave of technology will change the fundamentals, not just the process of recruiting. Finding new ways, such as skills-based recruiting, will need to become the norm. Successful universities will adopt new technology and adapt their process and culture to accommodate. Long-standing campus traditions about what makes an ideal candidate will change as these schools come to see as the end goal of recruiting finding quality talent who can perform in the advertised position. These changing traditions will allow institutions of higher education to evolve as employers and to best meet the needs of their university as well as the needs of their college towns.

CHAPTER 15

Student Expectations and Student Needs

How Effective College Towns Are Designed with Students at the Center

EUGENE L. ZDZIARSKI II

For a week during March or April every year, high school students across American enjoy Spring Break. They relax on a beach, travel to a ski slope, or just lounge around their house. For high school juniors and seniors, Spring Break is also peak time for college visits. College-bound students and their families load up the car and travel to a wish list of colleges and universities. Yet, when you talk to parents who have made these trips, it is not uncommon to hear a story about a student who was thrilled about a particular school he or she had always dreamed of attending, but on the trip, something changed. Appropriate planning was done ahead of time, a sequence of appointments was made, and the tour was scheduled. The family drove for several hours to get there, and when they finally pulled into the visitor parking lot, their child said, "We don't need to get out. I don't think I'm interested." When questioned about this sudden change in heart, the student replies, "It just doesn't feel right. I just can't see myself living here for four years."

There are many different guides published to aid students and their families in choosing a college, such as The Princeton Review guides and *US News & World Report*'s rankings, but few of them say anything about the college town that surrounds the campus as a factor in making a college decision. Yet students do have some expectations and needs concerning their college town. While these needs and expectations may not be the deciding factor in a student's college choice, they are factors that college administrators as well as city officials should note. If you ask students about their needs and expectations of their college town, rarely do they articulate them in explicit terms. Instead, they often describe elements of the atmosphere or environment within the community: "Residents in the community treat students like they're a nuisance," or "I don't know, I just don't feel safe walking in the community."

This chapter discusses five needs and expectations students have of their college towns: a sense of being welcomed, a sense of safety, a sense of fairness, a sense of responsibility, and a sense of engagement. These needs and expectations are based on more than thirty years of observations and interactions with students on a variety of campuses, public and private, urban and rural. If college administrators and city officials can work together and carefully tend to each of these "senses," they can create an effective college town designed with students at its center.

A SENSE OF BEING WELCOMED

One of the first things students expect from their college town is to be welcomed and valued by its residents. In some communities, a number of local residents may convey an attitude that college or university students are little more than spoiled children placing additional burdens on local community services. As young adults, students certainly need to be taught to be good citizens, but the existence of a higher education institution can have a significant positive impact on the local economy and the overall quality of life within that community. In effective college towns, civic leaders and college administrators act intentionally to create opportunities to welcome students and remind residents of the positive impact the college and its students can add.

A good example of this intentional effort to welcome students to their new community is RCity in Roanoke, Virginia. Every September, the Sunday night before classes begin at Roanoke College, first-year students are taken to Market Square in downtown Roanoke. Sundays are traditionally slow nights for downtown establishments, and many close early, but on this night every fall, the city and local businesses welcome new students and go out of their way to introduce them to the city. This event provides an opportunity to showcase the arts and culture available within the community as well as a wide variety of music venues and restaurants. Beginning in the Market Square, students are welcomed by the mayor, who acknowledges the important contributions the college and the students make to the community economically and socially and invites them to be active participants in Roanoke life. Then, armed with a map highlighting participating venues and a handful of wooden tokens, students spend the next several hours exploring the city. The available venues include local

New students at Roanoke College are welcomed to Market Square in downtown Roanoke during RCity. Roanoke College

art galleries, museums, and a variety of restaurants and music clubs. The wooden tokens are used at the various venues to purchase food and non-alcoholic beverages. RCity has become an important tradition that welcomes new students to the city of Roanoke.

Colleges in large metropolitan cities have also identified ways to welcome new students to the city and introduce them to the breadth of opportunities available. At DePaul University in Chicago, all new students are required to take the "Chicago Quarter" class. Chicago Quarter courses are for-credit classes designed to "acquaint first-year students at DePaul with the metropolitan community, its neighborhoods, cultures, people, institutions, organizations and issues."[1] From more than one hundred different Chicago Quarter options, students select a class focusing on a Chicago-related topic, such as art and architecture, business and industry, literature, science, politics, media, food, sports, social justice, spirituality,

Needs and Expectations of Students in College Town Collaborations

- Being welcomed
- Fairness
- Engagement
- Safety
- Responsibility

EUGENE L. ZDZIARSKI II

What is the single most important piece of advice you would give a higher education leader regarding town-gown collaborations?
Many college and university administrators need orientation and education about off-campus living rules and expectations.

ethnic identity, the natural environment, or music and theater. The city itself serves as classroom, text, and subject of inquiry. On various excursions into the city, students meet with city officials, local business owners, and citizens. Whether small college town or large metropolitan city, effective towns are intentionally creating opportunities to welcome new students and introduce them to the various opportunities available within their new community.

A SENSE OF SAFETY

Another expectation students, as well as parents, have of their college town is safety. With the violence reported on local news channels every day, it is hard for parents to send their students away from home to college. They want to be sure the campus and the surrounding community are safe. Just go to an orientation session held on any campus and listen to the questions students and parents ask. Many of them focus on safety. In effective college towns, both civic and higher education administrators are intentional about developing collaborative strategies to address student safety.

Since the shootings at Virginia Tech in 2007, emergency text messaging has become almost a universal method of communicating with students and other members of the campus community about potential safety threats on campus. In addition to knowing about potential threats on campus, students want to be advised of potential threats adjacent to campus. Also, the many students who live off campus in private housing that may not be adjacent to campus are equally concerned about potential threats in their neighborhoods.

Many cities and other municipalities have developed similar messaging systems for community members. Often these messaging systems have geo-mapping features that allow the system administrators to direct messages to individuals who live within a specific area or section of the community. In addition, these systems offer a variety of message options that citizens can choose to receive, such as weather alerts, road closings, and community events. Through collaborative partnerships, city officials and college and university administrators can articulate these campus and municipal messaging systems in order to address more effectively the safety of both students and community members. Colleges can actively market, and encourage students to register with, the municipal system so that students are aware of potential threats that may impact them in their local community, and so that city officials can alert residents living near or around the college of potential threats on campus.

In addition to integrated emergency messaging and alert systems, effective college towns engage their stakeholders. Whether a campus has a licensed law enforcement agency or campus security guards, maintaining a strong relationship with local police authorities is essential. However, this relationship goes beyond police personnel and involves stakeholders from both the campus and the community. One example is conducting regular district meetings with residents, students, and college administrators to discuss safety concerns and respond to questions concerning recent incidents within the district. While the meetings are open to anyone who lives within the police district, organizers are intentional in obtaining regular participation from key stakeholders such as neighborhood association officers, student government leaders, Greek organization leaders or other off-campus student representatives, and university administrators such as representatives from the office of the dean of students. Through such purposeful engagement and regular involvement in meetings, these stakeholders build relationships, not only with local and campus police but also with one another. They share their common concerns and issues with both on- and off-campus law enforcement officers so that they can work together to address these concerns. Whenever problems arise between neighbors and particular student groups, if they have previously developed a relationship, they are in a better position to resolve these problems collaboratively and often without direct police involvement.

EUGENE L. ZDZIARSKI II

What is the most important lesson learned from past college town collaborations you have observed or participated in?

City or town emergency management planning programs should integrate the participation of college administrators.

Another example of local and campus law enforcement strategically engaging stakeholders is through community coalitions created to address alcohol misuse and abuse. Stakeholders include senior university leadership responsible for policy development, municipal representatives, local bar and restaurant owners, key student leaders, and other community residents. Together coalition members work to address issues such as establishments that regularly sell or serve alcohol to underage individuals, alcohol sales promotions such as "chugging" and "beat the clock" contests that encourage abusive drinking habits, and other events that often involve high-risk drinking behavior.

A SENSE OF FAIRNESS

Except at smaller residential colleges, a majority of college students now live in neighborhoods and communities off campus. Students want and need affordable, adequately maintained housing. They and their parents frequently inquire about the local housing market, having heard stories about price-gouging property managers and "student ghettos." Effective college towns acknowledge this need to ensure a sense of fairness in the student housing market.

Off-campus student housing is dramatically different from the on-campus residence hall situation, and students are not often aware of or do not truly understand the implications of those differences. In the residence hall environment, each student has a separate contract, independent of roommates. These contracts typically run for the academic year and include all services such as electricity, gas, water, and trash. Many of them also include additional services such as cable and internet. In the off-campus environment, leases as well as services are associated with a particular dwelling and run typically for a calendar year, and services may be contracted with one or more of the residents in the dwelling. These dynamics are a frequent source of conflict for off-campus student renters. For example, when two or more students reside in a dwelling, are all parties included on the lease? If one of the students moves out, are all of the students held accountable for the lease's terms, or just those who remain in the dwelling? Similar issues arise with the utilities and services. These are issues that impact not only students but property managers and city services as well.

Ideally, property manager associations collaborate with university leaders to address these and many other issues. Frequently, these collaborative efforts lead to the development of town-gown organizations or even formal memorandums of understanding. One excellent resource for communities looking to develop such partnerships is the International Town & Gown Association. In addition to holding an annual conference and publishing a newsletter, the organization provides an online resource center through which city and college leaders share information and resources on leading practices for addressing town and gown issues.

While it is important for community and institutional leaders to work together to address problems, it is equally important to educate and inform students about tenant rights and responsibilities, particularly regarding the nuanced issues involved with student renters. One of the most common strategies is to conduct off-campus housing fairs. Such fairs involve students, campus administrators, property managers and owners, city services directors, and other local officials. Through these fairs students can not only identify off-campus housing options but learn about the responsibilities that come with signing a lease, obtaining city services, and complying with city codes and ordinances that affect off-campus student living. Typically, these fairs are scheduled early to mid-spring when students are beginning to make plans for housing for the next academic year. Some institutions, such as the University of Maryland, schedule two off-campus housing fairs, one in early spring for current students and another in midsummer for new students.[2] While the motivation for students and property managers to attend such an event centers on confirming housing arrangements for the following academic year, fairs provide an ideal forum for campus administrators and city officials to educate and inform both students and property managers about the rights, responsibilities, and expectations concerning off-campus living.

Effective town-gown planners recognize the challenges associated with the student housing cycle in their community and assemble the appropriate partnerships and establish processes to ensure a fair and equitable system for students and their community.

A SENSE OF RESPONSIBILITY

While students increasingly voice their expectation of fairness, they also need to assume some responsibility. When college students move into traditional, single-family neighborhoods, issues often arise with the late-night parties, loud music and drinking, and the traffic and trash they generate. The challenge with students living in traditional neighborhoods is that they are temporary residents. Students typically reside in a house or apartment during the school year and are absent during extended breaks or the summer months. Further, students often change residences from one school year to the next, rooming with different people as some students graduate, financial circumstances change, or roommate relationships form or fall apart. The temporary nature of student residency fosters little commitment on their part to develop and maintain positive relationships with their neighbors. Likewise, the neighborhood's permanent residents who have been through the cycle of students moving in and out of rental properties are frustrated with the ongoing problems many of the students bring to their community.

When addressing inevitable conflicts, it is helpful if those involved can approach them from a previously established relationship. Strategically, college administrators and city officials should create opportunities for students and neighbors to develop relationships before problems arise. For example, a neighborhood picnic held on an early evening the first week of school can bring permanent residents and students out of their houses and get them interacting with each other. With some joint city-college support for marketing and promoting the event, as well as for providing some basic picnic food such as hot dogs or hamburgers, such events can develop into annual neighborhood block parties where neighbors and students can share their concerns and expectations and offer suggestions on how to avoid some of the common problems that arise. In some college communities in which the academic calendar cooperates, these events can be combined with other programs such as National Night Out, "an annual community-building campaign that promotes police-community partnerships and neighborhood camaraderie to make our neighborhoods safer."[3] These picnics also provide ideal opportunities for mayors, city council members, and key college personnel to interact with students and neighbors and identify themselves as resources should a problem develop that requires additional assistance.

While establishing a relationship with your neighbor is a good starting point, it won't eliminate all the problems that arise between students and established neighbors. College administrators need orientation and education about off-campus living similar to what they receive about the on-campus environment. Another strategy that effective college towns use is creation of a "community ambassadors" program. Most often composed of off-campus student leaders, a community ambassadors program serves to build relationships between the institution and the neighbors who live around the campus.[4] This program provides education and engagement to teach students civic responsibility and inform them about city ordinances and college policies associated with off-campus living.[5] What makes this opportunity especially effective is that the ambassadors take this information directly to the students by going door-to-door in neighborhoods that have a high density of students. Through this approach the ambassadors interact not only with students but also with residents of the

Thoughts from a NASPA Leader on How to Involve Students Effectively in College Town Plans and Projects

STEPHANIE GORDON is vice president for professional development at NASPA (National Association for Student Personnel Administrators): Student Affairs Administrators in Higher Education, where she has been in the leadership for fifteen years.

What is the best way to engage students authentically in town-gown projects beyond their campuses?
Actually, it is easier now than perhaps at any time in the past generation to engage students in town-gown projects in their local communities. What we are observing is that many students *want* to become involved and will increasingly make the effort. Beyond what we have come to know as service learning, students now are designing and taking part in what is more accurately described as civic learning and democratic engagement. Whether through participation in town or city meetings, voter registration drives, or simply tutoring regularly in local schools, students are helping to shape a new college town experience.

What is the single most important piece of advice you would offer to a university or college president seeking to connect with students about town-gown issues and concerns?
We have found in working with students year after year that *people support what they help to create*, so to speak. Thus, the key for a new president, in particular, is to listen to students closely at least three times a year via a set of questions posed to everyone at their initial orientation, at the end of the first semester, and at the end of the second semester. Another key is then not simply to collect suggestions but to act on them.

What is one change you have noted about American college town culture during your years at NASPA?
It seems clear that, over time, open, trusting, and purpose-driven relationships between a town or city and its colleges reduce stress and improve mental health in both town and gown, and students are the ones who can benefit the most from this relationship.

neighborhoods and establish themselves as resources for both students and residents should a conflict arise. In addition, community ambassadors coordinate service projects designed to give back to communities in which students live—projects like trash collection, leaf raking, and snow removal. Through this kind of intentional outreach, students are reminded that they are more than students living off campus, but citizens of their community with responsibilities to that community.

A SENSE OF ENGAGEMENT

In effective college towns, the campus engages regularly and authentically with its community. Students and their neighbors interact, enjoy, and celebrate a shared sense of purpose in meaningful ways both on campus and off. One of the great benefits of living in a college town consists of all the opportunities for continuing education and cultural enrichment. Residents learn that the college or university is a place offering opportunities to hear a best-selling author discuss his or her new book, to see an inspiring theatrical performance, or cheer on young athletes at a collegiate sporting event. Thousands of higher education institutions offer special classes and short seminars for community members, whether to explore various aspects of the arts, to develop better business practices, or simply to learn how to use a personal computer.

Similarly, many students seek ways to engage with the community around them. They value opportunities to learn about its history and culture, and they respond to invitations to meet business and elected leaders. Effective college towns reach out to and connect students with these opportunities. Many cities have special holiday and cultural festivals that provide perfect opportunities to engage local students and recent alumni. Whether it is the annual Christmas light displays, such as UT Night at the Austin Trail of Lights, or a fall arts-and-crafts festival like Olde Salem Days, just outside the entrance to Roanoke College, students can become involved.[6] Even large metropolitan areas with dozens of higher education institutions are creatively capitalizing on this trend. For example, in Chicago the annual LGBTQ Pride Parade is a huge event and a daylong celebration through the streets of the city.[7] With more than 2 million people, thousands of businesses, and more than twenty colleges in the downtown area, competition for the limited number of spots in this annual event is high. However, each year, city officials and parade organizers commit at least one of the 150 parade slots for college students to collectively participate in this important community tradition.

EUGENE L. ZDZIARSKI II

What is something you would do differently if you were starting a town-gown project with the benefit of past experience?
Spend more time developing closer relationships with city administrators and elected representatives before a project or collaboration is proposed.

Sports offer another great way for students to participate in the local community. While most campuses have intramural sports programs, students, particularly juniors and seniors preparing to enter the workforce, are interested in finding ways to meet and network with young professionals in the local area. In many town-gown environments, parks and recreation departments market their leagues to college and university students in addition to local residents. Some communities, like the city of Syracuse for example, offer special registration rates for students.[8] Whether it is softball, soccer, or ultimate Frisbee local sports leagues provide opportunities for students to engage in entertaining and rewarding ways.

Finally, college towns offer students civic and political engagement. Whether by working with local political parties during a major election season or by serving as members of a campaign staff for a local race, students increasingly demonstrate an interest in contributing to change through political action. Even traditional associations like Rotary, Kiwanis, and Lions Club, to name a few of the more common ones, provide immediate experiences for students to engage with their communities through such student membership programs as Rotaract and Circle K. Proactive civic leaders ensure that these groups forge sustaining partnerships between the student chapters and local clubs. Through local arts and cultural events, sporting leagues, and political action groups, students are seeking engagement, and town-gown planners are realizing the sometimes-lifelong benefits that can be achieved as a result.

STUDENTS AT THE CENTER

Many senior student affairs officers are noting how articulate current students are in describing the atmosphere and that students want to know they are welcome and are considered a valuable part of the community. Along with their parents, they expect a reasonable sense of safety within the community and need confirmation that municipal leaders have incorporated them in their emergency planning. When it comes to housing and city services, students do not want to be taken advantage of, and they also understand that being part of the community means they have to assume some responsibilities. Perhaps most important, students want to engage in relationships that serve the greater good of the communities in which they live. Those college and university administrators who work effectively with civic leaders to meet these needs and expectations are creating the kinds of college towns at the center of this book.

CHAPTER 16

Las Vegas

Designing a College Town in the Shadow of Neon Lights

KIM NEHLS

No large community is complete without its university, both as a source of opportunities for individuals and as a radiating center for the subtle but powerful interplay of the intellect upon its activities.

Frank Kingdon, president of the University of Newark, 1936–1940

The city of Las Vegas evokes images of neon lights, casinos, glitz, drinking, clubs, and sinful excess. Rarely are there feature stories about the impact of higher education, and the city's slogan, "What happens in Vegas stays in Vegas," holds a second meaning to those who live in the state: community and educational development that happens in Vegas certainly does stay in Vegas. More than 30,000 students are educated annually at the city's flagship institution, the University of Nevada, Las Vegas (UNLV), and over 80 percent of students are Nevada residents. The local community college and the regional university, College of Southern Nevada and Nevada State College, respectively, both boast resident student populations over 90 percent. To be sure, the Nevada institutions of higher education are providing the state's population a means to earn a post-secondary degree. The five examples below, however, graphically illustrate ways that Las Vegas's college and universities reach far beyond educating the local population in order to understand that college towns are now found in unusual, sometimes very unusual, places. From the influential presidential debate in 2016 to a single student packing lunches for those in need, those campuses within the shadow of Las Vegas's neon lights are accomplishing town-gown objectives broader than classroom instruction.

BUILDING A NEW COLLEGE TOWN IDENTITY

The UNLV Presidential Debate 2016

On October 19, 2016, the University of Nevada, Las Vegas, hosted the third and final presidential debate between Hillary Clinton and Donald Trump. More than 71 million people viewed the debate, giving it the title of the third-most-watched debate in U.S. history, behind the first election debate of 2016 and the 1980 debate between Ronald Reagan and Jimmy Carter. To put this viewership number in perspective, later that year the historic Chicago Cubs' baseball victory in Game 7 of the World Series was viewed by 40 million sports fans. The audience size indicated the public's interest in that year's presidential election, but it also brought UNLV into the spotlight as an influential institution in the American higher education landscape as the debate mixed education, politics, and media power.

The debate strengthened the university's ties to its many external communities. UNLV collaborated with Clark County School District (CCSD) to organize a number of initiatives to educate the community about politics.[1] CCSD is the fifth-largest school district in the nation, with more than 300,000 students and an unusual mix of urban, suburban, and rural schools that encompass the vast diversity of southern Nevada. A meet-and-greet at Paradise Elementary School on the UNLV campus kicked off Debate Week, in which students, teachers, and parents asked questions and discussed the debate with CCSD superintendent Pat Skorkowsky, president and CEO of the Las Vegas Convention and Visitors Authority Rossi Ralenkotter, and UNLV president Len Jessup. Among the numerous debate activities featuring the institution and the community, the school district ran an essay contest challenging CCSD high school students to write about the merits of presidential debates. The winner of the essay contest, a junior from inner-city Las Vegas Chaparral High School, received a $1,000 scholarship to UNLV.

Although UNLV is known primarily for its national championship men's basketball team, the university's nationally ranked Sanford I. Berman Debate Team connected with community by establishing mentoring programs for local high schoolers throughout the year of the debate. In addition, the debate team hosted "Debaters Watch the Debate," in which UNLV and CCSD debate teams discussed and provided commentary online and on air during and after the primary and general election debates.[2] The partnership between UNLV and CCSD provided many other opportunities during the debate season, including debate-themed lesson plans for K–12 students created in collaboration with UNLV educators. The university offered a series of free lectures about the presidential debate to students and the public, collaborating with universities across the United States by featuring local guest lecturers as well as experts from Northwestern University, the University of Missouri, Central Michigan University, Northeastern University, and the University of Wisconsin.[3]

More than one thousand UNLV students, staff, and community members applied for official volunteer positions at the debate, which took place in the Thomas and Mack basketball arena—home to the university's Runnin' Rebels. A major highlight of the event was the presence of nearly five thousand journalists occupying UNLV's campus throughout Debate Week. Almost all major-network news stations broadcast directly from the university the day of the debate, allowing students and community members to experience media activities surrounding a national debate and to be interviewed on camera for local opinions and feedback about the educational, political, and commercial significance of the town-gown backdrop.

In retrospect, it is clear that UNLV students and faculty as well as many members of the greater community invested thousands of hours and significant resources in the 2016 presidential debate, far beyond the relatively short time the debate actually appeared on networks. These efforts were well rewarded. According to the local newspaper, UNLV's participation in the presidential debate generated an estimated $114 million in publicity for the university and Las Vegas.[4] Every screenshot of the live debate featured UNLV's logo on a drape behind the podiums, and every reporter broadcasting live from the university mentioned the institution by name multiple times during each live report. The publicity cannot be understated; it more than doubled the initial $50 million in expectations. Further, the debate not only focused national televised attention on the University but also helped drive a tenfold spike in traffic to its official website and a steady increase in applications for the following semester. Finally, beyond these financial and publicity gains, the debate provided tangible educational opportunities for students and community members, putting both UNLV and southern Nevada in a positive light by enhancing the identity of Las Vegas as an innovative college town.

UNLV and the National Football League

Until the establishment of the Golden Knights hockey team in 2017, Las Vegas had never been home to a professional team in any major sport. Capitalizing on the unlikely success of the NHL Golden Knights, who unexpectedly made it to the Stanley Cup Finals in their first season, Las Vegas's dream of professional football is also coming true. In 2017, the

Colleges and Universities in the Las Vegas Area

- Arizona College of Nursing, Las Vegas
- Asher College
- Brightwood College in Las Vegas
- Carrington College, Las Vegas
- Chamberlain University College of Nursing
- College of Southern Nevada
- DeVry University
- Heritage College
- Le Cordon Bleu College of Culinary Arts, Las Vegas
- Lincoln Christian University, Las Vegas
- Nevada State College
- Northwest Career College
- Pima Medical Institute, Las Vegas
- Roseman University of Health Sciences
- Touro University, Nevada
- University of Nevada, Las Vegas
- University of Phoenix

Nevada legislature passed a bill to raise $750 million in tourism taxes to serve as the primary funder for a new $1.9 billion, 65,000-seat NFL stadium to house the currently named Oakland Raiders, beginning in 2020. As previously mentioned, Las Vegas has long been a basketball town with the perennial success of the Runnin' Rebels and Hall of Fame coach Jerry Tarkanian. However, with the hiring of coach Tony Sanchez in 2014, UNLV football received a dose of local pride and an infusion of new spirit. Since moving to UNLV, Coach Sanchez has been a prominent figure in strengthening the football team's ties between the university and the local community with new uniforms, a new field, and a greater social media presence. One of Sanchez's strongest and most beneficial connections is with the Fertitta family, which donated $10 million to UNLV to help fund the 73,000-square-foot, two-level Fertitta Football Complex to serve as the practice fields for UNLV football.

The planned arrival of the Oakland Raiders team in 2020 and the construction of the Fertitta Football Complex reflect the hard work of many individuals, and represent original town-gown thinking on the part of the UNLV president and leadership team. The Nevada Board of Regents voted to approve the agreement to use the new stadium in an 11–1 vote, showing strong support for the UNLV-NFL connection. At the signing, proponents of the agreement predicted that the new stadium and facilities would propel the UNLV football program, as well as the city of Las Vegas, into the center of the national football stage, both at NCAA and NFL levels. The new stadium will create new jobs; garner additional

KIM NEHLS

What is a key to sustained and effective town-gown collaboration?
Sometimes the best town-gown relationships are not planned. The most memorable feeling of unity and togetherness between the city of Las Vegas and its higher education institutions happened in the aftermath of the October 1, 2017, mass shooting outside the Mandalay Bay Hotel. The key is to establish solid, trusting relationships prior to a crisis situation.

revenue, prestige, and tourism for Las Vegas; and enable UNLV to join a higher level of athletic competition—perhaps even to join a conference like the PAC-12 with the likes of Stanford, the University of Southern California, and the University of California, Berkeley. Such a coup would bring not only increased athletic but also heightened academic prestige to the university and the city of Las Vegas.

In conjunction with all the new sports teams hitting the Las Vegas strip—a new NFL team, new NHL hockey club, new women's NBA team, the national headquarters of the Ultimate Fighting Championship (UFC), and UNLV's football revival—the university is making strides to create majors, minors, and certificate programs to support students' future job prospects in these sports hospitality, management, and training areas. A graduate certificate in sports leadership was launched in 2016, and in 2018 a sports marketing class was added to the curriculum at the Lee Business School. Students are responding with increasing enrollments in these new career-related offerings, and their degrees have been designed to support the city's future needs.

Nevada State College

Also meeting the needs of the city, but in this case primarily for nursing and education, is Nevada State College, the newest addition to higher education in the Las Vegas valley. The higher education landscape of major metropolitan areas is often organized in a three-tier system with levels specializing in associate degrees (community or junior colleges), another focusing on bachelor's degrees (state colleges), and another emphasizing graduate degrees (research universities). In the early 2000s, thirty-eight of the forty major metropolitan areas in the United States featured a three-tier higher education system. Las Vegas was one of the two metropolitan areas without a three-tier system, as it lacked an institution focused on baccalaureate degrees. At the same time, however, Las Vegas was one of the fastest-growing cities in the nation, and with this population growth came an increasing number of high school graduates without options for post-secondary education. After studying the issue in 1999, the Nevada Board of Regents began planning for a state college in or near Las Vegas. By 2001 then-governor Kenny Guinn recommended state funding to help establish the state college, and the Nevada legislature approved $13 million in capital expenditures, $3.75 million in state general funds, and $650,000 in student registration fees to form the initial seed funding for the state college.[5] A confluence of state funds and student tuition thus made this founding possible, and in retrospect, this decision was as important as perhaps any other discussed in this chapter in shaping the higher education aspirations of a city long known for casinos and gambling.

Located on the outskirts of Henderson, Nevada State College (NSC) opened its doors in 2002 to its first class of 177 students. NSC intentionally focused its course offerings on nursing and education to fill personnel needs within the city. Since then, the fledgling state college has grown considerably. Following the initial funding, the Nevada legislature secured another $22 million to fund NSC operations in 2005 as well as an additional $9 million to finance the construction of the Liberal Arts and Science Building, which opened in 2008. In 2010, NSC's campus master plan was approved by the Nevada Board of Regents; it includes additional education classrooms and a town center area near campus featuring residential, retail, and commercial buildings. Less than a decade after welcoming its first class, NSC officially received accreditation from the Northwest Commission on Colleges and Universities in 2011.

The NSC student population grew from 177 in 2002 to more than 4,000 undergraduates in 2018. With this tremendous growth, state policy makers have continued their support of the college while NSC has experienced a

---

KIM NEHLS

What is the single most important piece of advice you would give to someone beginning a town-gown project in Las Vegas?

At first glance, the relationship between the hospitality-gaming industry and education appears adversarial. Anyone interested in bridging the two fields must be tenacious and believe in the power that the combination is greater than the sum of its parts. Las Vegas cannot achieve greatness as a city without both of these parts working together.

---

growing level of student support as well. The $54 million needed for construction of two new buildings were funded mostly by student fees approved by 75 percent of the student population. NSC opened those two buildings in 2016: the state-of-the-art Nursing, Sciences, and Education Building and the Rogers Student Center, which houses Nevada's largest digital library.

Also worth noting is NSC's fund-raising capacity for such a young institution. The college has achieved significant success in philanthropy, receiving large donations from prominent individuals and businesses throughout the Las Vegas valley, such as Cox Communications, Elaine Wynn & Family foundation, and NV Energy. Its first fund-raising campaign exceeded its goal of $10 million, reaching nearly $17 million. Donations helped fund 120 full scholarships for local students and bolstered NSC's School of Education with a new building and increased credibility as a relevant higher education option. Private dollars also made it possible for NSC to add such new programs as deaf studies and early-childhood education, which are focused on supporting city needs. Relatively quickly, NSC has come to be viewed as a critical provider of career and educational opportunities for local students, and at a cost affordable to families. Looking ahead, Nevada State College projects that it has the space and the facilities to expand its campus to a level of 22,000 students, many of whom will have the potential to serve the Las Vegas community with new career opportunities.

UNLV's Service to the Local Community

Las Vegas higher education institutions also reach the community through the public service work of its students and staff. UNLV offers a growing number of courses, including the mandatory First Year Experience seminar, in which students serve the local community as part of their college experience. Service-learning opportunities help students connect with the larger society of the city of Las Vegas, integrating relationships with UNLV's many community partners like Habitat for Humanity and a cluster of local animal shelters. Students can serve in short-term projects or develop more sustained projects with local community agencies. They also have the option to participate in out-of-classroom service with such university organizations as UNLVolunteer.[6] One such learning experience is known as Alternative Break. While these trips take place outside the valley, they are a valued opportunity for students to learn about different community and social justice issues, such as immigration in San Diego or homelessness in San Francisco, and bring home lessons learned to benefit Las Vegas. UNLV also sponsors numerous recurring traditions

KIM NEHLS

What is a lesson learned from recent town-gown initiatives in Las Vegas? Las Vegas is constantly reinventing itself with new themes, new hotels, new sports, and new slogans. The three public institutions in Las Vegas—University of Nevada, Las Vegas, College of Southern Nevada, and Nevada State College—must also constantly adapt. They should not be afraid to take risks.

such as Service Day and DASH (Delivering And Serving Hope). Occurring once every semester, Service Day involves nearly three hundred students serving up to fifteen local nonprofit organizations and has become one of UNLV's fast-growing and enriching traditions. DASH happens twice a month when students make sack lunches on campus and deliver them to nonprofits around Las Vegas, such as local food bank Three Square, which provides meals for those with food insecurity in Clark County and surrounding areas.

Finally, UNLV is also doing its part to help homeless teens within the Clark County School District in what some view as its most significant step toward creating a sense of college town engagement. Recently established in 2016, the UNLV Hope Scholars program provides homeless college students with secure housing as well as academic and financial support while they attend UNLV. Beginning immediately after the students' high school graduation, the support provides dorm rooms and campus employment for the HOPE Scholars while they acclimate to college. More than a dozen students are named Hope Scholars each year, and the program exemplifies a true community partnership among Title I HOPE of the Clark County School District, Nevada Partnership for Homeless Youth, Desert Sage Auxiliary, and the university.[7]

Higher Ed Responses to the Violent Mandalay Bay Hotel Shooting in 2017

One of the greatest community outreach opportunities for UNLV was spontaneous. On the night of October 1, 2017, a heavily armed gunman opened fire from a room in the Mandalay Bay Hotel on an unsuspecting a crowd at a country music festival on the Las Vegas strip. In less than fifteen minutes, the gunman shot more than 1,100 rounds into the crowd of 22,000, killing 59 and injuring more than 850 citizens before taking his own life. As of this writing, the incident remains the deadliest mass shooting in US history. The UNLV campus is located just a couple of miles from the area of the outdoor concert. During the immediate panic and mass confusion, thousands of frightened concertgoers stumbled out of the gates and fled the area. Many of the spectators—injured and noninjured—arrived on the UNLV campus seeking safety. As the crowds grew on campus near midnight, staff and campus police mobilized and opened the Thomas and Mack Center basketball arena.

Campus police gathered evacuees and brought them to the Thomas and Mack Center for safety. The officers located any "walking wounded" near campus as well as those confused and in shock. Police also assisted with security screening of all incoming victims to ensure no potential threats were allowed into the building since, at the time, it had not been ascertained that there was only one shooter. Student security officers at the Thomas and Mack Center maturely took on responsibilities and duties beyond position expectations. Through the night and into the morning, thousands of concerned Las Vegas citizens dropped off food, drinks, blankets, and clothing for the displaced. Some concertgoers stayed at the arena for days while they waited to make statements to the police and be reunited with loved ones. Trained medical and nursing faculty and staff from UNLV volunteered at the arena and at local hospitals to provide first aid and support to the injured. Blood drives were immediately organized.

In addition, clinical faculty members from the UNLV Psychology Department responded to a midnight call from campus police to go to the Thomas and Mack Center. Some faculty stayed through the morning hours, providing psychological first aid. By 9:00 the following morning, the UNLV-sponsored Community Mental Health Clinic was coordinating a crisis response to the incident for the greater Las Vegas community. First, a letter was sent to the Clark County School District through the College of Education, which provided resources and links for children under stress following the mass shooting and suggestions for parents in talking to their children following this traumatic event. The clinic staff also created a schedule of immediate appointments for free walk-in crisis counseling, and many of the UNLV student clinicians offered volunteer hours and staffed the clinic for the entire week for walk-ins. Student clinicians also provided post-crisis counseling, information, and resources in the student union. For two weeks following the tragedy, the clinic continued to provide free post-event counseling to walk-ins and responded to numerous media and community requests including continued information on psychological first aid, post-event crisis recovery counseling, and general information regarding mental health needs following a traumatic event.[8]

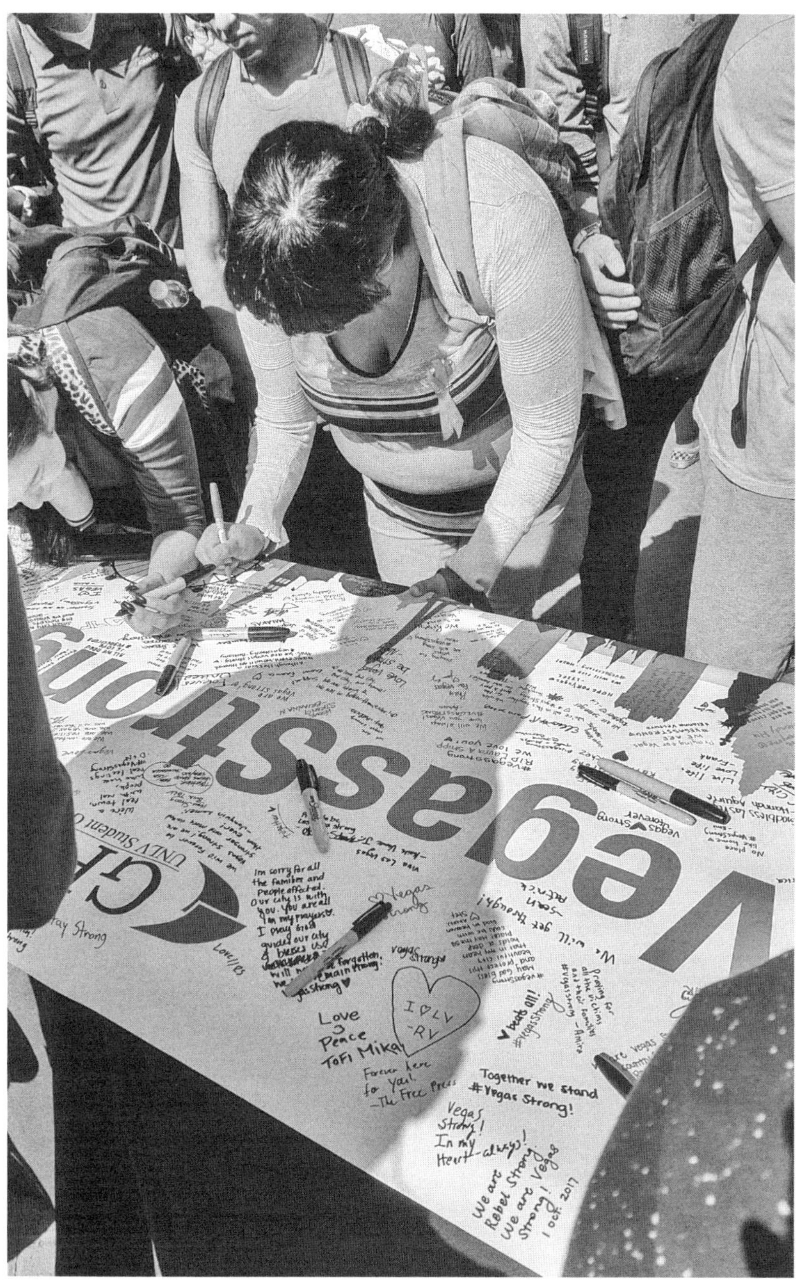

Students sign a #VegasStrong banner at the Remembrance Ceremony held at the University of Nevada Las Vegas following the October 1 mass shooting on the Las Vegas strip. Photo by Kimberly Nehls

The Community Mental Health Clinic continued to provide free counseling and therapy for those directly affected by the events of October 1 long after the tragedy took place. The ongoing free counseling was a direct result of a generous anonymous donor who paid for two thousand hours of services and support funding for two student clinicians to keep doors open through summer months to support the needs of the community as it heals. Another way that UNLV offered support during the healing process was through a remembrance ceremony held on campus one month following the shooting. Victims' families were recognized at the ceremony, as were students and staff who attended the concert and were affected by the event. Many attendees provided testimonials of the night and the impact that UNLV had on their sense of safety and well-being during a horrific experience. UNLV president Len Jessup read the names of the numerous campus safety officers, faculty, staff, and student workers who mobilized on the night of October 1 and throughout the weekend to assist concertgoers. The ceremony ended with chimes that rang fifty-nine times to recognize those who died that night. Following the remembrance ceremony, attendees were encouraged to sign #VegasStrong banners around campus. Many have commented on how this event helped create a new sense of community for both the city and the campus after a tragic, life course–altering event.

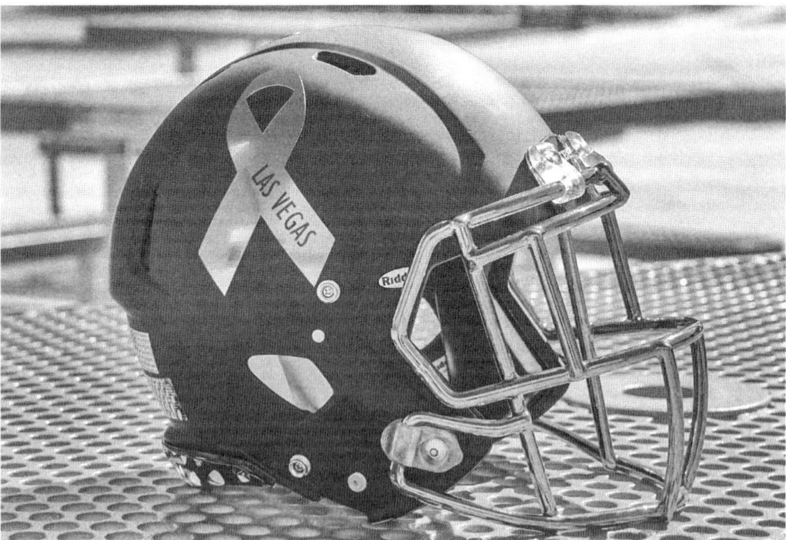

Photograph tweeted by @UNLVathletics three days following the tragic shooting on the Las Vegas strip. Photograph by Kimberly Nehls

LESSONS LEARNED

As mentioned at the beginning of this chapter, the city of Las Vegas is best known for the glitz and glamour of the Strip, but some perhaps more influential and lasting aspects of Las Vegas can now be viewed in the activities and partnerships that its college, university, and community now make happen. From the 2016 Presidential Debate to new NFL connections; to coursework and degree programs supporting local needs in sports, education, and nursing; and to students' community service and an unprecedented outpouring of community service on the night of an unspeakable tragedy, higher education has rallied to boost Las Vegas more than its neon lights ever could. The change is becoming appreciated regionally and nationally. Las Vegas colleges and universities are impacting social issues while bringing increasing prestige and publicity to the state. One of the keys to making all of this possible is having strong linkages among dozens of community organizations, the Visitors' Bureau, business representatives, concerned philanthropists, and the higher education institutions. Without these connections, the events highlighted in this chapter would not have been so successful. Higher education in Las Vegas is enriched by its multiple external communities, and those communities are learning the benefits of partnerships on a more powerful scale. Each campus may still fall in the shadow of the city's neon signatures, but more are now realizing how potent its colleges and universities have become.

CHAPTER 17

Remote and Ready to Partner

A Blueprint for Sustainable Town-Gown Partnerships in Rural Areas

ROBERT C. ANDRINGA

WHY SHOULD SMALL COLLEGES AND TOWNS SEEK GREATER COLLABORATION?

According to 2016 Integrated Postsecondary Education Data Systems (IPEDS) statistics there were *926 private, four-year colleges with fewer than two thousand students*. Too many overlook these small gems.[1] Another 195 had head counts of between two thousand and three thousand. Some of these nonprofit institutions reflect as many as two hundred years of history. They add to the admired diversity of American post-secondary education. So what does their future hold in the context of town-gown collaboration, and why should they join forces on a broader scale?

- Both the town and the campus lack financial resources to do all they desire.
- Economic development gains are possible when they link arms.
- Citizens could experience a higher quality of life with a nearby campus.
- Students need off-campus opportunities for work and entertainment.
- More capital projects could be funded with both campus and town investments.

A 2017 news report began: "College towns may be the way to combat a slumping local economy, according to a recent report from Brookings Institution and *The Wall Street Journal*. Researchers looked at sixteen places where overall job growth was strong despite manufacturing employment declining more in those regions than in the U.S. overall. They found that half of those places were also homes to colleges."[2] Beth Bagwell, executive director of the International Town & Gown Association, agrees: "College towns tend to provide stability during economic downturns and may help combat a slumping local economy."[3] If small-college presidents can convince civic leaders and their constituencies that the region will remain more profitable and productive through economic ups and downs, collaboration with the local college or university will benefit the common good.

At the same time, small campuses and small towns face many challenges, some similar and some very different. Several of the presidents interviewed for this chapter offered the following as challenges for small campuses:

- Financial impossibility to relocate their main campus to higher-density areas
- Location and reduced pools of students in the rust belt of Middle America in contrast to the sunshine and growth areas of the West and Southeast
- Stress on campus leaders with must-do tasks that leave little time for executing significant collaboration ideas
- The often-distracting allure of online and distance learning as the silver bullet for sustainability
- Few college departments that offer significant benefits for regional growth
- Marketing for new students, most of whom today prefer the cities
- Small-scale athletic programs that have difficulty attracting top athletes and large numbers of spectators
- Modest endowments or major donors to frontload collaboration[4]

The same presidents counted the following as difficulties encountered by small towns seeking higher education partners:

- Some mistrust of higher education and its value in the current era
- Frustration that college property is not subject to taxes
- Lack of leaders in town with experience dealing with higher education

- Few opportunities for meaningful internships linked to student majors
- Few part-time job opportunities for students and college families
- Low tax revenues to invest in culture-changing collaboration
- Loss of young people who leave town for greener pastures[5]

My own observations, drawn from several years as the leader of a national higher education association, are optimistic about seven benefits to be derived from rural and remote town-gown collaboration:

1. These communities reflect the values of friendship, caring, service to neighbors, civic pride, and the like, which many people still seek in choosing places to live and to raise their families.
2. More and more people struggling with transportation, safety, living costs, and the stress of big cities are looking for alternatives. A small town with a small college is attractive to many.
3. It takes only a few visionaries in those towns and on those campuses to make things happen, and they can do it more quickly than in larger environments.
4. Both the town and the campus need some distinctive features to attract people and revenue. Collaboration that sets each of them apart is a natural path to pursue.
5. Technology is developing so quickly that location becomes less controlling a factor than in past decades. Especially for colleges, online learning gives a hope that income from it can offset the higher costs of the ground campus. And online learning makes it possible for faculty and students seeking advanced degrees to earn credits from hundreds of institutions.
6. The relatively lower costs of housing and other living expenses make it easier for campuses to recruit faculty and staff to their small communities.
7. The history of mergers—especially of campuses some distance apart—seems to demonstrate that the human and other costs are beyond the interests or capacity of small college boards, presidents, faculty, and alumni.

Fifteen Small College Towns with Best Quality of Life, 2016

1. Flagstaff, Arizona
2. Bozeman, Montana
3. San Luis Obispo, California
4. Claremont, California
5. Grand Forks, North Dakota
6. Fayetteville, Arkansas
7. Bloomington, Illinois
8. Oxford, Mississippi
9. Bloomington, Indiana
10. Logan, Utah
11. Lafayette, Indiana
12. Lawrence, Kansas
13. Binghamton, New York
14. Burlington, Vermont
15. Charlottesville, Virginia

Source: "20 Great Small College Towns with Great Quality of Life," Best Choice Schools, accessed October 21, 2018, https://www.bestchoiceschools.com/20-great-small-college-towns-with-great-quality-of-life/.

To put it bluntly, survival is a strong motivator for trying new things. With options somewhat limited for both small-town leaders and campus administrators, at least exploring significant collaboration seems like a winner. Both groups need to realize the diamonds in their own backyards and make harvesting them a priority. Change can be tiring and continually difficult, but the alternatives are uniformly negative.

SUCCESSFUL COLLABORATIONS BEGIN WITH PRESIDENTS

Small towns depended on volunteers to contribute their talents on town councils, civic clubs, churches, synagogues, and school boards. Usually holding down other jobs, few of them have the time or the authority to commit their town to major collaboration with their college. But the college president does have sufficient authority, staffing, faculty leaders, and budget flexibility, and knows that the future of the campus depends on being in a town that is attractive to employees and students.

For most of these institutions, the idea of relocating to a more urban area is out of the question. They do not have the money to relocate the entire campus, and who would purchase a campus in a town of only three thousand citizens? Leaders need to lay out a vision with new ideas, and they must start with the obvious:

- The cost of living is more affordable for faculty and staff in a small town. This is becoming no small deal for employees of universities in major cities. Consider housing costs alone, let alone transportation and other living costs.

- Many families appreciate the safety and "traditional values" more often experienced in small towns. I grew up in one of these small towns (without a college) and wouldn't trade that experience for anything. People get to know people through regular interaction. Such interaction builds trust. And change requires trust.
- The internet allows the campus and its employees to feel more in touch with the world. And Amazon shopping reduces to almost zero the need to walk through stores found only in large cities.
- True, faculty on these campuses can feel isolated from peers in their disciplines. Again, technology helps maintain connections. And libraries depend far less on bragging about umpteen books on the shelves. Networks of faculty sharing ideas and the fruits of their labor will only improve as technology advances.

My interviews with presidents, trustees, and multiple small-town mayors across the country have convinced me that the college leaders in rural areas are in the best position to dream big, conduct successful due diligence, and implement plans that are win-wins for the college and local community. Here are a few innovative ideas that were shared with me as I prepared this chapter:

- The local high school partners with the college's education department faculty and students to bring best practices to K–12 classrooms.
- The college intentionally designs internships that advance its curriculum while simultaneously addressing local labor market shortages.
- The town council and mayor partner with key faculty members to identify issues and trends relating to, for example, the local environment, housing, and safety.
- The college encourages its business students to actually run a business, or several, to help the local town while earning academic credit. In return, the town provides mentors from among current business owners.
- The town's limited health care services partner with a growing nursing or occupational therapy program to benefit citizens who would otherwise lack these services.

- The college band partners with one or more local high school bands for training, career development, and performances.
- Church staff from several local denominations provide some of the spiritual life activities for students, even serving as chaplains and counselors on campus.
- A farmer donates considerable land to a golf course developer who decides to give the town its first golf course and club in return for the college starting a major in golf course management with guaranteed on-the-job experiences.
- The college explores a major in senior living services in collaboration with a national senior living corporation that wants both a training center and administrative office in that region.

SMALL COLLEGE SUCCESS STORIES: THREE NEW STRATEGIES

A few years ago, I invited several leaders in higher education to brainstorm together about rethinking the pathways to healthy futures primarily for small colleges. We came up with twenty ideas. One of the ideas was for a college to "adopt" its small town and explore all sorts of fruitful partnerships. Allowing every faculty member to leverage learning in and out of the classroom was but one of the ways a growing culture of imagination and creativity could bring new life to these communities. A consulting firm even offered to put the ideas on a website.[6]

Most campuses that I know about have student internships in town businesses, hospitals, and K–12 schools. They welcome off-campus citizens to campus concerts and athletic events. In the summers, they run sports camps for area junior and senior high school students, not incidentally to plant seeds in their mind about attending college there. The president and others build bridges by joining local service organizations, serving on the school board, and providing leadership in local churches, parishes, and synagogues.

Play More Golf

In my inquiries with a few small-college presidents, I heard from President Todd Voss of Southern Wesleyan University in Central, South Carolina, with an enrollment of nine hundred traditional students and a growing online population of seven hundred. President Voss is doing some things others could replicate. Here is a partial summary of Southern Wesleyan's collaborations with the town of Central:

- A golf practice range open to the public on campus land is a student-run business; this project could not have been licensed, funded, or implemented without town support.
- A collaborative project to build a living community for people over age fifty-five capitalizes on the nearby golf range, right next to campus. Such projects are great for the town and add new intergenerational relationships on campus.
- A special-needs living and learning facility with Southern Wesleyan students living with and mentoring special-needs friends on the path to independent living.[7]

Return to Your Roots Geographically

Nyack College was originally founded in 1882 in New York City. Its move in 1897 to the town in New York that would become its namesake was precipitated by the need to find an adequate campus facility not available or affordable in Manhattan. Yet, nearly a century later, in 1995, the college opened a branch campus back downtown. Both of Nyack's campuses now enroll a diverse mix of students, and both campuses are experiencing steady enrollment growth. President Michael Scales explained Nyack's decision:

> To truly understand what many call Nyack's "return" to New York City, one must realize that in many ways Nyack never left the city. Our student demographic has long reflected the global character of the metropolitan New York area, and our commitment to serve the underserved, including students from immigrant populations, has always been part of our DNA. Nyack did not break into a new marketplace when we launched our Manhattan Campus in 1995. We went home. We reconnected our past with our future.[8]

Bring the College to the Town

Several suburban communities in major metropolitan areas are wooing colleges from afar to start a campus in their towns. The number of these invitations is growing, based on my research for this chapter, yet small towns reaching out to small colleges is not always a city council's priority. One exception is Huntington University–Arizona, a branch of Huntington University, based in the small town of Huntington, Indiana. Huntington decided to export its successful digital arts program to the Valley of the Sun, where Arizona State University with its 100,000 students was a potent lure. After seven years of working with suburban leaders, President Sherilyn Emberton offered this assessment of the strategic decision:

Huntington University opened a new location in Peoria, Arizona, in the fall of 2016 in close collaboration with the city of Peoria. The Arizona campus focuses on bachelor degrees in animation, broadcast media, film production, graphic design, and other digital media arts. The home campus is located in Huntington, Indiana, where it was founded in 1897. Enrollment at the Arizona location quadrupled in just two years, and the campus served more than one hundred degree-seeking students in the 2018–2019 academic year. Huntington University, Arizona Center for Digital Media Arts

> As a newly hired president of Huntington University, I was given the opportunity to continue the design and implementation of this project by our board of trustees and former university president. The university community took two years to define the scope of the curriculum, secure a suitable site, and close on the partnership agreement with the city. Along the way, we observed the success and failure of other academic expansions. Our team took away valuable lessons and had the support of an Arizona community that ultimately desired success for us both. We have continued to learn as we grow.[9]

It is too early to determine whether the investment in faraway cities by small colleges will pay off, but it is easier to recruit large groups of students to live in the sun belt than in the rust belt. One key will be the percentage of students at Huntington who still prefer the more intimate, rural, and remote campus experience. Whatever the case, small colleges must find ways to distinguish themselves amid increasing competition and declining enrollment pools.

FIVE KEYS TO BUILDING SUCCESSFUL PARTNERSHIPS IN RURAL AREAS

1. Without a vision, nothing will happen. An effective first step is for college trustees to adopt a goal to maximize learning, research, and service through creative collaboration with off-campus entities. The next step is to invite interested partners to identify themselves.
2. Invite civic leaders to meet regularly to build trust by collaboratively assessing needs, then organize task forces of representatives from both the campus and the community to explore the most promising strategies in more depth.

The Fifteen Top Rural Colleges, 2016

"For many students, their ideal college campus is away from the city. Whether they feel at home in a more rural setting, or they're looking to escape the hustle-and-bustle, there's a certain serenity that comes with attending a college isolated from the major metropolitan areas.

In this ranking, we looked at the best colleges which are located in rural campuses. By definition, these colleges will be outside of major city limits and may even be surrounded by undeveloped land."

1. Hamilton College, Clinton, New York
2. Sewanee–The University of the South, Sewanee, Tennessee
3. Thomas Aquinas College, Santa Paula, California
4. Saint Johns University, Collegeville, Minnesota
5. DeSales University, Center Valley, Pennsylvania
6. Saint Mary's College of California, Moraga, California
7. Houghton College, Houghton, New York
8. Marlboro College, Marlboro, Vermont
9. Principia College, Elsah, Illinois
10. Louisiana State University and Agricultural & Mechanical College, Baton Rouge
11. St John's College, Santa Fe, New Mexico
12. Erskine College, Due West, South Carolina
13. Emory and Henry College, Emory, Virginia
14. Stevenson University, Stevenson, Maryland
15. Wilmington College, Wilmington, Ohio

Source: Kaeli Nieves-Whitmore, "The 25 Best Rural Colleges–2016 University Rankings," College Raptor, accessed October 21, 2018, https://www.collegeraptor.com/find-colleges/articles/college-comparisons/best-rural-colleges/.

---

3. Set up communication channels, including a website and social media, for anyone to study the plans under consideration and offer comments on them.

4. When creative ideas achieve a consensus of campus and local community leaders, pursue funding from foundations and corporations. The goal should be to entice these organizations to build sites locally to leverage the talents on campus.

5. Leaders and conceptualizers will eventually need to engage, and trust, implementers to accomplish strategic objectives. These individuals will need to be given the authority to complete the myriad tasks signaling ultimate success. Leaders who endure and prosper in this environment are able to maintain a big vision without succumbing to the tyranny of the urgent.

Increasingly, students, faculty, administrators, and alumni are seeing "the good life" in less populated areas, and a local college adds almost immeasurably to the quality of life available to these seekers. College presidents and trustees in these communities realize that they need to be distinctive to compete. Their local communities cannot be liabilities when recruiting new generations of faculty and students, so they must design creative, win-win collaborations. Most will need to rethink how their liberal arts curricula can be repackaged to appeal to more pragmatic students while at the same time keeping their costs down. Presidents and mayors both realize that there are no shortcuts or secret pathways to long-term success but that partnering with neighbors may be the smartest, simplest, and safest way to start.

CHAPTER 18

Collaboration Is Complex

Five Lessons from Higher Education Consortium Directors for College Town Planners

PHILLIP DICHIARA

INTRODUCTION: HOW SOCIAL NETWORKS HAVE CHANGED US

Few will debate that the new American college town must be both virtual and concrete, leveraging the advantages of technology while not abandoning essential face-to-face human contact. Yet a case can be made that the traditional foundation of town-gown interactions should now be rethought in light of changes brought about by our better understanding of organizational behavior and by advances in web-based social networks and related technologies. In fact, one may argue that the operational foundation on which American town-gown collaborations have been based is no longer adequate. We must reconsider and support new solutions and opportunities. Social networks are having a growing impact. They are fundamentally democratic and voluntary, and college towns are a "social enterprise" that cannot expeditiously progress or be effectively governed by a purely hierarchic social model.[1]

There is no doubt that *command control*, the principal management and decision-making model, has a long and successful history. Most current college towns' interpersonal leadership remains tied to top-down, autocratic—presidential—oversight. The conflict between these two approaches—democratic and autocratic—is still subtle, but over time we will likely observe that we have unconsciously and unproductively surrendered significant and essential common ground: control and oversight, spurious in many circumstances, become more important than inherently democratic and natural productive decision-making processes. The opportunity for acceptable compromise becomes restricted in closed-door sessions by the most senior "decision makers," whether academic or civic. By supporting both informal and formal discussions long before a specific joint project is identified, we can build upon the common ground of earlier-established trust. Until we recognize that the careful development of trust is an asset that must be consciously cocreated, we will not consistently succeed in resolving complicated and sticky issues.

A successful model for collaborative thinking and project development can be found in the ongoing work of many academic *consortia*. These are often loose but also legally incorporated arrangements among academic entities whose goal is to collaborate for better educational outcomes, lower operating cost, and more reasonably scaled research and overhead costs. Currently, more than one hundred consortia operate nationally. They offer useful lessons for emerging college towns and their strategic development. They also affirm that a lesser-used means for getting things done, called *heterarchy*, deserves more attention. Simply put, heterarchy involves ongoing, often intensive interactions across autonomous groups that are, in the case of consortia, often termed *communities of practice*. Heterarchy, rather than command control, is more accommodating when a social enterprise must conduct projects across multiple independent organizations.[2] Emerging college towns should consider looking to these consortia for experience in establishing an environment in which everyone has a vote and a voice via social media. Certainly there are circumstances in which traditional hierarchies are necessary and work well, but they should not be the only process considered or employed. Collaboration is far more powerful than currently understood, in part because it is employed without adequate expertise. It has become painfully obvious to many presidents, provosts, mayors, and other elected officials that collaboration is an honored concept but that few practice it dependably or over a sustained period of time.

PHILLIP DICHIARA

Single most important piece of advice: When the going gets tough in developing a new collaboration or partnership, many of us tend to fall back on what we already know. Given the pace of change, this is a trap that must be avoided if we are to bring fresh thinking and leadership to the table.

THE DEMANDS OF COLLABORATION ON TOWN-GOWN PLANNERS

There is no single perfect recipe for designing a college town consortium. The consortium model does, however, provide guidance in some areas that are particularly sensitive. As articulated by Jim Collins, in a follow-up monograph to his landmark book, *Good to Great*: "Social sector leaders are not less decisive than business leaders as a general rule; they only appear that way to those who fail to grasp the complex governance and diffuse power structures common to the social sectors. For a business, financial returns are a perfectly legitimate measure of performance. For a social sector organization, however, performance must be assessed relative to mission, not financial returns."[3]

Trust

Aligning strategic goals can be exciting, yet establishing successful work processes can be tedious. Collaboration requires that both be done in an environment conducive to mutual respect and shared responsibility for positive outcomes. Without a strong and intentionally maintained foundation of trust, success will probably be limited to modest or inconsequential improvements.

Members of the Boston Consortium

The Boston Consortium was established in the fall of 1995 by the chief financial officers of eleven Boston-area colleges and universities. The consortium currently comprises the following institutions: Babson College, Bentley University, Berklee College of Music, Boston College, Boston University, Brandeis University, College of the Holy Cross, Emerson College, Harvard University, Massachusetts Institute of Technology, Northeastern University, Olin College, Rhode Island School of Design, Suffolk University, Tufts University, Wellesley College, and Wheaton College.

The institutions' diversity is reflected in their operating budgets, which range from $37 million to $1.5 billion, and annual research expenditures, which range from zero to about $351 million. The combined endowment of the seventeen current consortium members totals more than $11 billion. The combined payroll is more than $1.2 billion, and the total FTE (full-time equivalent) count is approximately 45,000 employees, making the group one of the largest employers in the area. The total student head count is approximately 122,000.

College Town Leadership Lessons from Consortium Practices

- Trust
- Patience
- Engagement beyond simple participation
- Decisional sovereignty
- Collaborative results
- Regularly updated mission

As the Teagle Foundation monograph *Collaborative Ventures* contends: "There are benefits of Trust's presence. Willingness to take risk: People have to feel safe and have to experience positive results before they are willing to take on riskier ideas. At the very least, there should not be a penalty for failure. With regard to Valuing and Rewarding Collaborative Work, the dominant culture of academe is one where individual's work within a department is valued and rewarded. Working outside of these departments (and across multiple institutions) while being valued and rewarded for cooperation is a challenge."[4]

Rarely does initiating collective action perfectly mesh with the preceding interests of an individual participant organization. As a result, individual institutions may opt out of a particular undertaking, establishing doubts about future collective success. The essential lesson that must be learned is that real collaboration requires some compromise of individual institutional decisional sovereignty. When done with care, a gentle movement evolves to build common ground, which effectuates the trust upon which future successes may be had.[5]

Patience

Enduring partnerships do not develop quickly or without hard work. They require time and skill to persuade all key stakeholders to speak the same language and agree on goals *and the means to achieve them.*[6] Academic and civic partners developing a collaborative, consortium-like vehicle must ensure that face-to-face contact recurs at appropriate time intervals. Scheduled forums for informal communication slowly but effectively encourage better *inter*institutional understanding. It is lack of familiarity that discourages and undermines trust. Simply discussing intraorganizational activities among and between town or college departments may initially appear superficial, but the first step to a collective vision is observing and understanding what already exists that drives a particular organization's vision. Finding common ground and building upon it takes time, as fear of the process will likely need to be dispelled before adequate trust can be built to construct a shared vision. In the current moment, there is a growing need to take the time and patience necessary to familiarize ourselves with the possibilities for interconnectedness in a college town.

Engagement beyond Simple Participation

College town projects, particularly complex ones, will likely be challenged in their development over time if participants perceive them to have benefits primarily accruing to the college or university rather than also to the city or town. Where that notion exists, it must be explored and, over time, addressed.[7]

Academic brand and civic reputation add additional layers of context and influence. These can complicate collaborative relationships at any level. Broader involvement of academic administrators and corresponding-level civic leaders, enhanced by social networks and driven by face-to-face dialogue, can, however, bridge such obstacles. Some presidents have noted the irony that loose federations structured as consortia can often be more effective than formally assembled senior managers of academic and town or city offices because they are not limited by tight organizational norms and traditional leadership models. Civic authorities, given the political nature of their roles, are hyperalert to who "talks a good game" versus who actually practices it. Attendance at meetings is a simple but often quite accurate indicator of which institutions are serious about fulfilling the joint mission.

Decisional Sovereignty

Depending on participant definitions, consensus agreement is often defined and implemented as the acceptable middle ground between two extremes of a "I don't fully agree but I can live with it" mentality. Most states maintain higher education–based political advocacy associations among their private colleges and universities whose role it is to ensure that legislation and regulation reflect the interests of that constituency. Those agencies that expand to include services not unlike the typical consortium are revealing examples of how compromise can work in multiple circumstances. Not every member fully agrees with every action and decision, but unless there is no acceptability whatever, compromise is a collective agreement that an act of unity of purpose is necessary. What is true both for educational consortia and college town organizations is that those that succeed and endure over many years reflect the fact that occasional displeasure with a particular approach is an inevitable part of doing business as a voluntary social enterprise. Decisional sovereignty is the right of a single organization to decide and act unilaterally. College and university leaders learn through these projects that some compromise of decisional sovereignty is necessary to meet the larger need for continued advancement and maintenance of common ground. However, final authority is so tightly woven into many management and leadership models that the notion of authentic collaboration is overlooked until the middle to late stages of planning. When collaboration is neglected, it can be a threat to the overall enterprise. In response, some institutions may simply abandon participation in current and possibly future joint efforts.[8]

Collaborative Results

Even for-profit companies are moving to product cocreation. They have established "engagement platforms" to involve customers, employees, and stakeholders in a systematic and continuous process of value discovery. It takes an even greater leap of faith to do so when working across multiple organizational entities. Consortia have generally mastered this challenge, and lessons are available for the emerging town-gown business models. It is important to acknowledge that cocreation can be discontinuous, made more complicated by staffing churn and the sometimes-limited involvement of senior administrators who feel uncomfortable in this milieu. Depending on one person to complete most of the plan, however comfortable they may be with that disproportionate role, is dangerous for long-term collective output. In this writer's experience, successful town-gown planners enjoy the social nature of work, including shared work responsibility.[9]

Regularly Updated Mission

Participating members of college towns and consortia come and go over time, and promotions, retirements, and the inevitable churn of staff can result in a disintegration of the collective understanding of the original common ground articulated by the founders. However, the connective tissue of an enduring collaboration requires solid and creative management at both the senior and the front-line decision-making level. For senior academic administrators and experienced city planners, sustained involvement can be difficult to achieve. Ideally, upper-middle and department managers will have been given the authority to negotiate the contributions to be made by the college or the town without splintering significant project goals. Splintering can follow inadequate understanding or lack of familiarity with key issues.

More formal interorganizational collaboration will need to be documented, communicated, and approved. Much information will inevitably flow upward as the content of the dialogue begins to produce actionable options for both the campus and the external community. It is at this moment that documentation can assist the parties in understanding what is missing that prevents continued progress.

BRINGING THE PIECES TOGETHER: LESSONS ACADEMIC CONSORTIA CAN OFFER COLLEGE TOWN PLANNERS

Primacy of a Long-Term Outlook

It is essential to focus relentlessly on the longer term and the bigger picture. This focus prioritizes face-to-face discussion and interpersonal reflection on shared mission from the outset.

In the case of faculty, they more naturally tend to share research interest and join together in related activities than do college and university presidents and business administrators. While each profession within academe has several highly competent, national peer-professional organizations, silos remain despite efforts at cross-communication. There are often equally ambivalent relationships between departments, including finance, human resources, facilities, and the other major divisions of nonacademic oversight. If internal connections are weak, a future must be articulated to overcome the limitations of less developed relationships between and with local authorities and internal stakeholders.[10]

Learn Deep Collaboration

Leaders on both sides should look beyond simple collaborative transactions that are otherwise important in the early days of a new college town model or consortium. While a form of preliminary success, such transactions become limiting when they block the organizational behavior and the difficult learning necessary for more complex undertakings from taking place. Hard lessons learned from failures at middle- and upper-middle-management levels can pay downstream and recurring dividends. Once again, it will be necessary to remember that collaboration is inherently a tedious and time-consuming effort. Clearly, it is far less time-efficient than the traditional command-control model, but its long-term advantage has been confirmed by the breadth and professionalism of the work installed across and between collaborating independent organizations.[11]

Over time, with informed guidance at all levels of responsibility, collective confidence on campus and in the town or city begins to build and deepen, and this can, in fact, lead to impatience for future successes. To address this impatience, leaders need to reinforce a collective focus on

PHILLIP DICHIARA

Most valuable lesson learned: It has been inspiring to observe that the overwhelming majority of individuals involved in collaborative efforts find, after a cycle of blood, sweat, and tears, that institutional camaraderie is a source of both joy and reward.

long-term strategies rather than short-term advances. College town leaders will need to reflect on the degree of freedom needed for emerging projects to succeed and endure. New approaches and different techniques may eventually become necessary.

Expect Dual Citizenship

Emerging town-gown initiatives, along with successful existing ones, must learn how to encourage a form of "dual citizenship" by which participants develop loyalties to both sides. Establishment of deep collaborative relationships across and between academic and civic colleagues must be undertaken intentionally. Decision making should begin at the lowest responsible level of authority and move to the highest, smoothly and with trust among all parties. Senior management oversight and ultimate responsibility is not eliminated, but it is enhanced by a wide depth and breadth of involvement essentially nonhierarchical. What distinguishes dual citizenship is the expectation that decisions must be agreed upon by those whom the changes most directly impact.

Small Groups Are Complex Systems

The ability and time that civic and campus-based groups devote to processing information and generating meaning is essential for their long-term success. The interaction between such groups in addressing a common problem reveals the complex systems in which they are embedded. In the end, the desire to leverage the formal and informal opportunities of emerging college towns will require patience and the "consent of the governed." Reliance on hierarchy and its associated processes will, in this writer's view, not expedite progress but rather can undermine it. Successful campus–local community initiatives value critical thinking and independence of thought. Authority and autocracy may be able initially to achieve order and control, but they will not sustain good citizenship behaviors over the long term as successfully as will freedom of choice and commitment to a common cause.

CHAPTER 19

A College Town Legal Primer

The Most Frequently Asked Questions, and Answers, about Campus-Community Partnerships

JAMES E. SAMELS AND JAMES MARTIN

HISTORICAL LEGAL CONTEXT OF COLLEGE TOWNS

This chapter offers administrators and civic leaders the tools, strategies, and perspectives to help colleges, universities, and municipalities optimize, and monetize, the benefits of creating a new model of college town while proactively navigating the associated legal pitfalls. Contemporary college towns are best characterized by thoughtful, carefully sequenced, collaborative planning efforts that produce mutually profitable results. This cooperative process fosters an atmosphere where both education and business ventures can flourish and generate significant opportunities to revitalize downtowns. Working together through codevelopment and co-utilization, colleges and towns can conserve resources by achieving economies of scale, efficiencies in operation, and nonduplication of facilities, programs, and services. There are scores of reasons why cities and towns have a growing appetite for attracting college and university campuses to their community. Institutions of higher learning are frequently among the largest employers, they provide scholarships for local high school graduates, and in many instances they help defray the actual costs of fire and public safety protection, solid waste disposal, and public works projects. The complex dynamics of town-gown relationships have emerged into bold relief over the past several decades. We have learned from both what has gone right in the past and what has gone wrong. As readers will discover in numerous chapters of this book, hundreds of higher education institutions across all geographic regions are now engaging with their partner towns and cities.

Conversely, when town-gown relations go sour, there can be plenty of blame to go around. In some instances, institutions may have been less than forthright with municipal officials about plans for expansion and redevelopment. These tensions are often exacerbated by nagging problems of noise, traffic, a scarcity of parking, and gentrification of housing stock. Over time, many campuses learn that transparency and mutual trust provide a useful framework for avoiding the downside of uncoordinated planning. Since the body of law governing town-gown relationships is still evolving, college and university counsel must be cognizant of state statutes and municipal ordinances, bylaws, and licensing and permitting regulations. Intelligent college planning provides more nimble and responsive collaboration, including payment *in lieu of taxes* to help mitigate the direct fiscal burden placed on host communities by their respective college or university. As well, college and municipal corporation counsel must be up-to-date on the body of law that governs higher education, and in particular, constitutional statutory and judicial authority—provisions of the law that exempt nonprofit and public institutions from arbitrary moratoriums on growth and development.

Unhappily, the reality for some towns and cities is that their resident higher education institutions may have conflicting needs that can generate considerable controversy. If not timely and properly addressed, these difficulties can result in long-standing feuds and legal horror stories. In traditional college towns like Amherst, Princeton, or Ann Arbor, town-gown relations have been harmonized over perhaps a century or more. Yet, for most other aspiring college communities, without a long history of higher learning, special care must be given to learning about the partner's perspectives, motivations, and immediate objectives. This can mean facilitating numerous town hall conversations and dozens of smaller, candid, one-on-one exchanges. What follows is a 360-degree environmental scan and synthesis of the legal environment that surrounds college town planning, programming, codevelopment, and cobranding. This distillation of the legal framework behind college towns offers summary best practices, lessons learned, and challenges to anticipate.

Zoning, Permitting, and Licensing

Local cities and towns have the power to promulgate rational zoning, permitting, and licensing regulations. These laws and regulations can seriously impede a college or university's plans for growth. Challenges to zoning and land use can take a variety of forms, ranging from constitutional challenges that involve a heavy burden to seeking an exception, variance, or amendment to the zoning ordinance. Most state constitutions prohibit creating classifications that burden certain groups of people unless there is a rational public purpose. A municipality's zoning ordinances and application may not deprive institutions of the use of their land to the extent that this constitutes a "taking."[1]

The courts are increasingly asked to balance the autonomy higher education institutions have over the use of their land against the reasonable needs and interests of urban, suburban, and rural communities and the right to use and enjoy surrounding property. "As a consequence of their inherently beneficial nature," the New York Court of Appeals has asserted, "educational institutions have long 'enjoyed special treatment with respect to residential zoning ordinances and have been permitted to expand into neighborhoods where nonconforming uses would otherwise not have been allowed.'"[2] In *Trustees of Union College v. Members of the Schenectady City Council* (1997), the New York Court of Appeals cited the failure to balance competing interests in holding that an ordinance's exclusion of educational uses in the historic district was unconstitutional: "In failing to provide any means whereby Union College's proposed educational uses might be balanced against the public's interest in historical preservation, City Code §264-8 serves no end that is substantially related to the promotion of the public health, safety, morals or general welfare, and as such is unconstitutional."[3]

In some cases, towns and universities can become legal adversaries when a city attempts to block an institution's growth. George Washington University is an example of an institution that has faced multiple lawsuits in its attempts to expand its residential and academic facilities. One such case is illustrative. The university is located in a partly residential neighborhood. District of Columbia zoning law permits university use in residential areas as a special exception only when approved by the Board of Zoning Adjustment (BZA). When the local community challenged the university's planned construction of dormitories and academic buildings near campus, the BZA responded by making provision of additional living quarters on campus a requirement for approving any further on- or off-campus nonresidential expansion. The university challenged this order in court. In *George Washington University v. District of Columbia Board of Zoning Adjustments*, 831 A.2d 921 (D.C. 2003), the U.S. Court of Appeals for the District of Columbia remanded the case to the board on one issue involving the separation of powers. On other aspects, the D.C. court ruled that the board's order that the university provide additional on-campus housing was neither arbitrary nor capricious. The court found that the BZA's threat to stop construction of all nonresidential building was a permissible use of its powers because it provided an appropriate incentive for the university to comply with the BZA's order.

As a general rule, higher education institutions are bound by local law;

Eleven Legal Best Practices for College Town Planners

- Zoning, permitting, and licensing
- Downtown housing
- Town-gown planning
- Public and private codevelopment
- Payment in lieu of taxes
- Environmental issues
- Economic, workforce development, and technology internships
- Campus police and local law enforcement collaborations
- Disaster management plans
- Social media management
- Later-life college communities

however, many state legislatures have enacted express statutory or regulatory exceptions to prevent towns and cities from imposing an arbitrary moratorium on college and university construction and improvements. For example, Massachusetts passed the Dover Amendment to grant educational institutions autonomy over the use of their property. Section 3 of the Dover Amendment (Massachusetts General Laws, Chapter 40A) provides: "No zoning ordinance or by-law shall . . . prohibit, regulate or restrict the use of land or structure . . . for educational purposes on land owned or leased by the commonwealth or any of its agencies, subdivisions or bodies politic or by a religious sect or denomination, or by a nonprofit educational corporation."

Boston College invoked the Dover Amendment in its lawsuit against the city of Newton for its refusal to grant a construction permit to build three interconnected buildings. A January 2001 land court decision stated that the city's "zoning regulations may not reasonably be applied to the middle campus project" and the denial of the college's petition to build the project "is legally untenable under the Dover Amendment and therefore beyond the authority of the Board." The decision was upheld by the appeals court and became final after further appellate review was denied by the Massachusetts Supreme Judicial Court.[4]

Zoning cases involving higher education can turn on how the term *educational use* is interpreted. For example, in *People ex rel. Cooper v. Rancho Santiago College* (1990), the city of Santa Ana sued Rancho Santiago College to enjoin operation of a weekly swap meet on college property. This case involved the interpretation of California Government Code, section 53094, which allows a school district to declare a city zoning ordinance inapplicable to a proposed use of its property, but does not include within this exception a proposed use for "nonclassroom facilities." The California Court of Appeal upheld the lower court's injunction against the college's proposed commercial activity on college property in violation of the city's zoning laws. In reaching this result, the court noted that if an institution "could exempt itself from a city's zoning controls simply by receiving some remunerative return for use of its property, section 53094 would become meaningless."[5] Nonetheless, colleges need to know that they may be subject to local zoning, permitting, and licensing restrictions even when exempted from taxation by their nonprofit status. For example, zoning laws do not exempt college property from meeting fire and safety codes or accessibility requirements mandated by Section 504 of the Rehabilitation Act of 1973 or the Americans with Disabilities Act. Beyond land use and occupancy issues, student conduct and behavior downtown or elsewhere off campus can trigger the promulgation and enforcement of restrictive conditions. It is no surprise that these conditions can easily find their way into restrictive covenants in college project licensing and permitting.

Downtown Housing

Zoning and land use regulation must be taken into account in the development of housing policy in order to maximize harmonious town-gown relations and to minimize the likelihood that college expansion projects will end up in litigation. If not handled strategically, expansion of college and university housing can erode positive relationships with neighboring communities when increases in property values drive out long-term residents. The better course for educational institutions to take is to find ways to partner with the community in developing properties both for its own use and for affordable neighborhood housing. According to the Center for Urban and Regional Policy at Northeastern University, universities have used several models in partnering with communities around housing:

1. Financial contributions to assist in the production or preservation of housing
2. Employer-assisted housing for university and staff
3. Direct production of affordable housing for community residents
4. Housing development and planning assistance using university resources targeted at specific communities or neighborhoods.[6]

In its "Primer on University-Community Housing Partnerships," the center warns that an effective collaboration cannot be created overnight.[7] The primary ingredient in developing a successful partnership is establishing an environment of mutual trust and respect, often needed to overcome past suspicion and animosity.

Town-Gown Planning

The collaborative planning model involving civic leaders that this book is predicated on means having honest conversations about intentional real estate development goals and strategies aimed at mutually rewarding results for the campus and the downtown merchant population. One of the primary purposes of zoning and permitting is to achieve the highest and best use of the real estate based on comparable sales, replacement value, and capitalization of income approaches to valuation, appraisal, collaboration, and monetization of new development projects. Land use issues cover a full range of questions regarding educational, cultural, scientific-technological, residential, athletic-recreational, and preservation-focused purposes for land. By planning together with higher education institutions, cities and towns can anticipate college growth and provide for the zoning, permitting, and licensing of foreseeable campus expansion. Indeed, municipalities and colleges can frequently retrofit existing structures, thereby saving millions in capital and financing costs; downtowns can be reengineered, transforming river mill cities into the pistons of the new bricks-and-clicks economy.

The decision to site a campus downtown can often cause college or university officials to become more sensitive to the impact their facilities have on the surrounding community and its own downtown revitalization efforts. This is an important college town planning lesson for local developers. From a branding perspective, cities and towns typically increase their real estate value by aligning with higher education institutions. These decisions can be independently verified by appraised value in the tax assessment process. When education is located downtown, more students and visitors spend discretionary money on restaurants, bookstores, and boutiques, businesses thrive, and downtown becomes revitalized. In the initial stages of the downtown college town development process, the construction phase brings solid job growth. After that, the academic and housing facilities and increased services needed to support them create even more sustainable employment.

In some cases, these collaborations have revitalized communities by creating an *urban downtown renaissance*. The water crisis helped unite the Flint, Michigan, community and sharpened the entire state university system's focus on public health, wellness, community revitalization, and urban renewal and led to new international public health collaboration opportunities. The city of Flint immediately focused on the water crisis and, remarkably, achieved a shared sense of resilience and ingenuity, and the will to create a sustainable, postindustrial metropolitan ecosystem. This later-stage downtown revitalization process has focused on the reengineering of the FirstMerit Bank building and the Riverfront Residence Hall and Conference Center. Significantly, with the acquisition of these two structures, the University of Michigan–Flint (UM-F) has created a vibrant college town vibe for the benefit of its students, faculty, and the larger Flint community. For example, UM-F's Department of Theatre and Dance hosts productions open to the public—alongside exciting venues like the Flint Institute of the Arts and Buckham Gallery that promote local artwalks within the emergent creative economy.

By growing its downtown presence by approximately 25 percent, the Riverfront Residence Hall and Conference Center stands out as a beacon of cultural enrichment and civic pride. As an urban area reaping the benefits that a new kind of college town identity can bring, Flint is becoming a magnet for millennials and retirees who want to reside near a forward-thinking metropolitan area. In our view, the reinvigorated downtown will attract several more waves of young professionals seeking to experience an urban revival as it is happening.

Public and Private Codevelopment

In joint-venture contractual arrangements, the partners share both the risks and the rewards. One side may give up some control in exchange for capital outlay, credit enhancement, or other forms of collateral—for example, a greater share of the investment risk for a greater share of control. As such, public-private partnerships are becoming increasingly common in higher education. For example, the New Jersey Economic Stimulus Act of 2009 allows a public institution to partner with a private company. One institution that has taken advantage of this opportunity is Rowan University in Glassboro, New Jersey. With the $350 million Rowan Boulevard project, Rowan University offers a remarkable best-practice case study in public-private partnerships. The project involved a multiuse building and parking garage to be owned and operated initially by a private developer and leased to the university. Under the terms of the partnership agreement, ownership of the classrooms will eventually revert to Rowan while the developer continues to own and manage the parking garage. Strolling down Rowan Boulevard, one can observe firsthand the downtown renewal with student housing, bookstores, cafés, other retail stores, and eventually several restaurants and a craft brewery, cobranded nationally with Marriott, Barnes & Noble, and regionally with Pete's Crab House and Sports Bar.

In Akron, Ohio, what has changed over the past decade is the collaborative codevelopment of its downtown via a creative partnership between the university and the city's civic leaders. After several key land swaps, the downtown area now boasts multiple brand hotels, retail shops, cafés, and fine-dining options. These several venues are connected through the revitalized Towpath Trail, with existing links to Akron's main attractions such as its art museum and zoo. Staying ahead of the millennial curve, the university recently invested in a downtown student housing facility to address, as Glassboro has, the goals and needs of young professionals who want to live and work where urban revival is ubiquitous.

Payment in Lieu of Taxes

Beyond the realm of land use and occupancy disputes, cities and towns provide municipal services without full payment of taxes on the same basis as commercial enterprises. This sets the stage for payment in lieu of taxes. Critically important to most campuses are municipal services, such as police and fire protection and refuse disposal, that are primarily funded by property tax revenue. Public and nonprofit educational institutions are exempt from property tax, yet they receive these services. In recent years, some municipalities have asked nonprofit educational institutions to make a voluntary payment in lieu of taxes (PILOT). In other cases, colleges and universities have sometimes made PILOTs to the city or town voluntarily. Connecticut and Rhode Island have a PILOT program mandating that the state reimburse a city for the nontaxable property occupied by tax-exempt institutions such as universities. However, the state does not reimburse the city for its PILOTs for all the potential taxes lost.

PILOTs help institutions develop good working relationships with municipal government and the surrounding community. The city of Boston, for example, adopted guidelines for a PILOT program that apply to institutions from the educational, medical, and cultural sectors owning property valued in excess of $15 million. The guidelines provide that PILOT contributions should be 25 percent of what the institution would be expected to pay in real estate taxes if the exempt property were taxable, with a 50 percent PILOT deduction for qualifying community programs that uniquely benefit Boston residents. "Of the 19 colleges and universities in Boston," the *Boston Globe* reported, "14 paid less than what was requested in fiscal year 2017, which ended in June. . . . The total value of the land owned by the 19 colleges is $7.2 billion, according to city data. If that property was taxable, the city would be entitled to $223.7 million. Instead, the city requested PILOT payments totaling $26.9 million from colleges and universities and received $13.4 million."[8] In fiscal year 2016, the city of Boston reported that forty-nine nonprofit institutions met the PILOT criteria. Of the 23 colleges, universities, and schools on the list, only five paid the full amount of the requested PILOT. Some institutions cite in-kind contributions as a rationale for paying less than the requested amount. Others may consider themselves in circumstances of financial exigency.[9]

Environmental Issues

Preserving conservation land, disposing of hazardous waste, and toxic mitigation can embroil an institution in complex litigation under federal, state, and municipal law and impose costly cleanup duties. It is recommended that institutions be proactive by conducting environmental compliance audits. The American Council on Education and the National Association of College and University Business Officers are among the organizations that work with the US Environmental Protection Agency to develop tools to assist colleges in managing compliance with environmental laws. The "Environmental Management Guide for Colleges," issued by the EPA's Office of Environmental Stewardship in October 2007, provides a helpful guide to developing a management system to balance the competing demands of compliance with the efficient use of resources while meeting the mission of the educational institution.

Environmental wetlands, toxic mitigation, and remediation present issues all subject to federal, state, and municipal regulation and enforcement. For example, the Environmental Protection Agency works with institutions of higher learning on smart-growth development approaches and sees these institutions as resources in their capacity as developers, teachers, researchers, providers of technical assistance, and community members. "Over the last several decades," the EPA notes,

> colleges and universities have transformed into economic engines, and their economic impact extends beyond traditional campus boundaries. As institutions serving students, faculty, and staff, they need to maintain and expand their facilities. They are typically responsible for providing classrooms, offices, research space, laboratories, administrative offices, and housing, as well as transportation facilities that include parking lots, buses, bike racks, and bikes. Their expansion affects surrounding neighborhoods and often the larger region.[10]

Smart-growth strategies support environmentally friendly development patterns. Useful examples include:

- Compact development that lessens the demand for the conversion of undeveloped land and thereby helps to protect working lands and habitat
- Mixed-use development that expands transportation choices and decreases automobile use
- Reusing existing properties such as brownfields and underused sites[11]

As urban land development increases, mitigation and rehabilitation of contaminated properties have become increasingly common. Goodwin College in Connecticut has reportedly cleaned and repurposed several brownfield properties as part of its neighborhood stabilization and revitalization initiative and to meet the college's need for more space. This remediation and reuse of brownfields has brought economic, educational, and environmental benefits to the surrounding community.[12]

Economic, Workforce Development, and Technology Internships

Colleges and universities can bring expertise, research, and resources to municipalities with inadequate budgets. Student internships are increasingly a win-win in that students get to apply their theoretical knowledge to actual professional situations and then return to the classroom with an enhanced sense of purpose. Municipalities can always use an extra hand, and positive student experiences within municipal agencies may help inspire the next generation of municipal workers. In these times of fiscal frugality and budget shortfalls, colleges and cities are looking for additional ways to collaborate and in the process do more with less. In these instances, it would be wise for provosts and academic administrators to remain aware of the legal implications that the many different models of internships can trigger.

Drexel University

Drexel University in Philadelphia has declared its aim to be one of the top civically engaged universities. Committed to the welfare of surrounding neighborhoods, the university supports engagement in the following three areas: research and academic programs that directly benefit communities, public service internships for students and faculty, and business practices that support local and regional economic development. The university recognizes that "civic engagement not only unites neighborhoods [but] educates students in problem solving, understanding diversity, good citizenship, and leadership."[13] Drexel University's Center for Neighborhood Partnerships offers residents of an inner-city Philadelphia neighborhood free services such as internet coaching, help in finding work, legal aid, and money management advice.[14]

Wagner College–Port Richmond Partnership

On Staten Island, New York, the Wagner College–Port Richmond Partnership is a best-practice model of a new town-gown strategy.[15] The partnership involves a collaboration among the college and more than two dozen nonprofits, schools, medical centers, health and wellness organizations, churches, and helping agencies focused on health, education, immigration, and the economy. The partnership's mission is to develop sustainable relationships among members of the Port Richmond and Wagner College communities in order to enhance student learning and raise civic awareness while also supporting collaborations that address significant challenges and establish measurable results in five high-need areas: arts, education, health, economic development, and immigration. The partnership encourages the development of collaborative programs that contribute to school improvement, economic growth, health care enhancement, and immigration reform; that play a significant role in advancing research and inquiry about pressing community issues; and that build mutually beneficial curricular and cocurricular internship placements for Wagner College students to broaden their experiences and strengthen a wide variety of community-based services.

A memorandum of understanding (MOU) was signed in the spring of 2009, officially establishing the Partnership. Based on an agreement between Wagner College and several organizations and institutions in Port Richmond, the partnership was designed to extend Wagner's commitment to learning-by-doing, as well as to rejuvenate an economically distressed community. Since the partnership's inception, the number of participating organizations has reportedly doubled, and through regularly scheduled meetings, partners have worked closely together to tap existing community assets by continuing to build significant, sustainable, and increasingly ambitious partnerships. To date, 40 percent of Wagner College undergraduate students have at least one community internship experience in which they work with and learn from the residents of Port Richmond.[16]

MetroLab Network

MetroLab Network is a group of more than thirty-five city-university partnerships focused on bringing data, analytics, and innovation to city government. Its members include thirty-eight cities, four counties, and fifty-one universities. Its mission is to pair university researchers with proximate city policy makers to undertake research, development, and deployment projects that improve infrastructure, public services, and environmental sustainability. Some of the largest challenges the organization is currently addressing include traffic congestion, crime, economic growth, climate change, and delivery of city services. As the group's website explains, "MetroLab network's city-university partnerships are mutually beneficial relationships in which the university is the city's R&D department and the city is the test-bed. Faculty and students get access to real-life laboratories to test approaches that are aimed to address city priorities and challenges. Cities and their residents benefit from the university's technical expertise to help solve those challenges."[17]

Examples of current collaborative projects include:

- Baltimore Falls Reduction Initiative: City of Baltimore and Johns Hopkins University
- Engineering Smart Cities: Arlington County, Virginia, and Virginia Tech
- Evaluating and Expanding the Impacts of Downtown: City of Burlington and University of Vermont
- Geospatial Determinants of Health Outcomes: City of Detroit and Wayne State University
- Urban Water Mitigation Project: City of Baltimore and University of Baltimore[18]

Campus Police and Local Law Enforcement Collaborations

Collaborations between campus police and local law enforcement agencies are increasingly becoming a standard practice for universities and colleges, as reflected in the 70 percent of campus law enforcement agencies that have MOUs with local law enforcement.[19] The University of New Hampshire and the Durham Police Department offer best-practice examples of collaboration between a municipal police department and campus police. Their collaboration involves the following key elements (among others):

- An MOU providing authority for both police agencies operating within the community
- Obtaining accreditation from the Commission for Accreditation on Law Enforcement, which helps ensure that both local police and campus police are responding similarly and according to the same procedures
- Local and campus police routinely cohost trainings for their staff and area agencies.
- Local and campus police routinely collaborate on state and federal grants to maximize the changes resulting from obtaining funds.
- Local and campus police routinely collaborate on major special-event management.[20]

Disaster Management Plans

All higher education institutions now need a disaster management plan that coordinates closely with those of municipal and federal agencies. To work most effectively, coordination between colleges and institutions must begin long before a disaster strikes. Four standard phases include:

1. Mitigation: preventing emergencies or minimizing their effects
2. Preparedness: plans for response and rescue operations, evacuation, stocking food and water
3. Response: actions taken to save lives and prevent further property damage
4. Recovery: actions taken to return to normal[21]

Municipal agencies come to the aid of a college in times of crisis. Conversely, colleges can coordinate emergency information and provide support services when their city is in need. The University of Michigan–Flint performed an exemplary role in responding to the crisis of lead in the city's water. In doing so, the university mounted a multitiered response included creating a $100,000 funding opportunity for faculty researchers, filtering its own water, handing out portable filters to the university community, distributing supplies to Flint residents, providing free lead screening, offering a free course on the crisis, and conducting a city-wide mitigation effort including mapping the city's water supply.[22]

Social Media Management

Social media can enhance the communication between a college community and its city or town. In the critical area of safety, for example, the most dramatic need comes in times of violence when the word needs to get out instantaneously to go into lockdown mode and to get word to campus and town police. The ability to send messages by text and by reverse 911 are both relatively recent technological tools that can help in a variety of emergency situations ranging from a shooter on campus to a natural disaster such as a fire or flood.

An app called LiveSafe offers but one of many examples of technologies that can help in routine ways to create safer communities. It can be set up to notify both campus and town police simultaneously and gives the sender the option to report anonymously. Pictures and videos can be sent with the notification. It contains a list of emergency resources. It can send someone's location to safety officials in an emergency. This app also allows users to send their planned route home to a friend, monitor their location while in transit, and check in with others virtually until arrival at their destination.

Later-Life College Communities

Some college towns have added senior-living communities on or abutting the campus. Seniors benefit from significant, ongoing educational opportunities and cultural offerings provided by the higher education institution. Students are enriched by intergenerational learning, and the town or city benefits from the added revenues. The Village at Penn State in State College, Pennsylvania, is a prime example of an elder village. The Village at Penn State defines itself as a university-based community. Besides proximity, the Village offers advance notice of priority seating at entertainment and cultural events; special passes to the golf course; environmental education; and nature programs, among others. Independent-living residents get lifetime priority access to onsite health services at predictable rates. Personal care and nursing care are available.

Another example is Lasell Village in Newton, Massachusetts. Sponsored by Lasell College, Lasell Village includes apartments, a supported-living unit, and a skilled-nursing facility. Residents can take advantage of both Lasell Village amenities and Lasell College courses. Lasell Village offers all of the following: retirement living, support services, short-term rehabilitation and long-term care, and lifelong learning. The complex is composed of fifteen residential buildings connected by enclosed walkways, with a central building offering a full range of amenities including dining and banking facilities. Each residential building includes at least one common space dedicated to continuing education and physical fitness. Although college-affiliated retirement communities are becoming more common, Lasell Village was the first to feature a mandatory, formal, and individualized continuing-education program for its residents.

A third model provides students rent-free housing in an elderly retirement home in exchange for committing a specified number of hours to elderly nursing-home residents. "In exchange for small, rent-free apartments, the Humanitas retirement home in Deventer, Netherlands," for example, "requires students to spend at least 30 hours per month acting as 'good neighbors.'"[23] This intergenerational model is currently in use in Cleveland, Ohio, and Lyons, France. In the mid-1990s, Spain began housing students in the homes of older people. So far, the program, International Association of Homes and Services for the Aging, has spread to more than twenty-five cities.[24] These intergenerational programs offer students the benefit of low-cost housing and elders the benefits of companionship.

FUTURE CHALLENGES, FUTURE BENEFITS

The presence of a college or university can reshape a town. If it is intentionally managed, the combination of higher education and municipality becomes greater than the sum of the parts. Colleges stimulate economic expansion, cultural enrichment, and accessible research opportunities. Colleges also bring competing needs for land and increased demand on environmental resources and municipal services. Still, civic leaders should not be viewed as natural enemies of college and university counsel. Rather than withdraw from municipal issues, college and university counsel should regularly share useful information with a broad range of municipal agencies in order to avoid the unfortunate consequence of meeting the mayor for the first time in an adversarial proceeding. To avoid this mishap, provosts, chief student affairs officers, and even presidents should actively participate in town hall meetings. This openness can build a trusting relationship that will survive the test of conflicting needs and expectations. Finally, when in doubt, leave litigation out. Even though the university may win its zoning challenge in court, it may also lose the support of neighborhood residents, who will rightly fear displacement, a loss in property values, and increased traffic. Beyond immediate public relations, however, it will be wise to remember that the larger, more important objective is not simply a new residence hall or technology patent but a web of enduring relationships that form a new model for American college towns.

CHAPTER 20

Get Ready

College Towns Two Generations from Today

JOEL GARREAU

Is Deep Springs College—the smallest and possibly most remote institution of higher learning in the United States—the future of college towns? To be sure, its "college town" would be Bishop, California, an hour by car over a mountain pass from where Deep Springs sits in its lonely high-desert splendor between the White and Inyo mountain ranges.[1]

But hear me out.

The world is going through the biggest revolution in three generations in how it builds cities. I call it the Santa Fe–ing of the planet. Places are erupting worldwide that are urbane without ever being anything like what we have thought of as "urban." Many are far beyond today's old-fashioned cities or even large metropolitan areas. This Santa Fe–ing is the opposite of suburbanization. This is not sprawl. It involves equal and opposite effects—dispersion *and* aggregation. It is people—students, alumni, citizens, tourists—coming together in the nicest places they can discover, no matter how distant.

Our ever-accelerating digital trends are the drivers. These Santa Fe–like places excel at providing the rare and valuable: the things we *cannot* digitize. Think spectacular natural surroundings—*and* face-to-face contact. The more intense the digital juggernaut, the more these new spaces develop specific identities. Santa Fe, New Mexico, itself is the long-standing example. It has world-class opera, charming architecture, distinguished restaurants, quirky bookstores, major diversity, and multiple colleges. Yet it is compact. Only 70,000 people, far from the nearest major metro. Here, small is beautiful and in new ways.

Places like Santa Fe are now dotting the planet, like stars in a night sky. US Census data show them to be among the fastest growing in the country. People are magnetically attracted to them globally, from Morocco to Croatia. How can this possibly be?

Commencement at Deep Springs College, with the Owens Valley in central California as backdrop. Deep Springs College. Photograph by A. Jackson Frishman.

All cities throughout human history have been shaped by whatever the state-of-the-art transportation device was at the time. Railroads produced places like Chicago, from the intraurban rail of the "L" to the vast wealth from processing the bounty of the hinterlands in the Yards. The automobile produced places with multiple urban cores—edge cities—like Los Angeles and Detroit.

Then along came the jet passenger plane. Those who are baseball fans may not realize how vastly different the game has become since the arrival of air travel. Where was the southwestern-most major league baseball team in 1955? St. Louis, Missouri. One could not maintain a major league schedule farther away from the Northeast than that, as players were moved by train. As a result, a vast swath of the country all the way to the Pacific became "Cardinal Nation." St. Louis became the "home team" for much of the South and West. Then jets changed all that. Airlines helped world-class metros to rise in Dallas, Denver, Houston, Atlanta, and Phoenix.

Today, we add the internet, and what has the internet wrought? The Santa Fe–ing of the world: the astounding rise of places the entire point of which is face-to-face contact in marvelous locales. Digital acceleration has transformed all built environments. There are nearly one hundred classes of real estate out of which you build cities, according to the late William J. Mitchell, the former head of the architecture and planning department at

MIT, and every one of those classes is being transfigured faster and more fully than occurred as a result of the automobile. For example, these new Santa Fe's are full of people who

- *Are not anchored to office towers.* They can work from anywhere. (And their Sisyphean curse is—anywhere they are, they're working.) As a result, millions of square feet of commercial real estate in legacy downtowns and edge cities stand empty or are being converted to residential space.
- *Have much different needs for homes.* If you only had to visit headquarters two or three days a week, might that affect your choice of residence? Might the coasts and mountains start looking good to you? If you had to be in the main office only two or three days a month, might the Caribbean start looking good to you?
- *Do not need malls.* We are going through a monumental freight revolution. Things are coming to us, rather than us going to things. Santa Claus now travels in a Big Brown truck, and things arrive overnight—year-round.

However, these new Santa Fe's are not just in remote places. They frequently start as romantic weekend getaways. Folk prefer urbane and sophisticated, but they are not crazy about the downsides of urban to which they have become accustomed. Which is why you can see the explosive growth of these towns from the Big Sky Country of Montana to the Gold Country of the California Sierras, from the Hill Country of Texas to the Piedmont of North Carolina, and even to the jagged coasts of New England.

And in certain new models of American college towns.

It's as if we're waking from our two-century-long fever dream with Industrial Age cities. We originally flocked to those cities for jobs. But what we now find attractive—and lucrative—is a blend of the eighteenth-century Agrarian Age and the twenty-first-century Information Age. Think Monticello with broadband. As Thomas Jefferson was thoughtful enough to found in the nearby foothills of the Blue Ridge the University of Virginia, in the early twenty-first century that creation has yielded a very powerful package. You could see this Santa Fe–ing take off in the data more than a decade ago. Where was the fastest-appreciating real estate metro in the United States reported in 2007?[2] Wenatchee, Washington. Homeowners were getting rich.

Where is Wenatchee, Washington? Three hours east of Seattle, on the dry side of the Cascades, and this explains a lot. The Seattle metropolitan area is full of great jobs—Amazon, Microsoft, the Gates Foundation—but it rains all the time. So some folks went out and discovered Wenatchee which has 300 days of sunshine a year and fine skiing, but also something new—with implications for the future of American college towns: People went there for rain-free weekends and they, Sunday after Sunday, began to say, "*Why are we leaving?*"

Everyone had a supercomputer in their pocket, so more workers travelled to Wenatchee on Thursdays and came back on Tuesdays. And that was the revolution. At that point, they were spending more time living and working in Wenatchee than in Microsoft's Edge City of Redmond. Does this mean even greater numbers will travel even greater distances to be alone and live remotely? Not necessarily, but this is not the point. Humans continue to require face-to-face connections, and that is one reason why college town planners and civic leaders are recognizing that the town-gown settings that provide creative, sustainable face-to-face contact will flourish, and the ones that fail to do so will fade into insignificance.

This is why some college towns are not thriving. Students—and faculty—enjoy concentrated, walkable spaces that display integrity, vibrancy, and look nothing like sprawl. These towns and cities provide urbane measures of sound and sight and scent well beyond the usual

Fastest-Growing College Towns

2013	2016
Raleigh, North Carolina	Greeley, Colorado
College Station, Texas	Auburn, Alabama
Las Cruces, New Mexico	Fargo, North Dakota
Gainesville, Florida	Fort Collins, Colorado
San Marcos, Texas	Iowa City, Iowa
Columbia, Missouri	Wilmington, North Carolina
Fayetteville, Arkansas	Savannah, Georgia
Flagstaff, Arizona	Bryan-College Station, Texas
Auburn, Alabama	Boulder, Colorado
College Park, Maryland	Clarksville, Tennessee

Sources: "America's 10 Fastest Growing College Towns," National Real Estate Investor, September 11, 2013, https://www.nreionline.com/node/31602/gallery?slide=10; John Egan, "The 12 College Towns That Are 'Growing like a Weed,'" Lawn Starter, April 4, 2016, https://www.lawnstarter.com/blog/city-rankings/fastest-growing-college-towns/.

definition of urban, and they will become more accessible with the rise of self-driving cars and countless forms of artificial intelligence. Some of the fastest growing metros worldwide are places like Wenatchee. The data show it. The main question for higher education planners is which colleges and universities are best positioned to capitalize. For example, census flags Georgetown, Texas, as one of these wildly attractive new places. Where is it? In the lush Hill Country with a quaint and walkable Old Town. Who benefits? Hello, Southwestern University. Hello, University of Texas-Round Rock, and, for that matter, hello Wenatchee Valley College.[3] Today it may simply be just a two-year school, but soon an ambitious president-in-waiting will discern and learn to control the powerful forces gathered within it.

This technology-driven premium on face-to-face interaction still privileges selectively, however. In the nineteenth century, a vast swath of colleges were romanticized as Arcadian glades, to be placed as far from the perceived poisons of the evil cities as possible. Success, however, was intermittent because college-town planners are now learning that rural locales are by no means the only model for succeeding at face-to-face. Another one is being utilized by my own university, Arizona State—the largest public research university in America and one of the fastest growing—surrounded by vast and colorful skies, mountains, and lush Sonoran desert.[4] Around its main campus, it is partnering on numerous fronts with the once-suburban town of Tempe to build walkable and engaging places that emphasize face-to-face, and around its downtown Phoenix campus, ASU also is contributing remarkably to revive a city that lacked a higher education identity.

All of this is to show that when the critical element is a game-changing, technology-enhanced premium on face-to-face, the creation of new kinds of college towns can be achieved through a variety of innovative, planning strategies. Put differently, Cambridge and Palo Alto no longer hold a monopoly on this type of growth. Keep in mind that competitors will be thinking very broadly about what constitutes the "college" in this new "college town," and future success stories may actually involve "knowledge enterprise" towns. Credible scenarios exist in which the current college and university campus format becomes dated and is left behind, even though it is difficult to imagine a future in which there are no institutions creating new knowledge and finding innovative uses for it. For example, new "colleges" that make Santa Fe the smart-person mecca it is today are the Los Alamos National Laboratory, the birthplace of the atomic bomb, and the Santa Fe Institute, a host for multidisciplinary complexity studies.[5] These generators of intellectual capital are prime examples of "knowledge enterprises" that new college towns will seek to incorporate into their evolving brands.

We now can return to Deep Springs College as the future of college towns.[6] Let's consider it not simply today, but also twenty years ahead when electric cars and artificial intelligence are common. Consider what being the smallest institution of higher learning in the United States means. At any given moment, the number of students on its 2,500-acre "campus" is fewer than thirty.[7] Even including faculty and staff, everyone at Deep Springs is not more than fifty individuals, and they are the only inhabitants of this high-desert California valley. Land-line phone service is spotty and mobile service is non-existent, as is television. Internet is by satellite. "Remote" and "rural" does not fully capture this new town, and yet, clearly, Deep Springs is "urbane." Its students study an eclectic curriculum that includes ancient Greek, genetics, biology, music, philosophy, political science, mathematics, literature and international relations. Two-thirds of its graduates earn degrees beyond the baccalaureate, and over half earn a doctorate. Deep Springs alumni have been awarded Rhodes and Truman Scholarships, three MacArthur "genius grants," two Pulitzers, and one Emmy.

This is in part because Deep Springs has embraced its isolation as central to its sophisticated educational experience. In the words of its founder, Lucien Lucius Nunn: "Gentlemen, for what came ye into the wilderness? . . . You came to prepare for a life of service, with the understanding that superior ability and generous purpose would be expected of you."[8] Deep Springs was learning-by-doing generations before that became a buzz phrase. The college describes itself in the following pragmatic ways:

> Deep Springs operates a cattle ranch and 155 acre alfalfa farm. The college sells both hay and beef cattle for a modest income, but the ranch and farm are maintained primarily for educational purposes.
>
> The ranch keeps about 200 head of beef cattle which graze throughout the valley and in the White Mountains. Working with the ranch manager, students perform much of the necessary ranch work, from herding cattle to shoeing horses to delivering calves. . . .
>
> Students often have the opportunity to tackle special short-term agricultural projects based on their own interests.[9]

Suppose, however, that in 2040, this reality sounds like nirvana to a growing percentage of the projected US population of 380 million, people who somehow managed to miss this kind of opportunity when they were undergraduates.[10] In this scenario, let us assume that the college will con-

Deep Springs College students and staff moving cattle. Wikimedia Commons

tinue to value its isolation but will also see the benefits in expanding its collaboration with Bishop, its local college town. Let us further suppose that electric cars and artificially intelligent aircraft can make the current four-to-six-hour drive to Deep Springs and Bishop from Los Angeles, Las Vegas, or San Francisco not only less taxing but even enjoyable. If so, and if face-to-face contact coupled with transformative technologies is shaping the experience in new American college towns, Deep Springs will be viewed as a pioneer and prototype.

Notes

Chapter 1. The New American College Town

1. Rawn, “Campus and the City,” 105.
2. Rawn, “Campus and the City,” 106–7.
3. Van Agtmael and Bakker, *The Smartest Place on Earth*, 207.
4. Davis, “There’s an Antidote to America’s Long Economic Malaise.”
5. Davis, “There’s an Antidote to America’s Long Economic Malaise.”
6. Susan Henderson, conversation with authors, March 9, 2017.
7. Morris, “What the iPhone Wrought.”
8. Rockwood and eds., “Always-On Education”; ADP Research Institute, “Evolution of Work 2.0.”
9. Hoffman, “Social Networks Will Help Education to Realize Its True Potential.”
10. Eugene Zdziarski, email to authors, August 14, 2017.
11. Phillip DiChiara, email to authors, August 14, 2017.
12. McKinnon, “Higher Ed Leaders Renew Their Vows.”
13. Douglas Belkin, “More U.S. Colleges Are Dropping Out,” *Wall Street Journal*, July 20, 2017, A-3.
14. Heathcote, “Urban Outfitters.”
15. Universum Top 100, “The Most Attractive Employers in the U.S.”
16. Kevin Drumm, email to authors, August 15, 2017.
17. Perry and Wiewel, “Ivory Towers No More,” in Perry and Wiewel, eds., *The University as Urban Developer*, 315.
18. Perry and Wiewel, “Ivory Towers No More,” 315.
19. Hale and Vina, “University Challenge.”
20. Tracee Reiser, email to authors, August 10, 2017.
21. Michael Winstanley, email to authors, August 16, 2017.
22. “Fort Kent Named 27th Business-Friendly Community,” *Bangor Daily News*, June 24, 2014, http://bangordailynews.com/bdn-maine/community/fort-kent-named-27th-business-friendly-community/.
23. Gerry Boyle, “Jumpstart: Colby-Led Collaboration Is Revitalizing Waterville’s Main Street and Shaping the City and the College for the Future,” *Colby Magazine* (Winter–Spring 2017): 27, 29, 30, 31.
24. “Morrisville State Welcomes Two Business Partners Approved under Start-Up NY,” Morrisville State College News Center, March 11, 2015, http://www.morrisville.edu/news/Article.aspx?id=22147#.WxLSGlOUvOR.
25. “Northern Essex Community College—Dr. Ibrahim El-Hefni Allied Health & Technology Center,” Mass.gov, accessed July 1, 2018, https://www.mass.gov/service-details/northern-essex-community-college-dr-ibrahim-el-hefni-allied-health-technology.
26. “New Outdoor Space Will Connect NECC with Lawrence Downtown,” *Northern Essex Community College Newsroom*, June 22, 2016, https://www.necc.mass.edu/newsroom/2016/06/22/new-outdoor-space-will-connect-necc-with-lawrence-downtown/
27. *The Best 382 Colleges, 2018 Edition.*

28. "The Princeton Review's 27th Annual College Rankings Revealed on Company's Site and in its Book, The Best 384 Colleges, 2019 Edition Available August 7th," *MarketWatch*, August 6, 2018, https://www.marketwatch.com/press-release/the-princeton-reviews-27th-annual-college-rankings-revealed-on-companys-site-and-in-its-book-the-best-384-colleges-2019-edition-available-august-7th-2018-08-06.

29. "Loyola University New Orleans Ranked No. 1 in the Nation for Town-Gown Relations by the Princeton Review," Loyola University New Orleans Press Release, Loyola Office of Public Affairs, External Relations Department, August 6, 2018, http://www.loyno.edu/news/story/2018/8/6/4126.

30. Greg Jarobe, "What Makes Lone Star College–University Park the 'Innovative College'?" Affordable College, August 30, 2016, http://www.affordablecollege.org/post/what-makes-lone-star-college-university-park-the-innovation-college.

31. Northwestern Medical BRANDVOICE, "Should You Retire to a College Town?"

32. Smith, "What the New Wave of Wireless Tech Can Do For Your Campus."

33. Bernico, "Complicating the Digital Divide."

34. Peters, "Tapping the Mighty Mississippi and Coastal Tides with Underwater Turbines."

35. Angel, *Planet of Cities*, 304.

36. "Responding to the Change in How Infrastructure Is Developed," *Think: Infrastructure Forum: A Discussion Series Presented by HNTB* (January 24, 2012), 8.

37. Mill Cities Leadership Institute, "About," Lawrence CommunityWorks, accessed July 28, 2017, https://www.lawrencecommunityworks.org/site/about-lawrence-community-works/.

38. "A Community Gateway," *Lafayette*, accessed July 2, 2018, https://www.lafayette.edu/college-town/community-gateway/.

39. Ian Whitaker, "UNLV Has Designs on a More Collegiate Feel," *Las Vegas Sun*, October 26, 2015, https://lasvegassun.com/news/2015/oct/26/unlv-has-designs-on-a-more-collegiate-feel/; "Grafton Hopes to Become a 'Collegetown,'" *Grafton News*, September 23, 2010.

40. "Memorandum of Understanding—SUNY Canton and SUNY Potsdam," SUNY Canton Online, accessed July 1, 2018, http://www.canton.edu/shared/pdf/Shared-Services-MOU.pdf.

41. "Why CAAT at Macomb Community College?" Center for Advanced Automotive Technology, accessed July 3, 2018, http://autocaat.org/About_CAAT/Why_CAAT_at_Macomb_Community_College/.

42. "Elko Campus," Great Basin College, accessed June 1, 2018, http://www.gbcnv.edu/campus/elko.html.

43. "De Anza College," Wikipedia.org, accessed July 28, 2018, https://en.wikipedia.org/wiki/De_Anza_College.

44. Jacobs, "50 Fittest College Towns in America, 2016–2017."

45. "Employment," Charlotte Checkers, AHL Internet Network, accessed June 1, 2018, http://gocheckers.com/team/employment.

46. Dixon, "The Best Minor League Baseball Towns of 2016."

47. "Community Colleges near Round Rock," CollegeSimply, accessed June 1, 2018, http://www.collegesimply.com/colleges-near/texas/round-rock/community-colleges/.

48. McMichael, "More Civilians Calling Military Bases Home."

49. Cary, "Best Military Bases to Retire Near."

50. Gavrich, "Golf College Towns."

51. Lott, "Get Smart!"

52. "About Us," Barnes & Noble College, accessed June 1, 2018, https://www.bncollege.com/about-us.

53. Wahba, "Exclusive: Barnes & Noble Seeks Big Expansion of Its College Stores."

54. Maya Sweedler, "Hotel Developers Head Back to School: Lodging-Industry Investors Turn to Properties in College Markets, Rooms for Homecoming," *Wall Street Journal*, August 28, 2018, https://www.wsj.com/articles/hotel-developers-get-into-school-1535454001.

55. Nancy Trejos, "Graduate Hotels Graduates into a Bigger Chain," *USA Today*, January 4, 2018, https://www.usatoday.com/story/travel/roadwarriorvoices/2018/01/04/graduate-hotels-graduates-bigger-chain/1002913001/.

56. Sweedler, "Hotel Developers Get into School."

57. "Impact Statistics: The Craft Brewing Industry Contributed $67.8 Billion to the U.S. Economy in 2016, more than 456,000 Jobs," Brewers Association, 2018, https://www.brewersassociation.org/statistics/economic-impact-data/.

58. Durisin, "Why Everyone Is Going Crazy for Craft Beer."

59. Lone Star College, "Minuti Café and Coffee Shop," accessed February 25, 2019, http://www.lonestar.edu/minuti-cyfair.htm; Canton State University of New York, "Computer Labs," accessed February 24, 2019, http://www.canton.edu/it/pc_facilities.html; Canton State University of New York, "Cyber Café Menu," accessed February 24, 2019, http://www.canton.edu/ca/dining/cyber_cafe.html; St. Louis Community College, "Center for Workforce Innovation," https://www.stlcc.edu/workforce/center-for-workforce-innovation/.

60. "The 50 Best College Towns to Live in Forever."

61. Murgia, "The Truth about Children and Social Media."

62. Tsukayama, "Teens Spend Nearly Nine Hours Every Day Consuming Media"; Murgia, "The Truth about Children and Social Media."

63. Pinker, The Village Effect, 282.

Chapter 2. Fostering an Effective Town-Gown Relationship

This chapter was cowritten by Michael Fox and Beth Bagwell, and Beth would like to acknowledge and thank Michael for his primary authorship.

1. Bruning, McGrew, and Cooper, "Town-Gown Relationships."

2. Nichols, *University-Community Relations*; Torres and Schaffer, *Benchmarks for Campus/Community Partnerships*; Gavazzi, *The Optimal Town-Gown Marriage*.

3. Goodman et al., "Identifying and Defining the Dimensions of Community Capacity to Provide a Basis for Measurement."

4. Gavazzi and Fox, "A Tale of Three Cities," 189.

5. Smith, "'Studentification': The Gentrification Factory?"; Torres and Schaffer, *Benchmarks for Campus/Community Partnerships*; Snyder, de Brey, and Dillow, "Digest of Education Statistics, 2015."

6. Crystal Burnette, Hailey Palmer, and Crossie Cox, "Clemson University and the City of Clemson—A Case Study in Collaboration," paper presented at the International Town & Gown Association Annual Conference, Chicago, 2016.

7. More details are available at University of Colorado–Boulder, "Off-Campus Housing & Neighborhood Relations," accessed May 15, 2018, http://ocss.colorado.edu.

8. David Ziomek, Nancy Buffone, and Tony Maroulis, "Blurring the Borders between Campus and Community: Creating a Town-Gown Committee for Shared Success," paper presented at the Annual International Town & Gown Association Conference, Chicago, 2016.

9. Lisa Dvorak, Bob Klett, Margaret Yackel, and Rosanne Proite, "ACT San Marcos: The Evolution of Solutions," paper presented at the Annual International Town & Gown Association Conference, Chicago, 2016.

10. Emily Allen, "Colorado State University & the City of Fort Collins: A Town/Gown Collaboration," Grand Forks [ND], September 16, 2015, http://www.grandforksgov.com/home/showdocument?id=8292.

11. Jeannie Ortega and Emily Allen, "Collaborative Partnerships: The Art of Using Town-Gown Relationships to Address Issues Surrounding Noise, Alcohol, Neighborhood Conflicts, and Common Student Pitfalls," paper presented at the United Kingdom Town & Gown Association Conference, November 15–16, 2016, Nottingham.

12. Suchitra Webster and Janet Lillie, "Data Driven Community Relations: Using Student Mapping Data to Advance the Conversation," paper presentation at the Annual International Town & Gown Association Conference, Eugene, OR, May 30–June 2, 2017.

13. Ziomek and Maroulis, "Blurring the Borders between Campus and Community."

14. "The ITGA Certificate in Town-Gown Relations Offered at the Annual Conference," International Town & Gown Association, 2018, accessed January 28, 2019, http://www.itga.org/certificateprogram.

15. Smith and Fox, "A Studentification Guide for North America."

16. Gavazzi, *The Optimal Town-Gown Marriage*.

17. Fox, Town and Gown.

18. Fox, Town and Gown.

Chapter 3. Urban-Serving Universities

1. Approximately 56 percent of all US college students (9.5 million) go to college in the fifty-two US metros with more than one million people, and more than a quarter (27.6 percent, or 4.7 million) attend school in just the nation's ten largest metros. New York, Los Angeles, Chicago, Boston, and Philadelphia have the largest student populations in the country. Florida, "The Reality of America's College Towns."

2. The Coalition for Urban Serving Universities defines a USU as a higher education institution "located in metro region with 450,000+ population; minimum of 10M research; offers doctoral programs." "About," Coalition of Urban Serving Universities, accessed October 15, 2018, http://usucoalition.org/about/overview.

3. Diner, *Universities and Their Cities*.

4. While USUs serve many beneficial roles, they also face many challenges. First-generation and low-income college students must overcome multiple barriers to completing college. Urban-serving universities have lower retention and graduation rates than traditional colleges and universities, and students often

require more services—for example, advising, mentoring, culturally specific supports—to succeed. These demands place pressure on already-strained budgets and are driving a focus on early and integrated interventions that keep students on track to graduation. Major foundations including Gates and Lumina are working with USUs across the country to develop degree maps, new advising strategies, and more effective articulation agreements with two-year colleges to help more students complete college in a timely fashion with limited debt.

5. Florida, "The Reality of America's College Towns." Florida notes that the vast majority of students attend college where they live. A much smaller proportion of students—the wealthy and most accomplished—move away to residential colleges.

6. Urban location and access to employment and jobs have also made USUs attractive to international students, who represent a key student enrollment growth area.

7. The Association of Public and Land-Grant Universities reports enormous growth in networks, organizations, journals, and awards centered on "university engagement" since 1990. While no more than a dozen networks, organizations, journals, and awards focused on engagement in the mid-1990s more than forty exist today. Prominent among these are the Coalition of Urban and Metropolitan Universities and the Coalition of Urban-Serving Universities, an affiliate of APLU. Laurie Van Egeren, "Scanning the Engagement Landscape: University Engagement by the Numbers," Association of Public & Land-Grant Universities and Council on Engagement & Outreach, September 2015, accessed February 2, 2019, http://www.aplu.org/members/councils/engagement-and-outreach/scanning-the-engagement-landscape.pdf.

8. Craft et al., "Anchoring the Community."

9. Craft et al., "Anchoring the Community," iii.

10. PSU's Capstone program has been well documented in the engagement literature. In fact, to mark the twentieth anniversary of PSU's implementation of the program, the Coalition of Urban and Metropolitan Universities dedicated an entire issue of the journal *Metropolitan Universities* to PSU's engagement agenda. See "Curricular Innovation: Engaged Capstones at Portland State University," special issue, *Metropolitan Universities* 26, no. 3 (January 2016).

11. The Carnegie Foundation's Classification for Community Engagement is elective, meaning that it is based on voluntary participation by institutions. It involves data collection and documentation of important aspects of institutional mission, identity, and commitments and requires participating institutions to invest substantial effort. It is an evidence-based documentation of institutional practice to be used in a process of self-assessment and quality improvement. The documentation is reviewed to determine whether the institution qualifies for recognition as a community-engaged institution. The classification runs on a five-year cycle. Currently, 240 US colleges and universities have the classification.

12. PSU defines strategic partners as business and civic entities that typically engage with multiple colleges and tap into a range of university assets, including faculty research, student labor, career services, contract research and service, and demonstration planning and development initiatives. Because of their complexity and the partners' strategic and political importance, these multifaceted partnerships require coordination, management, and regular reporting.

13. Storm Cunningham, "19 Higher-Education Anchor Institutions Pledge to Help Revitalize 5 New Jersey Cities," *Revitalization: The Journal of Urban, Rural & Environmental Resilience*, no. 53 (June 15, 2017). https://revitalization.org/article/19-new-jersey-colleges-universities-form-anchor-institution-coalition-help-revitalize-5-cities/#.XG7puZNKhTY.

14. Office of Research and Strategic Partnerships, Portland State University, 2014.

15. PSU's Engagement Agenda, as articulated in its current Strategic Plan, includes the following priorities: (1) support lifelong community engagement; (2) make PSU's engagement more visible and accessible; (3) enhance internship opportunities; (4) enhance PSU's role as an anchor institution by advancing strategic partnerships. "Strategic Plan," Portland State University, accessed October 20, 2018, https://www.pdx.edu/strategic-plan-extend-our-leadership-in-community-engagement.

16. "Public Engagement Council," Regents of the University of Minnesota, accessed October 20, 2018, https://engagement.umn.edu/about-engagement/public-engagement-council.

17. "Collaboratory: Track•Report•Connect•Plan," Institute for Community & Economic Engagement, University of North Carolina at Greensboro, accessed October 20, 2018, https://communityengagement.uncg.edu/the-collaboratory/.

18. Craft et al., "Anchoring the Community."

19. For the PSU-BPS partnership, Portland State won the prestigious McGrath Community Engagement Award in 2016 from the Association of Public and Land-Grant Universities.

Chapter 4. How College Towns Have Become Regional Economic Drivers

1. Peter Behr, "Bethlehem Steel Files for Bankruptcy," *Washington Post*, October 16, 2001, https://www.washingtonpost.com/archive/business/2001/10/16/bethlehem-steel-files-for-bankruptcy/ba652f60-f009-46c8-864e-20df5a8d2584/?utm_term=.41bf31a3f261.

2. "Community and Economic Revitalization in Bethlehem," The Intersector Project, accessed June 14, 2018, http://intersector.com/case/steelstacks_bethlehem/.

3. "Lehigh and Bethlehem Expand Their Partnership," *Lehigh University News*, November 17, 2015, https://www1.lehigh.edu/news/lehigh-and-bethlehem-expand-their-partnership.

4. Pearson, "Community Schools," accessed February 3, 2019.

5. "Lehigh University Center for Community Engagement," Lehigh University, accessed December 15, 2017, https://www.lehigh.edu/~inengage/.

6. Kelly Hochbein, "A Partnership for Better Mental Health," *Lehigh University News*, January 29, 2015, https://www1.lehigh.edu/news/partnership-better-mental-health.

Chapter 5. The Public Purpose of Higher Education

1. "Civic Action Plan Library," Campus Compact, accessed June 1, 2018, https://compact.org/actionstatement/civic-action-plans/.

2. "Connections," Connecticut College, accessed May 16, 2018, https://www.conncoll.edu/connections/.

3. "Holleran Center for Community Action and Public Policy," Connecticut College, accessed May 12, 2018, https://www.conncoll.edu/academics/majors-departments-programs/majors-and-minors/holleran-center/; "Community Learning and Engagement," Connecticut College, accessed May 12, 2018, https://www.conncoll.edu/community-partnerships/; "The Otto and Fran Walter Commons for Global Study and Engagement," Connecticut College, accessed May 12, 2018, https://www.conncoll.edu/academics/global-focus/.

Chapter 6. Starting from Scratch

1. "Best College Rankings: National Liberal Arts Colleges," *U.S. News and World Report*, 2017, accessed June 14, 2018, https://web.archive.org/web/20170608031511/https://www.usnews.com/best-colleges/rankings/national-liberal-arts-colleges.

2. Detweiller, "From Learning to Life."

3. Richard Longworth, "Liberal Arts and the Post-Industrial Midwest," *Midwesterner*, The Chicago Council on Global Affairs, September 16, 2014, https://www.thechicagocouncil.org/themidwesterner/liberal-arts-and-post-industrial-midwest.

4. Belkin, "To Save Themselves, Small Colleges Offer Lifeline to Their Hometowns."

5. Catherine Kerley, "Albion Businesses Look to 2018 with Renewed Hope," *Albion Recorder* (January 4, 2018), 1.

6. Schultz, *Boomtown USA*.

7. Lorin Ditzler, "The Power of the Porch," *The Review* (Michigan Municipal League), September–October 2017, http://www.mml.org/resources/publications/mmr/issues/sept-oct2017/Review_Sept-Oct_2017_Release.pdf, 16–18.

8. Lorin Ditzler, "Chemistry Professor's Blues 'Experiment' Catalyzes Small Town Culture Revival," *Daily Yonder*, June 7, 2017, https://www.dailyyonder.com/chemistry-professors-blues-experiment-catalyzes-small-town-cultural-revival/2017/06/07/19109/.

Chapter 7. A Plan for Brooklyn

1. "About," Opportunity Insights (formerly The Equality of Opportunity Project), accessed October 15, 2018, https://opportunityinsights.org/policy/.

2. "Saint Francis College," The Upshot, *New York Times*, accessed October 20, 2018, https://www.nytimes.com/interactive/projects/college-mobility/saint-francis-college.

3. Joseph Berger, "Frank Macchiarola, Called the 'Standard' for a New York Schools Chief, Dies at 71," *New York Times*, December 18, 2012, https://www.nytimes.com/2012/12/19/nyregion/frank-macchiarola-highly-regarded-new-york-schools-chancellor-dies-at-71.html.

4. "About," Brooklyn Chamber of Commerce, accessed October 20, 2018, http://www.ibrooklyn.com/about-us.

5. "History and Mission," St. Francis College, accessed October 20, 2018, https://www.sfc.edu/about/historymission.

6. For a discussion of Franciscan Charism, see "Module 1—Charism," Association of Franciscan Colleges and Universities, accessed February 28, 2019, http://franciscancollegesuniversities.org/portfolio-view/module-1-charism/.

7. "About," Association of Franciscan Colleges and Universities, accessed October 10, 2018, https://franciscancollegesuniversities.org/.

8. "The Inauguration of President Miguel Martinez-Saenz: St. Francis College to Celebrate 19th President—Jan. 17–27," *St. Francis College News*, December 15, 2017, https://www.sfc.edu/cf_news/view.cfm?newsid=778.

9. "About," *Lyrics from Lockdown*, accessed October 20, 2018, http://www.lyricsfromlockdown.com/.

10. "College Opportunities for the Formerly Incarcerated," Academics, St. Francis College, accessed October 20, 2018, https://www.sfc.edu/academics/institutescenters/postprison.

Chapter 8. Right Place, Right Time

1. "Institutional Profile: New Jersey City University, 2015–2016," State of New Jersey, Office of the Secretary of Higher Education, 2016, accessed February 6, 2019, https://www.nj.gov/highereducation/IP/IP2016/PDF/NJCU.pdf.

2. "NCJU School of Business to Relocate to Jersey City's Financial District," *NJCU Newsroom*, February 4, 2015, http://newsroom.njcu.edu/news/njcu-school-business-to-relocate-to-jersey-citys-financial-district.htm.

3. Briana Vannozzi, "NJCU to Relocate School of Business to Heart of Jersey City's Financial District," *NJTV News*, April 15, 2015, https://www.njtvonline.org/news/video/njcu-to-relocate-school-of-business-to-heart-of-jersey-citys-financial-district/.

4. Vannozzi, "NJCU to Relocate School of Business."

5. Matthew Speiser, "NJCU Business School Plans to Turn 'Wall Street West' into Learning Environment," *NJ.com*, posted February 10, 2015, http://www.nj.com/hudson/index.ssf/2015/02/njcu_opening_new_downtown_business_school_this_fal.html.

6. Nicholas Zeitlinger, "NJTV to Broadcast Business News Segment from Jersey City University," *NJ.com*, posted June 2, 2016, http://www.nj.com/hudson/index.ssf/2016/06/njcu_to_work_with_njtv_on_new_weekly_business_segm.html.

7. Erika Solorzano, "NJCU Breaks Ground for New $50 Million Dormitory at 'West Campus,'" *NJ.com*, May 14, 2015, http://www.nj.com/hudson/index.ssf/2015/05/njcu_breaks_ground_for_west_side_student_resident.html.

8. Solorzano, "NJCU Breaks Ground for New $50 Million Dormitory."

9. "The Hampshire Companies, Claremont Companies and Circle Squared Alternative Investments Celebrate Groundbreaking of University Place in Jersey City," Circle Squared Alternative Investments, September 12, 2016, http://www.circlesquaredalts.com/the-hampshire-companies-claremont-companies-and-circle-squared-alternative-investments-celebrate-groundbreaking-of-university-place-in-jersey-city/.

10. PILOT, or payments in lieu of tax, are "federal payments to local governments that help offset losses in property taxes due to non-taxable Federal lands within their boundaries." See "Payments in Lieu of Taxes," U.S. Department of the Interior, accessed February 28, 2019, https://www.doi.gov/pilt.

Chapter 9. Community College Towns

1. Carey, "On the Immense Good Fortune of Higher Education."

2. Filion et al., "The Successful Few."

3. Jon Connolly, email to author, August 30, 2017.

4. Filion et al., "The Successful Few."

5. Filion et al., "The Successful Few," 328. Twelve of the nineteen top downtowns in the 2004 study were in college towns.

6. Adhya, "College Towns as a Model of Sustainable Placemaking."

7. Paul Young, email to author, August 30, 2017.

8. Florida, *Rise of the Creative Class*.

Chapter 10. How Planners Work

Portions of this chapter appeared earlier in "In Perfect (Imperfect) Harmony: Keene State College and Keene Rebalance Community Relations Through Historic Preservation" by Jay Kahn in *Planning for Higher Education Journal* 39, no. 3 (April-June 2011), a special themed issue entitled Integrated Planning to Ensure the Preservation of Campus Heritage.

1. Phillip Faulkner, "Heritage Commission Report to City Council on the KSC Alumni Center," City of Keene Heritage Commission, 2008; Heritage Commission, Ord. No. 0-2002-05, § 0817.4, 7-18-2002, Secs. 2-835-2-862, City of Keene, NH, 2010.

2. "Alumni Center at Keene State College," Weller and Michel Architects, Inc., accessed October 20, 2018, http://www.wapm.com/portfolio/alumni-center-at-keene-state-college/.

3. Klopott, cited in Kahn, "In Perfect (Imperfect) Harmony," 163.

4. Faulkner, "Heritage Commission Report."

5. Kahn, "In Perfect (Imperfect) Harmony."

6. Freeman Klopott, "College Looking at Other Options," *Keene Sentinel* (December 6, 2007), n.p.; Jake Berry, "City Okay with College Plan," *Keene Sentinel* (March 14, 2008), n.p.

7. Ordinance 2010-07, relating to establishment of the Sustainable Energy Efficient Development (SEED) Overlay, City of Keene, July 2010.

Chapter 11. How Architects Envision College Towns Today and Tomorrow

1. "About," DLR Group, accessed June 4, 2018, http://www.dlrgroup.com/about/.

2. "Work: Pinnacle Bank Arena," DLR Group, accessed June 7, 2018, http://www.dlrgroup.com/work/pinnacle-bank-arena/.

3. Robby Korth, "Lincoln's Pinnacle Bank Arena Blends Retro, Modern to Create New Haymarket Identity," *Omaha World-Herald*, May 22, 2013, https://www.omaha.com/news/lincoln-s-pinnacle-bank-arena-blends-retro-modern-to-create/article_4693361e-1f15-54f9-bf94-0000eab59924.html.

4. Melissa Lindberg, "DLR Group's University of Nebraska Arena Project: Designer Forum," *Floor Daily*, accessed June 6, 2018, https://www.floordaily.net/floorfocus/dlr-groups-university-of-nebraska-arena-project-.

5. Fain, "Completion Comes First."

6. Benedictine University, "Benedictine's New Goodwin Hall Open for Business Education, Innovation," *Cision PR Newswire*, October 22, 2015, https://www.prnewswire.com/news-releases/benedictines-new-goodwin-hall-open-for-business-education-innovation-300164985.html.

7. "SCC's Newly Renovated Library Now Open," *SCC News*, August 17, 2016, https://news.scottsdalecc.edu/post/2016/08/sccs-newly-renovated-library-now-open.

8. Mariel Williams, "Performing Arts Center Dedicated," *Temple Daily Telegram*, October 13, 2017, http://www.tdtnews.com/news/article_6a6e78dc-b08d-11e7-b765-330fe879cbf8.html.

9. "Housing: Panoramic Residences," California College of the Arts, accessed July 15, 2018, https://www.cca.edu/students/housing/halls/panoramic.

10. This project was led by Stuart Rothenberger prior to joining DLR Group.

11. "Salve's O'Hare Academic Center Debuts Renovated Classroom Wing," *SALVEtoday*, September 8, 2015, http://today.salve.edu/ohare-academic-center-debuts-renovated-classroom-wing/.

12. Additional best practices to consider:

Handling deferred maintenance for physical and programmatic quality

- Oberlin College: Bibbins Hall
- Santa Barbara College: Humanities Building
- Oklahoma State University: College of Human Sciences

Place-making and "curb appeal"—enhancing wayfinding and the visitor perspective

- Kent State University: Franklin Hall
- Lake Erie College: Austin Science Center
- University of Wyoming, Laramie: Rochelle Gateway Center

Fundraising and partnerships—evolving strategies and innovations

- Riverside College: Nursing and Allied Health Education Building
- St. Catherine University: Interior Design Studio at Market Square Design Center
- Arapahoe Community College: Sturm Collaboration Campus

Learning spaces, instruction, and research—remodeled and repurposed

- University of Northern Iowa, Schindler School of Education
- Case Western University: Mandel School of Applied Social Sciences
- Hillsdale College: Allan P. Kirby Jr. Center for Constitutional Studies and Citizenship

Libraries and learning commons—transforming collections into collaboration

- Diné College, Shiprock Campus: Senator John D. Pinto Library
- Harbor College, Los Angeles Community College District: Library and Learning Resource Center
- University of Nebraska, Lincoln: C. Y. Thompson Library and Learning Commons

Arts and cultural centers—promoting community and diversity

- Playhouse Square: colocation of professional performing arts, public broadcasting and higher education for Kent State University Cleveland Urban Design Collaborative, Case Western Reserve University Theater, and Cleveland State University Arts and Theater
- University of California, Los Angeles: Yitzhak Rabin Hillel Center for Jewish Life
- University of Minnesota: Cultural Center

Residence halls—teaching old facilities new tricks and building new
College of St. Benedict, St. Joseph, MN: Student Townhome Community
University of Colorado, Denver: Auraria Student Lofts Residence Hall
University of Texas Austin and Austin Community College: University Towers Residence Hall Renovation

Student centers and services—focusing on convenience, diversity, and wellness
Swarthmore College: Dining & Community Commons
Laramie County Community College, Cheyenne, WY: Pathfinder One-Stop Student Center
Los Angeles Southwest College, Los Angeles CC District: Student Union

Chapter 12. What Mayors Think

Kate Rousmaniere, James Martin, and James E. Samels would like to thank the following mayors for contributing their time and advice to this chapter:
Todd D. Barton, Crawfordsville, Indiana (Wabash University)
Tim Kearney, Borough of Swarthmore, Pennsylvania (Swarthmore College)
Steve Patterson, Athens, Ohio (Ohio University)
Kate Rousmaniere, Oxford, Ohio (Miami University)
Jerry Smith, DeKalb, Illinois (University of Northern Illinois)
Jim Throgmorton, Iowa City, Iowa (University of Iowa)
Lucy Vinis, Eugene, Oregon (University of Oregon)

1. Waltz, *Theory of International Politics*, 192.

2. Fox, *Town and Gown*. The International Town & Gown Association (ITGA) offers invaluable resources on town-gown relations. Fox's work speaks specifically to municipal and governmental relations in town-gown work. See also the handbook by Kemp, *Town and Gown Relations*.

3. Barber, *If Mayors Ruled the World*.

4. Fallows and Fallows, *Our Towns*.

Chapter 13. Money Matters

1. "About the Ignite Program," Grinnell College, accessed April 15, 2018, https://www.grinnell.edu/about/offices-services/community-enhancement/ignite/about.

2. "Pete Brownell: Giving Back to Those Who Give All," NRA Ring of Freedom, accessed May 19, 2018, via Internet Archive Wayback Machine, https://web.archive.org/web/20170617152723/https:/www.nraringoffreedom.com/our-members/pete-brownell/.

3. Seltzer, "Grinnell's Gun Connection."

4. "UCI Receives $200 Million gift to Name College of Health Sciences and Launch Major Integrative Health Initiative," *UCI News*, September 18, 2017, https://news.uci.edu/2017/09/18/uci-receives-200-million-gift-to-name-college-of-health-sciences-and-launch-major-integrative-health-initiative/.

5. Teresa Watanabe, "UC Irvine Aims to Transform Public Health with Record-Breaking $200-Million Donation," *Los Angeles Times*, September 18, 2017, http://www.latimes.com/local/lanow/la-me-uc-irvine-donation-20170918-story.html.

6. Michael Hiltzik, "A $200-Million Donation Threatens to Tar UC Irvine's Medical School as a Haven for Quacks," *Los Angeles Times*, September 22, 2017, http://www.latimes.com/business/hiltzik/la-fi-hiltzik-uci-samueli-20170922-story.html.

7. Steven Novella, "Quackademic Medicine at UC Irvine," *Science-Based Medicine*, September 20, 2017, https://sciencebasedmedicine.org/quackademic-medicine-at-uc-irvine/.

8. Seltzer, "Does $200 Million Quack?"

9. Melissa Korn and Christina Rexrode, "Banks Pay Big Bucks for Top Billing on College Campuses," *Wall Street Journal*, January 28, 2018, https://www.wsj.com/articles/banks-pay-big-bucks-for-top-billing-on-college-campuses-1517148001.

10. Seltzer, "Funneling Students to Bank Fees?"

11. "Durbin Urges Wells Fargo to Halt Any Plans to Expand Presence on College Campuses," Dick Durban: United States Senator, Illinois, March 7, 2018, https://www.durbin.senate.gov/newsroom/press-releases/durbin-urges-wells-fargo-to-halt-any-plans-to-expand-presence-on-college-campuses.

12. Ball State University Miller College of Business Center for Business and Economic Research (CBER), "Memorandum: Recent Studies of Muncie and Related School Corporations," March 15, 2017, CBER Data Center, https://projects.cberdata.org/reports/MuncieSchools-20170315.pdf.

13. Seltzer, "A University-Run School District?"

14. Stephanie Wiechmann, "Ball State Formally Begins Muncie Schools Takeover," *Indiana Public Media*, May 17, 2018, https://indianapublicmedia.org/news/ball-state-formally-begins-muncie-schools-takeover-147767/.

15. Seth Slabaugh, "Teachers Union Hopeful after Ball State Takeover Presentation," *Star Press*, May 17, 2018, https://www.thestarpress.com/story/news/local/2018/05/17/teachers-union-hopeful-after-ball-sate-takeover-presentation/619238002/.

16. Seltzer, "A University-Run School District?"

17. Seltzer, "Problems beyond the $306M Dorm."

18. Seltzer, "Bethune-Cookman Sues Over Expensive Dormitory Deal."

19. Seltzer, "Developer Countersues Bethune-Cookman."

Chapter 14. Hidden Opportunities and Challenges in the College Town Job Market

1. Elise Stevens, "The History of Old Main," Penn State World Campus, October 30, 2012, https://blog.worldcampus.psu.edu/2012/10/the-history-of-old-main/. See also "Penn State's Historic Old Main," About Penn State, PennState, accessed June 20, 2018, http://www.psu.edu/ur/about/oldmainhistory.html.

2. Thelin, *History of American Higher Education*, 68.

3. Gumprecht, *American College Town*, 1.

4. Thelin, 357–358.

5. For further discussion, see Evan Comen and Michael B. Sauter, "The Largest Employer in Every State," *24/7 Wall St.*, March 17, 2017, http://247wallst.com/special-report/2017/03/17/largest-employer-in-every-state/; Jeff Desjardins, "Walmart Nation: Mapping the Largest Employers in the U.S," *Visual Capitalist*, November 17, 2017, http://www.visualcapitalist.com/walmart-nation-mapping-largest-employers-u-s/.

6. "News & Announcements," Carnegie Classification of Institutions of Higher Education, accessed July 1, 2018, http://carnegieclassifications.iu.edu/.

7. Tracy Hooker, email to author, September 1, 2017.

8. Greater Madison Convention & Visitors Bureau, "Rankings," Destination Madison, accessed July 8, 2018, https://www.visitmadison.om/media/rankings/; Mark Rickenbach, email to author, January 26, 2018.

9. Deborah Haynes, email to author, January 31, 2018.

10. Albert A. Liddicoat, email to author, February 9, 2018.

11. Tracy Hooker, email to author, September 1, 2017.

12. Mark Rickenbach, email to author, January 26, 2018.

13. Jessica Haynes, "Tourism Brings More Than $1 Billion to Washtenaw County, Report Says," MLive, January 4, 2018, https://www.mlive.com/business/ann-arbor/index.ssf/2018/01/tourism_in_washtenaw_county_br.html.

14. "Facts + Figures," University of Michigan: U-M + Ann Arbor, accessed July 1, 2018, http://communityrelations.umich.edu/facts-figures/.

15. Town Gown Initiative Team, "Guiding Concepts for the Town-Gown Initiatives Team," International Town & Gown Association, accessed July 28, 2018, http://www.itga.org/userfiles/files/TGIT.pdf.

16. Abel and Deitz, "Do Colleges and Universities Increase Their Region's Human Capital?"

17. Abel and Deitz, "How Colleges and Universities can Help Their Local Economies."

18. David Lewis, email to author, January 19, 2018.

19. Lewis, email to author, January 19, 2018.

Chapter 15. Student Expectations and Student Needs

1. "Chicago Quarter (Autumn)—Discover & Explore Chicago," DePaul University, Liberal Studies Program, accessed July 29, 2018, https://academics.depaul.edu/liberal-studies/first-year-program/Pages/chicago-quarter.aspx.

2. University of Maryland, "Off Campus Living Fair," accessed February 21, 2019, https://www.oclf.umd.edu/.

3. "About us," National Night Out, National Association of Town Watch, accessed May 4, 2018, https://natw.org/about.

4. Examples of community ambassador programs include "Community Ambassador Program," Oregon State University, Office of Student Life, accessed May 7, 2018, http://studentlife.oregonstate.edu/ccr/community-and-u/community-ambassador-program; "Salam Ambassadors," Inside Roanoke, Roanoke College, accessed May 8, 2018, https://www.roanoke.edu/inside/a-z_index/student_affairs/departments/dean_of_students_office/salem_ambassadors; University of Albany's off-campus ambassadors, described in "UAlbany's Off-Campus Ambassadors Aim to Ease Town-Gown Relations," *timesunion*, August 24, 2015, http://www.timesunion.com/tuplus-local/article/UAlbany-s-off-campus-ambassadors-aim-to-ease-6461118.php; and "Off Campus Ambassadors," University of Florida Off Campus Life, accessed May 3, 2018, http://www.offcampus.ufl.edu/off_campus_ambassadors/.

5. Ehrlich, *Civic Responsibility and Higher Education.*

6. "The Event," UT Night at the Austin Trail of Lights, accessed July 28, 2018, https://austintrailoflights.org/the-event; "About," Olde Salem Days, accessed May 25, 2018, http://www.oldesalemdays.com/?page_id=527.

7. "2018 Pride Parade Line of March," Chicago Pride Parade, accessed July 28, 2018, http://www.chicagopridecalendar.org/lineup.html.

8. Katrina Tulloch, "Syracuse Spring Sports Leagues Begin Soon: Sign Up Now for Kickball, Ultimate Frisbee and Bocce," *Syracuse.com*, April 2, 2014, https://www.syracuse.com/entertainment/index.ssf/2014/04/syracuse_spring_sports_for_adults.html.

Chapter 16. Las Vegas

1. "COE Collaborations," UNLV College of Education, accessed October 20, 2018, http://education.unlv.edu/collaboration/.

2. "Life Lessons from the Debate," *UNLV News Center*, September 16, 2016, https://www.unlv.edu/news/article/life-lessons-debate.

3. "2016 Presidential Debate Lecture Series," University of Nevada, Las Vegas, accessed October 20, 2018, https://www.unlv.edu/2016debate/lectures.

4. Colton Lochhead, "Hosting Presidential Debate Worth $114M in Publicity for UNLV," *Las Vegas Review-Journal*, December 1, 2016, https://www.reviewjournal.com/news/politics-and-government/hosting-presidential-debate-worth-114m-in-publicity-for-unlv/.

5. "Mission & History," Nevada State College, accessed October 20, 2018, http://archive.nsc.edu/about/mission-and-history/index.aspx.

6. "UNLVolunteers," University of Nevada, Las Vegas, accessed October 20, 2018, https://www.unlv.edu/service/unlvolunteers.

7. Ana Ley, "UNLV Hope Scholars Program Aims to Connect Homeless Students to College," *Las Vegas Review-Journal*, July 9, 2016, https://www.reviewjournal.com/news/education/unlv-hope-scholars-program-aims-to-connect-homeless-students-to-college/.

8. Michele Rindels and Jackie Valley, "After Tragedy Comes Recovery: How Las Vegas Is Mobilizing to Heal a Wounded Community," *Nevada Independent*, October 15, 2017, https://thenevadaindependent.com/article/after-tragedy-comes-recovery-how-las-vegas-is-mobilizing-to-heal-a-wounded-community.

Chapter 17. Remote and Ready to Partner

1. "Undergraduate Enrollment," IES-NCES, updated May 2018, accessed February 21, 2019, https://nces.ed.gov/programs/coe/indicator_cha.asp.

2. Lizzie O'Leary and Cerise Castle, "Are College Towns the Cure for a Slumping U.S. Economy?" *Marketplace*, January 3, 2017, https://www.marketplace.org/2017/01/03/economy/could-college-towns-be-answer-slumping-economy.

3. Beth Bagwell, email to author, February 27, 2018.

4. I received comments from six college presidents in small towns via Survey Monkey in April 2018.

5. Presidents' comments via Survey Monkey, April 2018

6. Caylor Solutions, on its own initiative, created "20 Ideas for Higher Education." Number 11 on the list is "Adopt Your Town." See Christian Higher Education Futures Panel, Caylor Solutions, "20 Ideas for Higher Education," 20 Ideas.org, updated March 2014, accessed February 12, 2019, www.20Ideas.org/models-for-education/.

7. Todd Voss, email to the author, April 2, 2018.

8. Michael Scales, email to the author, April 4, 2018.

9. Scales, email to the author, April 4, 2018.

Chapter 18. Collaboration Is Complex

1. Lochridge and Rosenzweig, *Enlightenment Incorporated*, 78.
2. Fairtlough, *Getting Things Done*, 34.
3. Collins, *Good to Great and the Social Sectors*, 5, 10.
4. Armacost, *Collaborative Ventures*.
5. Rubin, *Collaborative Leadership*, 2–3.
6. Zimpher, "'Systemness.'"
7. Arrow, McGrath, and Berdahl, *Small Groups as Complex Systems*, 33.
8. Drath, *The Deep Blue Sea*, 31–61.
9. Ramaswamy and Gouillart, *The Power of Co-creation*, 35–70.
10. Saint-Onge and Wallace, *Leveraging Communities of Practice for Strategic Advantage*, 77–117.
11. DiChiara, "A New Way to Design and Deliver Higher Education Consortia."

Chapter 19. A College Town Legal Primer

1. Kaplan and Lee, *Law of Higher Education*, 1167–70.
2. See *Cornell University v. Bagnardi*, 68 NY2d 583 (1986), at 593.
3. See *Trustees of Union College v. Members of the Schenectady City Council*, 667 N.Y.S.2d 978, 91 N.Y.2d 161 (1997).
4. See *Trustees of Boston College v. Board of Aldermen of Newton*, 58 Mass. App. Ct. 794 (2003).
5. *People v. Rancho College*, 226 Cal. App. 3d 1281, 277 Cal. Rptr. 69 (1990); quotation at 1287.
6. "About," Dukakis Center for Urban and Regional Policy, accessed July 17, 2018, https://www.northeastern.edu/csshresearch/dukakiscenter/.
7. Bluestone, Maloney, and White, "A Primer on University-Community Housing Partnerships."
8. Laura Krantz, "City Asks for Payments; Most Colleges Don't Pay in Full," *Boston Globe*, August 18, 2017, https://www.bostonglobe.com/metro/2017/08/18/city-asks-for-payments-most-colleges-don-pay-full/KnZ5ZRx0QMhrB5FA6NJZxN/story.html.
9. "Payment in Lieu of Tax (PILOT) Program: Fiscal Year 2016 Payment in Lieu of Tax Program Results," City of Boston, accessed July 17, 2018, https://www.boston.gov/departments/assessing/payment-lieu-tax-pilot-program.
10. "Smart Growth and Colleges and Universities," US Environmental Protection Agency, accessed July 18, 2018, https://www.epa/gov/smartgrowth/smart-growth-and-colleges-and-universities.
11. Dalbey et al., "Communities of Opportunity," 11.
12. "About Goodwin: Redevelopment," Goodwin College, accessed July 17, 2018, http://www.goodwin.edu/about/redevelopment.
13. "University Civic Engagement," Drexel University, accessed July 17, 2018, http://drexel.edu/about/civic-engagement/.
14. N. J. Slabbert, "The Ever-Vexed Town-Gown Relationship," Governing the States and Localities, July 27, 2015, http://www.governing.com/gov-institute/voices/col-college-university-town-gown-relationship.html.
15. "Port Richmand Partnership," Wagner College, Center for Leadership and Community Engagement, accessed July 18, 2018, http://wagner.edu/engage/port-richmond-partnership/.

16. "Port Richmand Partnership,"

17. "About," MetroLab Network, accessed July 18, 2018, https://metrolabnetwork.org/about/.

18. "Projects," MetroLab Network, accessed July 18, 2018, https://metrolabnetwork.org/projects/.

19. Department of Justice, Office of Justice Programs, Bureau of Justice Statistics, *Campus Law Enforcement, 2011–2012* (2015).

20. Dean, "Town vs. Gown: From Conflict to Collaboration," 44.

21. "The Disaster Management Cycle," Global Development Research Center, accessed September 20, 2018, https://www.gdrc.org/uem/disasters/1-dm_cycle.html.

22. Martin and Samels, "Higher Ed to the Rescue."

23. Carey Reed, "Dutch Nursing Home Offers Rent-Free Housing to Students," *PBS Newshour*, April 5, 2015, https://www.pbs.org/newshour/world/dutch-retirement-home-offers-rent-free-housing-students-one-condition.

24. "Intergenerational Living," Global Living Network, accessed July 18, 2018, http://globalageing.org/intergenerational-living/.

Chapter 20. Get Ready

1. "Bishop, California," *Wikipedia*, accessed July 20, 2018, https://en.wikipedia.org/wiki/Bishop,_California; "Deep Springs College," *Wikipedia*, accessed July 20, 2018, https://en.wikipedia.org/wiki/Deep_Springs_College

2. This data can be found at Joel Garreau, "Edge City: Life on the New Frontier," The Garreau Group, 2007, accessed June 16, 2018, https://www.garreau.com.

3. "About," Wenatchee Valley College, accessed July 20, 2018, https://www.wvc.edu/about/index.html.

4. "A Year In Review," Arizona State University, accessed July 1, 2018, https://annualreport.asu.edu/.

5. Los Alamos National Laboratory, accessed July 30, 2018, http://www.lanl.gov/; Santa Fe Institute, accessed July 30, 2018, https://www.santafe.edu/.

6. "What Is Deep Springs?" Deep Springs College, accessed July 20, 2018, https://www.deepsprings.edu/about/.

7. Rory Carroll, "Deep Springs College: The School for Cowboys Gets Ready for Cowgirls," *The Guardian*, December 14, 2012, https://www.theguardian.com/world/2012/dec/14/school-for-cowboys-deep-springs-college.

8. Carroll, "Deep Springs College."

9. "Farm and Ranch Facilities," Deep Springs College, accessed July 20, 2018, https://www.deepsprings.edu/labor/farm-ranch-facilities/.

10. "Population Projections for the United States from 2015," statista: The Statistics Portal, accessed July 2, 2018, https://www.statista.com/statistics/183481/united-states-population-projection/.

Bibliography

Abel, Jaison R., and Richard Deitz. "Do Colleges and Universities Increase Their Region's Human Capital?" *Journal of Economic Geography* 12, no. 3 (2012): 667–91.

———. "How Colleges and Universities Can Help Their Local Economies." *Liberty Street Economics* (blog). Federal Reserve Bank of New York, February 13, 2012. http://libertystreeteconomics.newyorkfed.org/2012/02/how-colleges-and-universities-can-help-their-local-economies.html.

Adhya, Anirban. "College Towns as a Model of Sustainable Placemaking: Learning from Two Successful College Towns in Small Metropolitan Regions." *AIA Report on University Research*, vol. 5. Southfield, MI: Lawrence Technological University, College of Architecture and Design, December 1, 2011. https://www.brikbase.org/sites/default/files/aiab092657.pdf.

ADP Research Institute. "Evolution of Work 2.0: The Me vs. We Mindset." *Forbes* (April 25, 2017): 77.

Angel, Shlomo. *Planet of Cities*. Cambridge, MA: Lincoln Institute of Land Policy, 2012.

Armacost, Mary-Linda. *Collaborative Ventures*. New York: Teagle Foundation, 2002.

Arrow, Holly, Joseph McGrath, and Jennifer Berdahl. *Small Groups as Complex Systems*. London: Sage, 2000.

Barber, Benjamin R. *If Mayors Ruled the World: Dysfunctional Nations, Rising Cities*. New Haven: Yale University Press, 2013.

———. "To Save Themselves, Small Colleges Offer Lifeline to Their Hometowns." *Wall Street Journal*, December 21, 2016. https://www.wsj.com/articles/to-save-themselves-small-colleges-offer-lifeline-to-their-hometowns-1482316200.

Bernico, Matt. "Complicating the Digital Divide: Technological Innovation in a Small Town." *The Society Pages*, Cyborgology, October 19, 2015. https://thesocietypages.org/cyborgology/2015/10/19/complicating-the-digital-divide-technological-innovation-in-a-small-town/.

The Best 382 Colleges, 2018 Edition. New York: Princeton Review, 2017.

Bluestone, Barry, Richard Maloney, and Eleanor White. "A Primer on University-Community Housing Partnerships." Center for Urban and Regional Policy, Northeastern University, May 2003. Accessed February 12, 2019. https://community-wealth.org/sites/clone.community-wealth.org/files/downloads/paper-bluestone-maloney-white03.pdf.

Bruning, Stephen, Shea McGrew, and Mark Cooper. "Town-Gown Relationships: Exploring University-Community Engagement from the Perspective of Community Members." *Public Relations Review* 32, no. 2 (2006):125–30.

Carey, Kevin. "On the Immense Good Fortune of Higher Education." *Chronicle of Higher Education*, September 1, 2014. https://www.chronicle.com/article/On-the-Immense-Good-Fortune-/148541.

Cary, Jennifer. "Best Military Bases to Retire Near." *ClearanceJobs.com*, April 14, 2014. https://news.clearancejobs.com/2014/04/14/best-military-bases-retire-near/.

Collins, Jim. *Good to Great and the Social Sectors: A Monograph to Accompany* Good to Great. New York: Collins, 2005.

Craft, Andrea, Shari Garmise, Ali Modarres, David Perry, and Natalia Viillamizar-Duarte. "Anchoring the Community: The Deepening Role of Urban Universities." Coalition of Urban Serving Universities, 2016. http://usucoalition.org/documents/Anchoring_the_Community_APLU_USU_2016_Survey_Report_fnl.pdf.

Cunningham, Storm. "19 Higher-Education Anchor Institutions Pledge to Help Revitalize 5 New Jersey Cities." *Revitalization: The Journal of Urban, Rural & Environmental Resilience*, no. 53 (June 15, 2017). https://revitalization.org/article/19-new-jersey-colleges-universities-form-anchor-institution-coalition-help-revitalize-5-cities/#.XG7puZNKhTY.

Dalbey, Matthew, Kevin Nelson, Peggy Bagnoli, David Bagnoli, Martha Droge, and Anna Marie Cirino. *Communities of Opportunity: Smart Growth Strategies for Colleges and Universities*. Washington, DC: National Association of College and University Business Officers, 2007. https://community-wealth.org/sites/clone.community-wealth.org/files/downloads/report-dalbey-et-al.pdf.

Davis, Bob. "There's an Antidote to America's Long Economic Malaise: College Towns." *Wall Street Journal*, January 5, 2017. https://www.wsj.com/articles/theres-an-antidote-to-americas-long-economic-malaise-college-towns-1481558522.

Dean, Paul. "Town vs. Gown: From Conflict to Collaboration." *Campus Law Enforcement Journal* 47, no. 2 (March–April 2017): 44–46. Available at https://www.unh.edu/sites/default/files/departments/police_department/dean_kurz_town vsgown.pdf.

Detweiller, Rick. "From Learning to Life: The Long-Term Impact of Liberal Arts Education." *Council of Independent Colleges Conference*, Washington, D.C., January 2017.

DiChiara, Phillip. "A New Way to Design and Deliver Higher Education Consortia." In *Consolidating Colleges and Merging Universities*, edited by James Martin and James E. Samels, 159–72. Baltimore: Johns Hopkins University Press, 2016.

Diner, Steven J. *Universities and Their Cities: Urban Higher Education in America*. Baltimore: John Hopkins University Press, 2017.

Dixon, Amanda. "The Best Minor League Baseball Towns of 2016." *smartasset*, September 27, 2016. https://smartasset.com/mortgage/best-minor-league-baseball-towns-2016.

Drath, Wilford. *The Deep Blue Sea: Rethinking the Source of Leadership*. San Francisco: Jossey-Bass, 2001.

Durisin, Megan. "Why Everyone Is Going Crazy for Craft Beer." *Business Insider*, April 23, 2013. http://www.businessinsider.com/why-craft-beer-is-so-popular-2013-4.

Ehrlich, Thomas. *Civic Responsibility and Higher Education*. Westport, CT: American Council on Education; Oryx Press, 2000.

Fairtlough, Gerard. *Getting Things Done: Hierarchy, Heterarchy, and Responsible Autonomy*. Dorset, England: Triarchy Press, 2005.

Fallows, James, and Deborah Fallows. *Our Towns: A 100,000 Mile Journey into the Heart of America*. New York: Penguin, 2018.

"The 50 Best College Towns to Live in Forever." College Ranker. Accessed January 27, 2019. http://www.collegeranker.com/features/best-college-towns/.

Filion, Pierre, Heidi Hoernig, Trudi Bunting, and Gary Sands. "The Successful Few:

Healthy Downtowns of Small Metropolitan Regions." *Journal of the American Planning Association* 70, no. 3 (2004): 328–43.

Florida, Richard. "The Reality of America's College Towns." *CityLab*, September 8, 2016. https://www.citylab.com/equity/2016/09/americas-biggest-college-towns/498755/.

——. *The Rise of the Creative Class: And How It's Transforming Work, Leisure, Community, and Everyday Life*. New York: Basic Books, 2002.

Fox, Michael. *Town and Gown: From Conflict to Cooperation*. Municipal Knowledge Series. Union, Ontario: Municipal World Publishing, 2014.

Gavazzi, Stephen M. *The Optimal Town-Gown Marriage: Taking Campus-Community Outreach and Engagement to the Next Level*. North Charleston, SC: CreateSpace, 2016.

Gavazzi, Stephen M., and Michael Fox. "A Tale of Three Cities: Piloting a Measure of Effort and Comfort Levels within Town-Gown Relationships." *Innovative Higher Education* 40, no. 3 (2014): 189–99.

Gavazzi, Stephen M., Michael Fox, and James Martin. "Understanding Campus and Community Relationships through Marriage and Family Metaphors: A Town-Gown Typology." *Innovative Higher Education* 39, no. 5 (2014).

Gavrich, Larry. "Golf College Towns." *Carolina Living*. Accessed January 21, 2019. https://carolinaliving.com/lifestyle/golf/golf-college-towns.

Goodman, Robert M., Marjorie A. Speers, Kenneth McLeroy, Steve Fawcett, Michelle Crozier Kegler, Eugene Parker, Scott F. Smith, Terrie D. Sterling, and Nina Wallerstein. "Identifying and Defining the Dimensions of Community Capacity to Provide a Basis for Measurement." *Health Education & Behavior* 25, no. 3 (1998): 258–78.

Gumprecht, Blake. *The American College Town*. Amherst: University of Massachusetts Press, 2008.

Hale, Thomas, and Gonzalo Vina. "University Challenge." *Financial Times*, Life & Arts Section (June 25–26, 2016): 18.

Heathcote, Edwin. "Urban Outfitters." *Financial Times* (House & Home Section) (June 30–July 1, 2007): 1.

Hoffman, Reid. "Social Networks Will Help Education to Realize Its True Potential." In "The Wired World in 2016." Special issue, *Wired* (UK ed.) (November 2015): 125–26.

Jacobs, Kelley. "50 Fittest College Towns in America, 2016–2017." *Great College Deals*. October 2016. https://www.greatcollegedeals.net/fittest-college-towns-america.

Kahn, Jay. "In Perfect (Imperfect) Harmony: Keene State College and Keene, New Hampshire, Rebalance Community Relations through Historic Preservation." *Planning for Higher Education* 39, no. 3 (April–June 2011): 159–66.

Kaplan, William A., and Barbara Lee, *Law of Higher Education*. San Francisco: Jossey-Bass, 2007.

Kemp, Roger L., ed. *Town and Gown Relations: A Handbook of Best Practices*. Jefferson, NC: McFarland, 2013.

Kryza, Andy. "The 11 Best College-Town Breweries in America." *Thrillist*, September 22, 2016. https://www.thrillist.com/drink/nation/best-breweries-college-towns.

Lochridge, Scott, and Jennifer Rosenzweig. *Enlightenment Incorporated: Creating Companies Our Kids Would Be Proud to Work For*. Oakland County, MI: Dragonfly Organization Resource Group, 2009.

Lott, David. "Get Smart! College Towns near Amenity Communities in FL, SC, NC Make for a Rich Lifestyle." *Golf Course Home*, March 8, 2016. http://www.golfcoursehome.com/retire-to-college-towns-march-8-2016/.

Martin, James, and James E. Samels. "Higher Ed to the Rescue: Protecting Water Resources for the Next Generation." *University Business*, April 5, 2016. https://www.universitybusiness.com/article/fs-0516.

Martin, James, and James E. Samels, eds. *Consolidating Colleges and Merging Universities*. Baltimore: Johns Hopkins University Press, 2016.

McKinnon, Ryan. "Higher Ed Leaders Renew Their Vows, Seek the Market Area as Education Hub." *Bradenton Herald*, August 2, 2017. http://www.bradenton.com/news/local/education/article165043837.html.

McMichael, William H. "More Civilians Calling Military Bases Home." *USA Today*, September 17, 2014. https://www.usatoday.com/story/news/nation/2014/09/17/more-civilians-calling-military-bases-home/15809713/.

Morad, Renee. "The Transparency Paradox." *Transparent by Design*, a *Scientific American Custom Media* production (August 2017): 19.

Moretti, Enrico. *The New Geography of Jobs*. New York: Houghton Mifflin Harcourt, 2012.

Murgia, Madhumita. "The Truth about Children and Social Media." *Financial Times*, Tech World Column (June 17–18, 2017): 20.

Nichols, David. *University-Community Relations: Living Together Effectively*. Springfield, IL: Charles C. Thomas, 1990.

Northwestern Medical BRANDVOICE, "Should You Retire to a College Town?" *Forbes*, November 25, 2014. https://www.forbes.com/sites/northwesternmutual/2014/11/25/not-your-fathers-retirement-why-boomers-are-graduating-to-college-towns/.

Pearson, Sarah S. "Community Schools: The United Way." United Way of the Greater Lehigh Valley and Coalition for Community Schools. January 2010. http://www.communityschools.org/assets/1/AssetManager/Community%20Schools-%20The%20United%20Way%20-%20Short.pdf.

Perry, David. C., and Wim Wiewel, eds. *The University as Urban Developer: Case Studies and Analysis*. Cambridge, MA: Lincoln Institute of Land Policy; New York: Routledge, 2005.

Peters, Joey. "Tapping the Mighty Mississippi and Coastal Tides with Underwater Turbines." *Scientific American*, February 18, 2011. https://www.scientificamerican.com/article/tapping-the-mississippi-and-tides-with-turbines/.

Pinker, Susan. *The Village Effect: How Face-to-Face Contact Can Make Us Healthier, Happier, and Smarter*. Toronto: Random House Canada, 2014.

Ramaswamy, Venkat, and Francis Gouillart. *The Power of Co-creation*. New York: Free Press, 2010.

Rawn, William. "Campus and the City." In *Architecture for the Public Realm*, edited by William Rawn, 104–11. New York: Edizioni Press, 2002.

Rockwood, Kate, and editors. "Always-On Education." *Inc. Magazine* (July–August 2017): 88.

Rubin, Hank. *Collaborative Leadership: Developing Effective Partnerships for Communities and Schools*. Thousand Oaks, CA: Corwin Press, 2009.

Saint-Onge, Hubert, and Debra Wallace. *Leveraging Communities of Practice for Strategic Advantage*. Boston: Butterworth Heinemann, 2003.

Sanderson, Rachel. "The Man behind the $1,000 Puffa." *Financial Times*, House & Home Section (May 20–21, 2017), 2.

Schultz, Jack. *Boomtown USA: The 7-1/2 Keys to Big Success in Small Towns*. Herndon, VA: NAIOP: The Commercial Real Estate Association, 2004.

Seltzer, Rick. "Bethune-Cookman Sues over Expensive Dormitory Deal." *Inside Higher Ed*, January 26, 2018. https://www.insidehighered.com/quicktakes/2018/01/26/bethune-cookman-sues-over-expensive-dormitory-deal.

———. "Developer Countersues Bethune-Cookman." *Inside Higher Ed*, February 13, 2018. https://www.insidehighered.com/quicktakes/2018/02/13/developer-countersues-bethune-cookman.

———. "Does $200 Million Quack?" *Inside Higher Ed*, September 26, 2017. https://www.insidehighered.com/news/2017/09/26/uc-irvine-under-scrutiny-taking-200-million-school-health-couple-some-say-back-junk.

———. "Funneling Students to Bank Fees?" *Inside Higher Ed*, March 12, 2018. https://www.insidehighered.com/news/2018/03/12/durbin-scrutinizes-wells-fargos-contracts-colleges-new-data-show-how-bank-fees-hit.

———. "Grinnell's Gun Connection." *Inside Higher Ed*, February 19, 2018. https://www.insidehighered.com/news/2018/02/19/nra-presidents-donation-grinnell-prompts-policy-rewrite-and-soul-searching.

———. "Problems beyond the $306M Dorm." *Inside Higher Ed*, July 21, 2017. https://www.insidehighered.com/news/2017/07/21/bethune-cookman-confronts-questions-about-its-future-wake-financial-and-governance.

———. "A University-Run School District?" *Inside Higher Ed*, March 8, 2018. https://www.insidehighered.com/news/2018/03/08/ball-state-university-poised-historic-takeover-school-district-muncie-ind.

Smith, Darren. "'Studentification': The Gentrification Factory?" In *Gentrification in a Global Context: The New Urban Colonialism*, edited by R. Atkinson and G. Bridge, 72–89. Housing and Society Series. London: Routledge, 2005.

Smith, Darren and Michael Fox. "A Studentification Guide for North America: Delivering Harmonious Town and Gown Associations." Educational Events, American Planning Association, May 31, 2018. https://www.planning.org/events/activity/9151977/.

Smith, Frank. "What the New Wave of Wireless Tech Can Do for Your Campus." *Ed Tech: Focus on Higher Education*, September 8, 2015. https://edtechmagazine.com/higher/article/2015/09/what-new-wave-wireless-tech-can-do-your-campus.

Snyder, Thomas, Cristobal de Brey, and Sally A. Dillow. "Digest of Education Statistics, 2015." U.S. Department of Education, National Center for Education Statistics. Accessed January 27, 2019. https://nces.ed.gov/pubs2016/2016014.pdf.

Thelin, John R. *A History of American Higher Education*. Baltimore: Johns Hopkins University Press, 2004.

Torres, Jan, and Julia Schaffer, eds. *Benchmarks for Campus/Community Partnerships*. Providence, RI: Campus Compact, 2000.

Tsukayama, Hayley. "Teens Spend Nearly Nine Hours Every Day Consuming Media." *Washington Post*, November 3, 2015. https://www.washingtonpost.com/news/the-switch/wp/2015/11/03/teens-spend-nearly-nine-hours-every-day-consuming-media/.

Universum Top 100. "The Most Attractive Employers in the U.S." Special Advertising Supplement to *New York Times* (October 2012).

Van Agtmael, Antoine, and Fred Bakker. *The Smartest Place on Earth: Why Rustbelts Are the Emerging Hotspots of Global Innovation*. New York: PublicAffairs, 2016.

Vannozzi, Briana. "NJCU to Relocate School of Business to Heart of Jersey City's Financial District." *NJTV News*, April 15, 2015. https://www.njtvonline.org/news/video/njcu-to-relocate-school-of-business-to-heart-of-jersey-citys-financial-district/.

Wahba, Phil. "Exclusive: Barnes & Noble Seeks Big Expansion of Its College Stores." *Reuters*, May 8, 2014. https://www.reuters.com/article/us-barnesandnoble-college-exclusive/exclusive-barnes-noble-seeks-big-expansion-of-its-college-stores-idUSBREA470D420140508.

Waltz, Kenneth N. *Theory of International Politics*. Long Grove, IL: Waveland Press, 1979.

Winling, LaDale C. *Building the Ivory Tower: Universities and Metropolitan Development in the Twentieth Century*. Philadelphia: University of Pennsylvania Press, 2018.

Zimpher, Nancy. "'Systemness': A New Way to Lead and Manage Higher Education Systems." In *Consolidating Colleges and Merging Universities*, edited by James Martin and James E. Samels, 52–63. Baltimore: Johns Hopkins University Press, 2016.

Ziomek, David, and Tony Maroulis. "Blurring the Borders between Campus and Community: Creating a Town-Gown Committee for Shared Success" (conference presentation). International Town & Gown Association, Leading Practices Library. Accessed August 2, 2017. http://www.itga.org/resource-center.

Contributors

JAMES MARTIN was for many years a professor of English and a provost. He is also an ordained United Methodist minister. He was awarded a Fulbright Fellowship to study mergers in the University of London system, and he currently serves as a Senior Consultant at The Registry and as a Senior Contributor at HigherEdJobs.com. Martin also taught courses in the graduate program in Higher Education at Boston College.

Martin has coauthored seven previous books published by Johns Hopkins University Press: *Merging Colleges for Mutual Growth* (1994), *First among Equals: The Role of the Chief Academic Officer* (1997), *Presidential Transition in Higher Education: Managing Leadership Change* (2005), *Turnaround: Leading Stressed Colleges and Universities to Excellence* (2009), *The Sustainable University: Green Goals and New Challenges for Higher Education Leaders* (2012), *The Provost's Handbook: The Role of the Chief Academic Officer* (2015), and *Consolidating Colleges and Merging Universities: New Strategies for Higher Education Leaders* (2017).

A graduate of Colby College (AB) and Boston University (MDiv and PhD), Martin has written articles for *The Chronicle of Higher Education, London Times, Christian Science Monitor, Boston Globe, Trusteeship, CASE Currents*, and *Planning for Higher Education.*

JAMES E. SAMELS is the founder and CEO of both the Education Alliance and the Samels Group, a full-service higher education consulting firm. He is also the founding partner of Samels Associates, a law firm serving independent and public colleges, universities, and nonprofit and for-profit higher education organizations. Samels has served on the faculties of the University of Massachusetts and Bentley College and as a guest lecturer at Boston University and Harvard University. Prior to his appointment at the University of Massachusetts, Samels served as the deputy and acting state comptroller in Massachusetts, special assistant attorney general, Massachusetts Community College counsel, and general counsel to the Massachusetts Board of Regents.

Samels holds a bachelor's degree in political science, a master's degree in public administration, a juris doctor degree, and a doctor of education degree. He has written and cowritten a number of scholarly articles, monographs, and opinion editorials appearing in *The Chronicle of Higher Education, AGB Trusteeship, Christian Science Monitor, London Guardian, Boston Globe, Boston Herald, Boston Business Journal, Journal of Higher Education Management*, and *Planning for Higher Education.* He is the coauthor, with James Martin, of *Merging Colleges for Mutual Growth* (1994), *First among Equals: The Role of the Chief Academic Officer* (1997), *Presidential Transition in Higher Education: Managing Leadership Change* (2005), *Turnaround: Leading Stressed Colleges and Universities to Excellence* (2009), *The Sustainable University: Green Goals and New Challenges for Higher Education Leaders* (2012), *The Provost's Handbook: The Role of the Chief Academic Officer* (2015), and *Consolidating Colleges and Merging Universities* (2017), all published by Johns Hopkins University Press. Samels has previously consulted on projects and presented research papers at universities, colleges, schools, and ministries of education in Canada, China, France, Great Britain, Korea, Sweden, Thailand, and Turkey.

Robert C. Andringa served higher education as Education and Labor Committee Staff Director in the US House of Representatives; as a senior aide to Governor Al Quie in Minnesota; and as the CEO of the Education Commission of the States, headquartered in Denver. He served for twelve years as President of the Council for Christian Colleges and Universities, headquartered in Washington, D.C.

Aaron Aska joined the administration at New Jersey City University (NJCU) in June 2004 as Associate Vice President for Finance and Controller. In August 2008, after the completion of a national search, he was appointed Vice President for Administration and Finance. Previously, Dr. Aska held the title of Controller for seven years at Drew University, a small, private institution in Madison, New Jersey, where he gained his first experience with higher education, having previously worked for Price Waterhouse-Coopers.

As Vice President and Chief Operating Officer at NJCU, Dr. Aska provides strategic leadership and direction to the university in developing and implementing key aspects of its strategic plan, which includes aligning institutional resources with key academic initiatives, revamping the University Foundation's investment policy, and rebalancing its asset allocation. He was also instrumental in developing the first public-private partnership (P3) on campus, which is a 425-bed privatized student housing facility. During his tenure at the university, Dr. Aska has been involved in all phases of the University Place redevelopment project, from land acquisition, brownfield remediation, and ultimately development of the site. The west campus redevelopment project is intended to revitalize the western portion of Jersey City and provide a college town experience replete with academic and nonacademic facilities.

Dr. Aska holds a bachelor of science degree in accounting from Rutgers University, a master's in Management degree from the New Jersey Institute of Technology, and an executive doctorate in higher education management from the University of Pennsylvania. He is also a certified public accountant.

Beth Bagwell, MPA, is the Executive Director of the International Town & Gown Association. She has fifteen years of teaching experience and has worked in the nonprofit sector for over a decade. She holds a master's degree in public administration with a concentration in nonprofit management from Clemson University.

Ms. Bagwell also has a bachelor of arts degree in elementary and early childhood education from Lander University in Greenwood, South Carolina. Her work in the public sector and postgraduate position at the Strom Thurmond Institute of Government and Public Affairs at Clemson University helped prepare her for her current position with the ITGA, where she works with campus community partners and members from around the world.

Katherine Bergeron became the eleventh president of Connecticut College in January 2014. From her first months in office, she has focused on building the institution's academic, residential, community, and financial strength. She has supported the development of Connections, a bold new venture in interdisciplinary education designed to prepare twenty-first-century students for leadership in a rapidly changing, interconnected world. Connecticut College has also received some of the largest gifts in its history to improve financial aid and support career education, athletics, and the arts. Projects completed under her leadership include the renovation of the Charles E. Shain Library, the creation of the Walter Commons for Global Study and Engagement, and plans for the revitalization of the college's campus center and historic theater.

A Phi Beta Kappa graduate of Wesleyan University, Bergeron earned master's and doctoral degrees in music history from Cornell University and later wrote two prize-winning books on French music and culture. Before coming to Connecticut College, she was dean of the college at Brown University. She currently serves on the Editorial Advisory Board of "Liberal Education"; on the Executive Committee of the Council of Independent Colleges; on the Board of the Association of American Colleges and Universities; as a Commissioner for the New England Commission on Higher Education; and on the Board of Directors of the Eastern Connecticut Symphony Orchestra.

Kelly A. Cherwin has worked for HigherEdJobs.com since 2008 and is currently the Director of Editorial Strategy. After receiving her masters in business administration (MBA) degree from Loyola University Chicago in 2002, with a dual concentration in marketing and management and certification in ethics, she began working as the Director of Career Services at Career Colleges of Chicago. She later transitioned to Program Coordinator at the Illinois Institute of Technology (IIT) and in 2005 was appointed Director of Career Services at IIT's Stuart Graduate School of Business. Since 2003, Ms. Cherwin has also taught undergraduate and graduate business courses at IIT and Elmhurst College in organizational behavior, project management, strategic management, and ethics. Ms. Cherwin also holds a bachelor of science degree in biology-ecology, evolution, and behavior from the University of Minnesota–Twin Cities.

Phillip DiChiara has had the good fortune to have had a career that split his forty-three years of experience between senior positions in both higher education and health care. The common ground between them lies in his interest in system thinking, organizational behavior, and promoting operational excellence across and between competitor organizations in the form of interinstitutional collaboration. During a period of great change in health care, he was an active participant in Boston's Medical Academic and Scientific Community Organization, Inc., where efforts to coordinate operational needs were organized for collective action. At the time, the adage was "better to compete on quality than on the price of Band-aids." Phillip was Vice President for Operations at Beth Israel Hospital, having previously worked in Pennsylvania at the the Allentown Hospital and the Lehigh Valley Hospital Center. It was there that the impact of collective action beyond the traditional hierarchical organization structure influenced his work and approach to leadership.

He was recruited to form the Boston Consortium for Higher Education (TBC) as its first Managing Director and CEO. It was viewed as an experiment undertaken by the major private colleges in greater Boston. The board of the consortium consisted of the Chief Financial Officers of the sixteen members. Twenty-three communities of practice engaged upper-middle managers in collaborative projects to reduce nonacademic operating cost. The Boston Consortium was an influential player among the nations roughly 120 other consortia. DiChiara consulted with several organizations to share the experiences that had been collected. Of particular note was the role TBC played in forming Educators' Health. Now in its fifth year, it has successfully reduced what is often the second- or third-largest cost for colleges and universities: health insurance.

Lorin Ditzler is a city planning consultant.

Mauri A. Ditzler officially took office as the sixteenth president of Albion College on July 1, 2014. He brings with him a wealth of accomplishments in higher education built over a thirty-five-year career, including two decades as an administrator and, before that, fifteen years as an esteemed and national award–winning chemistry professor.

Ditzler came to Albion from Monmouth College in Illinois, where he served as president from 2005 to 2014. During his nine years there, he led initiatives that emphasized academic excellence, resulted in curriculum innovations, produced positive enrollment trends, and strengthened the college's relationship with its home community of Monmouth. One of Ditzler's signature achievements at Monmouth was the creation and implementation of a strategic plan, titled "Fulfilling the Promise," that recommitted the college to its founding principles—repurposed for the twenty-first century—and led to the largest capital campaign in the college's history.

Before Monmouth, Ditzler enjoyed six years as dean at Wabash College in Indiana, his undergraduate alma mater. At Wabash, he developed and helped raise more than $20 million in initial funding for the national Center of Inquiry in the Liberal Arts. Preceding his move into administration was a fifteen-year tenure as a chemistry professor at the College of the Holy Cross in Massachusetts. At Holy Cross, Ditzler led a team that created a chemistry curriculum, and he also published regularly—often with students as coauthors—and obtained major grants for research and laboratory facilities.

Kevin E. Drumm became the seventh president of SUNY Broome Community College in February 2010. In the past several years, he has overseen a dramatic transformation of SUNY Broome's campus, including:

- The $21 million Natural Science Center, opened in fall 2013, bringing the first new classrooms to the campus in fifteen years. The state-of-the-art, energy-efficient building houses the Biology, Chemistry, and Physical Science Departments.

- Opened in fall 2014, the new Student Village gave SUNY Broome students the opportunity for on-campus living for the very first time. The $18 million complex houses 336 students and a full-time director at the front of campus.

- The Darwin R. Wales Center completed a much-needed $4.6 million overhaul of a vintage-1956 building in June 2014. The space, considered the college's welcome center, is now accessible for the first time to people with disabilities, as well as energy-efficient and aesthetically pleasing.

Before coming to SUNY Broome, Dr. Drumm was president of the Northern Wyoming Community College District from 2004 to 2010. During his tenure at NWCCD, the district grew to enroll more than 5,500 students annually and also increased its operating budget from $24 to $35 million with 230 full-time staff and faculty. The district added more than 150,000 square feet of new facilities and raised more than $100 million in public and private funding.

Prior to becoming president of NWCCD, Dr. Drumm was Vice President for Enrollment/Student & Public Affairs at Springfield Technical Community College in Springfield, Massachusetts.

He has taught throughout his career and is also a graduate of the first American Association of Community Colleges Leadership Institute. He was educated at Berkshire Community College in Pittsfield, Massachusetts, transferring to Boston University for both his bachelor's and master's degrees, later completing his PhD in organizational studies and higher education at New York University.

Erin Flynn leads the Office of Strategic Partnerships at Portland State University (PSU). In this role she is responsible for designing and managing university-wide economic development and community engagement initiatives that advance strategic regional priorities related to economic development, innovation and entrepreneurship, community health, and urban sustainability. Dr. Flynn is Cochair of the PSU Partnership Council, a university-wide body that advances and communicates PSU's robust community engagement portfolio.

Over the course of her career, Erin has served as a policy and strategy consultant, a city government official, and a higher education executive. Erin excels at building bridges between the public sector, the private sector, and higher education to design and advance complex metropolitan agendas. At PSU she is point person on the Oregon Health and Sciences University (OHSU)–PSU Strategic Alliance, the Portland General Electric (PGE)–PSU Strategic Partnership, and PSU's extensive engagement with the city of Portland. On behalf of four regional anchor institutions—PSU, OHSU, Portland Community College (PCC), and Oregon Museum of Science and Industry (OMSI)—she currently spearheads Portland's "Innovation Quadrant." The IQ is envisioned as the geographic nerve center of a flourishing ecosystem that attracts talent, entrepreneurs, and investment and propels Portland to global prominence in the cross-collaboration of health, science, and product design.

Erin is actively engaged in state and regional economic and community development. In 2015 she was appointed by Governor Kate Brown to serve as chair of the Oregon Innovation Council, the state's innovation and entrepreneurship investment platform. Erin is also a board and Executive Committee member of Greater Portland, Inc., the metro region's public-private partnership for business recruitment and regional marketing. Prior to joining PSU in 2011, Erin served as Urban Development Director at the Portland Development Commission (2007–11). She moved to Portland from Boston, where she led a national consulting practice focused on regional economic and workforce development. Erin holds a PhD in political science from the Massachusetts Institute of Technology and a bachelor of arts in politics from the University of California, Santa Cruz.

Michael Fox is Professor and Chair of the Department of Geography and Environment at Mount Allison University in Sackville, New Brunswick, and the author of the book *Town & Gown: From Conflict to Cooperation* (2014). Michael also coauthored, with his colleague Darren Smith, *Studentification: A Guide for Delivering Harmonious Town & Gown Relations in North America.*

Michael teaches courses in community planning, place-based education, municipal affairs, and housing and recently concluded a term as Chair of the District Planning Commission for the Tantramar District of South-East New Brunswick. Michael has been a long-serving advisor to the town of Sackville's Housing Issues Committee, as well as to Acadia University and the town of Wolfville, Nova Scotia. He is a longtime member of the Town & Gown Association of Ontario and currently serves as the Canadian representative on the Board of Directors of the International Town & Gown Association.

Michael has been involved with university-community relations for nearly forty years and has served as Dean of Students at Bishop's University, Lennoxville, Quebec; Vice President (Student Affairs) at the University of Winnipeg; and Vice President (Academic & Student Affairs) at Mount Allison University. Michael began his long-held passion for town-gown relations during his undergraduate years as the Community Liaison Officer for the University Students' Council at Western University in London, Ontario.

Joel Garreau is Professor of Culture, Values, and Emerging Technologies, Office of the President, Arizona State University. He is a professional scenario planner formerly with Global Business Network; a Future Tense Fellow with New America in Washington, D.C.; and author of the best sellers *Radical Evolution: The Promise and Peril of Enhancing Our Minds,*

Our Bodies—and What It Means to Be Human, *Edge City: Life on the New Frontier*, and *The Nine Nations of North America*. In his former life he was a reporter and editor for the *Washington Post*. The author wishes to acknowledge the contributions to this piece of award-winning author and demographer Brad Edmondson, Deep Springs College '76.

Susan Henderson has served as the twelfth (and first woman) President of New Jersey City University (NJCU) since August 2012. Since her arrival, she has accomplished a range of transformational initiatives. She created the NJCU School of Business, relocated it to a state-of-the-art facility in Jersey City's financial district, and hired over half the faculty. During her tenure more than five new academic programs have been developed, as well as a new General Education program and Honors Program. She spearheaded the implementation of a $350 million project to redevelop the institution's West Campus to include student housing, shops, restaurants, and a pedestrian-friendly layout to aesthetically and economically revitalize the region.

In addition, Dr. Henderson has ensured that NJCU tuition and fees remain among the lowest of all four-year public colleges and universities in New Jersey, and implemented the NJCU Debt-Free Promise Program to make a college education accessible and affordable. Dr. Henderson serves on the Board of Directors of the Hispanic Association of Colleges and Universities; is Vice Chair of the DIII Presidents Council and a member of the Board of Governors of the National Collegiate Athletics Association; is a member of the Committee on International Education of the American Association of State Colleges and Universities; chairs the Academic Issues Committee for the New Jersey Presidents Council; and is on the Internationalization Commission of the American Council of Education. Her term as a Commissioner for the Middle States Commission on Higher Education began on January 1, 2018.

Andrew W. Hibel is a Cofounder and the Chief Operating Officer of HigherEdJobs.com, the leading academic job board. After starting their first jobs in higher education at Penn State University, Andrew and his cofounders, Eric Blessner and John Ikenberry, sought a better way to view and post jobs in higher ed. With this simple vision, they founded HigherEdJobs.com in 1996 and, since then, have helped employers and candidates find each other over the past twenty-two years. Andrew holds bachelor of arts and master of education (higher education) degrees from the University of Illinois, Urbana, and a juris doctor from Indiana University, Indianapolis.

Patrick Hyland Jr., AIA, designs for campuses, the arts, and interpretive environments for DLR Group. He has delivered several successful and award-winning design solutions to significant clients, including Penn State University, the Ohio State University, and the University of Mount Union. He has also worked on master plans and various facilities for Baldwin-Wallace University, Kent State University, and Westminster College. Patrick graduated with a master of architecture degree from the Yale School of Architecture. He earned his bachelor of architecture degree with distinction from Pennsylvania State University. He has taught undergraduate and graduate architectural and urban design studios at Kent State University and Penn State University. In addition to teaching, Patrick is active in the International Town Gown Association (ITGA) and has also served on design juries at Penn State University, Kent State University, the Ohio State University, and the University of Michigan.

Jay Kahn served Keene State College in New Hampshire as Vice President for Finance and Planning for nearly twenty-seven years and one year as Interim President. Previously he worked in Illinois higher education, first at the Illinois Board of Higher Education and then at Governors State University. He completed his doctorate in public policy studies at the University of Illinois–Chicago. With over forty-three years' experience in higher education, Dr. Kahn has served in volunteer leadership capacities with the National Association of College and University Business Officers and the Society of College and University Planning, and has chaired local hospital, chamber of commerce, and economic development boards.

Dr. Kahn is an honorary member of the American Institute of Architects–New Hampshire and of the Keene State College Alumni Association. Since retiring from Keene State College in 2016, he has been elected as a Keene City Councilor serving in 2016 and currently is in his second term as the region's State Senator. In that role, Senator Kahn is Chairman of the New Hampshire Senate Education and Workforce Development Committee, a member of the Finance Committee, and is a state-named Commissioner to the Education Commission of the States.

Liam Oliver Lair is Assistant Professor of Women's & Gender Studies at West Chester University (WCU). His previous teaching positions include Visiting Assistant Professor of Gender Studies at the College of St. Benedict/St. John's University in Minnesota and instructor in Women's and Gender Studies at Louisiana State University. He holds a PhD in women, gender, and sexuality studies from the University of Kansas. His teaching and research are rooted in feminist studies with a specific focus on sexuality, trans subjectivities, disability, and race. His publications include articles focused on how constructions of gender "deviance" were shaped by scientific racism, and on the embodied experience of working and researching in archival spaces. Dr. Lair has also worked with faculty, staff, and students to create safe and affirming spaces for trans and queer students at each of his previous institutions, and he continues this work at WCU.

Miguel Martinez-Saenz was appointed the nineteenth president of St. Francis College in Brooklyn, New York, in 2017. With a master's degree and a PhD in philosophy from the University of South Florida, he began his academic career as Assistant Professor of Philosophy at Wittenberg University in Springfield, Ohio. After earning tenure at Wittenberg, Dr. Martinez-Saenz accepted and held two administrative appointments: Assistant Provost for the First-Year Experience and Associate Provost for Academic Affairs.

Dr. Martinez-Saenz moved from Wittenberg to accept the position of Dean and Associate Provost for Student Success at St. Cloud State University, where he led a data analytics initiative that examines the factors influencing retention, with a special emphasis on the magnitude of these effects.

Dr. Martinez-Saenz's most recent appointment was at Otterbein University, where he served as Provost. In that position he led a number of efforts especially in the context of internationalization that included a three-year global arts initiative funded in part by the National Endowment for the Arts. He also helped lay the foundation for and developed partnerships with universities in South Africa, Costa Rica, Brazil, and Malaysia. Dr. Martinez-Saenz was an administrative Fulbright Scholar in 2016 through the Fulbright-Nehru International Education Administrators Program.

President Martinez-Saenz has been honored with a variety of accolades during his academic career, including the Ohio Latino Awards Educator of the Year, Insight into Diversity Visionary Award, and the Lillian C. Franklin Diversity Award.

Fred McGrail serves as Vice President for Communications and Public Affairs at Lehigh University. He leads a team responsible for community relations, federal and state relations, strategic communications, admissions marketing, university branding, media relations, creative services, and crisis communications.

McGrail has guided Lehigh University's efforts to build partnerships with city officials, community organizations, business leaders, and residents in order to contribute to the renaissance of Bethlehem, Pennsylvania, a postindustrial city once defined by the presence of Bethlehem Steel. Faculty, students, staff, and the leadership of the university are working together to have a significant impact on the city. Lehigh's efforts have focused on public health and safety, education, neighborhood stabilization, and economic development.

Kim Nehls served as the Executive Director of the Association for the Study of Higher Education (ASHE) from 2008 to 2018. ASHE is the premier scholarly society for higher education, and as its Executive Director, Dr. Nehls is responsible for a central office staff of five and more than two thousand ASHE members worldwide. She earned a Global MBA from Duke University, a PhD and a master's degree from the University of Nevada, Las Vegas, and bachelor's degrees from the University of Illinois, Urbana. Her research and professional interests include university philanthropy, leadership, and student engagement.

Dr. Nehls continues in a visiting faculty appointment at UNLV, where she teaches a range of classes from doctoral seminars in the College of Education to a global business strategy course. In addition, she regularly gives presentations at conferences and workshops and publishes on issues related to higher education.

As DLR Group's Campus Planning Leader, **Krisan Osterby, ASLA**, is responsible for the quality and relevancy of the firm's planning services. Her expertise includes comprehensive campus plans, strategic facilities plans, landscape master plans, and district redevelopment studies. For more than thirty years, Krisan has worked with every type of public and private higher education institution to integrate strategy with placemaking, including community and liberal arts colleges, historically black colleges and universities, and regional and land grant universities. Her implemented projects range from Alaska to Florida; she has also contributed to master plans in Canada, Great Britain, Hong Kong, India, and Iraq. She earned a Master of Landscape Architecture Degree with Distinction from the Harvard Graduate School of Design, received a Fulbright/ITT Fellowship in Planning in the Netherlands and is a registered Landscape Architect. Krisan is a frequent presenter on equity and engagement issues to the Society for College and University Planning (SCUP) and the International Town & Gown Association (ITGA). She also volunteers as a National Advisory Board member for Gustavus Adolphus College.

Tracee Reiser recently retired as Senior Associate Dean for Community Partnerships and Associate Director of the Holleran Center for Community Action and Public Policy at Connecticut College. She worked with students, staff, faculty, and community members for twenty-six years to create and implement innovative teaching and learning experiences that develop active citizenship, enhance scholarship, and contribute to advancing the quality of life in communities, both local and global. Reiser is a native New Londoner, and at Connecticut College she expanded initiatives to link community-based learning to the curriculum, helped create the Holleran Center for Community Action and Public Policy and the Center for the Comparative Study of Race and Ethnicity, and expanded student-led programs while building numerous partnerships between the college and its external community.

She secured grants and gifts from a wide range of public and private sources for college and community initiatives, and she was the first staff recipient of Connecticut College's Dr. Martin Luther King Jr. Service Award and the LGBTQ Advocacy Award. She cochaired the SECT Task Force on Racial Ethnic Balance in Schools that created and implemented the Regional Multicultural Magnet School and the Science & Technology Magnet High School. Reiser was also recognized as an Outstanding Community Collaborator by the NAACP.

As the Global Higher Education Sector Leader at DLR Group, **Stuart Rothenberger** collaborates with design and planning experts to set the direction and grow the firm's practice. He has served higher education clients almost exclusively throughout his career, delivering innovative design solutions that meet current and future needs of students and staff. His design portfolio features academic buildings, science centers, libraries, residence halls, dining centers, student unions, and facility master plans. Stuart is an active member of the Society of College and University Planners (SCUP), the Association of Physical Plant Administrators (APPA), and the National Association of College Auxiliary Services (NACAS). Beginning his career with the United States Air Force, he has completed planning and design services for a multitude of institutions, including Salve Regina University, Brigham Young University, Lehigh University, University of Pittsburgh, Villanova University, Cal Poly Pomona, Virginia Tech, and West Virginia University.

Kate Rousmaniere is Professor in the Department of Educational Leadership, Miami University, Oxford, Ohio, and, since 2015, Mayor of the city of Oxford. Her research centers on the history and politics of American educators. Her publications include *The Principal's Office: A Social History of the American School Principal* (2013), *Citizen Teacher: The Life and Leadership of Margaret Haley* (2005), and *City Teachers: Teaching and School Reform in Historical Perspective* (1997). Rousmaniere is a past president of the International Standing Conference for the History of Education, and of the American History of Education Society. Her current research centers on the history of university-town relations, particularly around issues of housing.

In 2011, after ending a nine-year term as Chair of her academic department, Kate was elected to the Oxford City Council, thereby pivoting her view of her community from the campus to the city. She was reelected in 2015 and then elected mayor by her Council colleagues. In a college town community where the university of 19,000 students more than doubles the full-time residential population, Kate has led the revitalization of town-gown relations with a particular emphasis on health- and arts-related initiatives. She is an active member of the International Town & Gown Association, which has helped Dr. Rousmaniere and other college town mayors develop strategies for communication, problem solving, and bridge building.

Rick Seltzer covers business and management as a reporter for *Inside Higher Ed*. He joined the publication in 2016 after working as a money and general-assignment reporter for the *Baltimore Business Journal*. Previously, he was a business reporter for the *Bloomington Herald-Times*, and he covered small business and health care for the *Central New York Business Journal*. Rick, a native of south-central Pennsylvania, started his career as a local beat reporter for the *Harrisburg Patriot-News*. He graduated from Syracuse University in 2008 after interning at the *Patriot-News* and the *Syracuse Post-Standard*.

John D. Simon is President of Lehigh University. During his time at Lehigh, Dr. Simon has worked to raise the university's national profile, grow its research infrastructure, expand its global programs, strengthen ties with the local community, and build on its long, proud legacy of distinction in teaching, research, and service. Under his leadership, the university has embarked on an ambitious strategy—known as the Path to Prominence—that will significantly expand Lehigh's undergraduate and graduate student populations, recruit new faculty, build new academic facilities, and launch an innovative college of health.

Dr. Simon came to Lehigh in 2015 from the University of Virginia, where he served as Executive Vice President and Provost. Previously,

Simon served as Vice Provost for Academic Affairs at Duke University from 2005 to 2011. He was Chair of Duke's Department of Chemistry from 1999 to 2004 and also held appointments in the Duke University Medical Center in both biochemistry and ophthalmology. He received his BA from Williams College in 1979 and his PhD in chemistry from Harvard University in 1983. After a postdoctoral fellowship at the University of California, Los Angeles, Simon joined the Department of Chemistry and Biochemistry at the University of California, San Diego, in 1985 and then moved to Duke University as the George B. Geller Professor in 1998.

Jefferson A. Singer is the Dean of the College and Faulk Foundation Professor of Psychology at Connecticut College. He has authored six books: *The Proper Pirate*; *Robert Louis Stevenson's Quest for Identity*; *Positive Couple Therapy: Using We-Stories to Enhance Resilience* (with Karen Skerrett); *Personality and Psychotherapy; Treating the Whole Person*; *Memories That Matter*; *Message in a Bottle*; and *The Remembered Self: Emotion and Memory in Personality* (with Peter Salovey), and has coedited (with Peter Salovey) a seventh book, *At Play in the Fields of Consciousness: Essays in Honor of Jerome L. Singer*.

Singer is the author of more than one hundred articles and book chapters in the fields of memory, personality, and clinical psychology. He received the 2010 Henry A. Murray Award for the Study of Lives from the Society for Personality and Social Psychology of the American Psychology Association. Dean Singer is a fellow of the American Psychological Association and past recipient of the Fulbright Distinguished Scholar Award to support research in the United Kingdom.

Allison Starer earned a master's degree in management from Lehigh University's College of Business and Economics in 2018 and received a bachelor of arts degree from Lehigh's College of Arts and Sciences in 2017, where she double-majored in political science and art history. Awarded a Strohl Research Grant, Allison traveled to cities across the United States to analyze how street art murals can positively affect community development and economic revitalization. She concentrated her senior thesis on the relationship between public art and urban identity.

While a student at Lehigh, Allison spearheaded a project to help bring murals to South Bethlehem, an endeavor that involved meeting with local business owners and commissioning artists. Allison continued her involvement with the Greater Lehigh Valley community by interviewing key leaders and influencers to gauge the pulse and gain insight into the relationship between the university and those who live and work in the surrounding community.

Wim Wiewel is Lewis & Clark University's twenty-fifth president. He took the helm on October 1, 2017, after nine years successfully leading Portland State University (PSU). Under his tenure, PSU became the largest and most diverse university in the state. Retention and graduation rates increased every year, while funded research went up 50 percent, and fund raising tripled. His leadership earned him a 2014 CASE (Council for Advancement and Support of Education) Chief Executive Leadership Award.

The recipient of a classic liberal arts education as a high school student in his native Amsterdam, Wiewel learned early on the value of a broad-based education rooted in critical thinking and analysis. The first in his family to go to college, he holds degrees in sociology and urban planning from the University of Amsterdam and a PhD in sociology from Northwestern University.

During his first year at Portland State, Wim secured a $25 million sustainability research grant from the Miller Foundation. He even invited students to tear up a section of the presidential house's yard to put in a permaculture garden. Wim received the 2012 inaugural Presidential Leadership Award from the US Green Building Council's Center for Green Schools. He also garnered a Climate Leadership Award from the national nonprofit Second Nature in 2013 for demonstrating innovative and advanced leadership in education related to sustainability and climate mitigation and adaptation.

A sociologist with a passion for strong cities, Wiewel has authored or edited nine books, including *Global Universities and Urban Development* and *Suburban Sprawl*, and his more than sixty-five articles and book chapters have appeared in such publications as *Economic Geography* and the *Journal of the American Planning Association*.

Eugene L. Zdziarski II is Vice President for Student Affairs at DePaul University in Chicago, Illinois. Dr. Zdziarski has more than thirty years of experience in higher education working with students in both private and public institutions, including Texas A&M University, the University of Florida, the University of Tennessee at Knoxville, and Roanoke College. He received his bachelor of science degree from Oklahoma State University, his master of science degree from the University of Tennessee at Knoxville, and his PhD from Texas A&M University.

Index

Page numbers in *italics* refer to figures and tables.